NATIONAL-LOUIS UNIVERSITY

3 2842 1810 4

D0095940

Critical Literacy

Studies in the
Postmodern Theory of Education

Joe L. Kincheloe and Shirley R. Steinberg
General Editors

Vol. 296

PETER LANG
New York • Washington, D.C./Baltimore • Bern
Frankfurt am Main • Berlin • Brussels • Vienna • Oxford

Cynthia A. McDaniel

Critical Literacy

A Way of Thinking, a Way of Life

PETER LANG
New York • Washington, D.C./Baltimore • Bern
Frankfurt am Main • Berlin • Brussels • Vienna • Oxford

National-Louis University
Lisle Campus Library
850 Warrenville Road
Lisle, IL 60532

Library of Congress Cataloging-in-Publication Data

McDaniel, Cynthia A.
Critical literacy / Cynthia A. McDaniel.
p. cm. — (Counterpoints: studies in the postmodern theory of education; 296)
Includes bibliographical references and index.
1. Critical pedagogy—United States. 2. Literacy—Social aspects—United States. I. Title.
LC196.5.U6M34   370.11'5—dc22   2006019010
ISBN 0-8204-7946-2
ISSN 1058-1634

Bibliographic information published by **Die Deutsche Bibliothek**.
Die Deutsche Bibliothek lists this publication in the "Deutsche
Nationalbibliografie"; detailed bibliographic data is available
on the Internet at http://dnb.ddb.de/.

Cover photo by Megan McDaniel
Cover design by Lisa Barfield

The paper in this book meets the guidelines for permanence and durability
of the Committee on Production Guidelines for Book Longevity
of the Council of Library Resources.

© 2006 Peter Lang Publishing, Inc., New York
29 Broadway, New York, NY 10006
www.peterlang.com

All rights reserved.
Reprint or reproduction, even partially, in all forms such as microfilm,
xerography, microfiche, microcard, and offset strictly prohibited.

Printed in the United States of America

◆◆ TABLE OF CONTENTS

◆ ACKNOWLEDGMENTS

Wanderer, your footsteps are the road, and nothing more;
Wanderer, there is no road, the road is made by walking.
                                    —Antonio Machado (1875–1939)

Many people—past and present—have influenced, inspired, and helped me on this journey. Paulo Freire made the road by walking, and I only wish I had discovered his work sooner. When I was feeling especially lonely and lost, some amazing scholars provided encouragement and wisdom: Jerome Harste, Dorothy Holland, Joe Kincheloe, Alan Luke, and Patrick Shannon. Their support renewed my Hope and I am extremely grateful to them. Several individuals have been guideposts along the way: Alida Allison, Carol Angell, Leif Fearn, Martha Bullitt Nastich, and Pam Ross. They have helped tremendously by providing mentoring, modeling, integrity, and honesty. Special thanks to Dana Grisham, my "academic mother," for everything—support, friendship, and advice. I appreciate the honesty and generosity of the future teachers (many of whom now have their own classrooms!) who participated in this study, especially the seven interviewees, who candidly shared their past experiences, current beliefs, and hopes for the future. I am also thankful for the support of my peers, the Critical Reading and Preparation group, as well as my two muses, Erika Daniels and Jennifer Hamby, who walked alongside me during many parts of this journey. And I received enormous help from the patient, knowledgeable people at Peter Lang—thank you. I am grateful for my family, who continued to care about and encourage me through (despite?) all my changes. This book is dedicated with love and great admiration to Katherine Elizabeth (the past) and Megan Elizabeth (the future). To everyone: thank you for helping me on my journey. "By walking one makes the road, and upon glancing behind one sees the path that will never be trod again" (Machado). And for all of us, the journey continues....Let us make every step meaningful.

CHAPTER 1
Introduction

1992: Wednesday night at a middle school campus in east San Diego County.

After fifteen months, we had finally reached the last ten-week cycle. Jim, Joe, John? I can't remember his name. But I can sure remember what he looked like—thick, straight salt-and-pepper hair framing a pasty, never-sees-the-sun face. I'll call him Ron. His wife, Sarah or something like that, always sat right next to him. I didn't think they should be together in the group because they habitually monopolized discussions with petty bickering, which seemed to be their way of communicating.

It was unusual to have a married couple in the program, but their daughter had been molested by their teenage son—so neither parent was an offender. Depending on the situation, perpetrators of child sexual abuse and non-offending spouses (like Ron and Sarah) were usually forced to complete this intense, county-sponsored program as part of their criminal punishment or family reunification plan. Adults molested as children (AMACs) attended voluntarily for various reasons. In my case, it was time to learn more about child sexual abuse in order to come to terms with the shame, pain, and fear I was dragging around.

Each Wednesday night session started with a meeting of the entire chapter in the junior high auditorium. Sitting on a cold, metal, fold-out seat surveying the crowd, I was always amazed at the diversity of the people—there's no such thing as a stereotypical child molester. When the opening announcements were over, counselors would lecture about how to break the cycle of sexual abuse and occasionally guest speakers would tell their gut-wrenching histories. Someone else's story always seems worse than your own.

Then we left the auditorium and met in a classroom—always two counselors and about ten to twelve members. We never learned much about the counselors' outside lives, but we knew they were volunteering their time. Stan was my favorite. Gruff but compassionate, he demanded that we face the truth, that we recognize the difference between reality and illusion, and that we stretch ourselves to do the impossible: change our ways of thinking about ourselves and others.

Our motley cohort had been together off and on since the beginning—men and women were separated during some cycles—and we knew each other's stories and personalities. Ron and Sarah seemed to derive a certain amount of self-satisfied pleasure from being "normal" parents among the rest of us who were deviant, misguided, and/or wounded. I was never a spill-your-guts type of speaker and I carefully maintained my composure throughout the program. My peer group and counselor evaluations at the end of each cycle typically reflected my extreme self-control and lack of confidence, with comments like "trust yourself," "you need to show your anger," and "don't laugh and smile when you're talking about something painful." However, I graduated to the next cycle every time.

Even though I was thirty years old, I still viewed myself as a girl rather than a woman, and I was extremely afraid of voicing my opinions. I had never raised my hand to ask or to answer a question or to voluntarily contribute to a conversation in my entire life, so when I was required to speak in our groups, my comments were as brief and restrained as possible. Despite my apprehensiveness during this time period, I embarked on a bold adventure in my real life—quitting my job as a legal assistant and enrolling full time at the community college. I wasn't sure where I would end up; but I had never attended college, although it had always been a dream.

Slowly gaining confidence, I began to see myself as a woman with worthwhile ideas, and more importantly, a positive role model for my five-year-old daughter. What seemed impossible just one year earlier became part of my everyday life. It would take a few years to graduate from community college, but I was only one week away from my first and most important milestone—completion of the sexual abuse program.

As we sat in a circle during our final group session, Ron complained that his daughter was not progressing quickly enough. Since their son had been removed from the home after molesting their daughter, Ron and Sarah desperately wanted everyone to cooperate and "get better" in order to reunite the family and resume a "normal" life. Ron was irritated that his daughter wasn't getting over the abuse and he even suggested that she had contributed to her own victimization.

It was near the end of the evening but we all listened intently as he explained his daughter's failure to progress and how hurtful it was to his son.

"What's the big deal?" he shouted. Ron's face was bright red.

I get scared when people yell.

"What the Hell is wrong with her?" Sarah sat quietly next to him.

"You," I thought. My face felt red and hot and tingly.

"Goddammit! She's making it hard for everyone!"

"You don't know how she feels!"

That was my voice.

I was a pressure cooker and the top had just blown off. I was sobbing and I was genuinely frightened. I honestly believed Ron might get up and hit me. But I needed to tell him how his daughter felt. He needed to hear how alone and horrible and filthy and awful it feels to be sexually violated and then violated again by the people you trust who are supposed to love you and take care of you but they don't believe you or don't understand you or they make you feel dirty. Ron started yelling back at me and the entire group, but Stan ordered him to listen. I don't know whether or not Ron actually listened, but I continued to tell him how your whole life changes and you can't trust anyone and there's no safety anywhere and you don't want anyone to touch you—not even in a nice or loving way.

When it was time for the session to be over, Stan provided some brief closing comments. Afterward, a few group members consoled me or thanked me for speaking out, but I was still crying and truly afraid that Ron would hurt me. Over the next week, I kept replaying the incident in my mind. I couldn't believe I actually stood up to him. I also worried about completing the program. Would I be "held back" because of my outburst?

The following Wednesday night, Sarah graduated with us; but for once, Ron wasn't standing next to her. He was "retained" to repeat the cycle. Did he learn anything? I sure hope so—for his children's sake. I think everyone felt a sense of accomplishment as we stood in front of all the members in the program to receive our certificates of completion. After that, the counselors handed back our written evaluations. On my paper, Stan had only written two words: "gutsy lady."

This event was a turning point and a rebirth for me. Since then, I have earned degrees in English and education, but my "certificate of completion" from the child sexual abuse program is still my most significant achievement. You may be wondering why a book about critical literacy begins with a story about a painful personal experience. I decided to share this information because it is crucial to my eventual discovery of critical literacy. Consider a recent conversation with my friend "Donna," whom I've known for twenty years:

"What's your book about?" asked Donna.

"Well, basically it's about questioning the status quo," I said. "It's also about social action. Trying to save the world and all that."

"Isn't that a personality thing? You think it can be learned?" she asked.

"Yeah, I think it can be learned because I've been on both sides."

"Really? I thought you'd always been a determined person," she said, acting surprised.

"Yeah. Determined but ignorant."

"What made you change?" Donna asked.

The answer popped into my head immediately, but I was trying to think of a way to frame my response. Sexual abuse as a child and a young adult. But more than that. Having absolutely no opinion about anything growing up, and then having a child—wanting to be stronger and smarter—wanting my daughter to think for herself and have confidence. At that point, I knew on some level I would have to make radical changes. But it would be a while before I was ready.

So my response to Donna was, "I decided to change after several major events: my mom died when I was six months pregnant with Megan, and as much as I adored my mom, I had a sense of freedom to become a 'real' adult. Of course, my perspective on life seemed discombobulated after Megan was born; I went from being certain about my viewpoints to aware of my ignorance and more interested in the world beyond my immediate existence. And strange as it seems, the sexual abuse program forced me rethink my black and white approach to life; in this case, about good and evil. I interacted with sexual perpetrators who had committed crimes, but who were also real people with feelings and good qualities."

I went on to tell Donna that my new awareness was a turning point because I finally recognized my lack of understanding about the world and my need to pursue an education. I was thirty years old—an age at which many people have completed their formal education or do not plan to attend college for various reasons.

I include personal information in this book to illustrate my transformation because critical literacy—the topic of this book—is a way of life, a way of thinking, not simply a teaching method. I have assumed a variety of roles in adulthood—mother, full-time homemaker, secretary, legal assistant, full-time college student, tutor, and teacher. Through the process of reaching my goal of full-time college English professor, the path I forged eventually led to critical literacy, which imbues all aspects of my life.

Critical literacy can be grossly simplified as questioning the status quo[1] and transforming oneself and/or one's world. However, there are a variety of definitions of critical literacy, and Shannon (1995) offered a concise, understandable explanation,

> Critical perspectives push the definition of literacy beyond traditional decoding or encoding of words in order to reproduce the meaning of text or society until it becomes a means for understanding one's own history and culture, to recognize connections between one's life and the social structure, to believe that change in one's life, and the lives of others and society are possible as well as desirable, and to act on this new knowledge in order to foster equal and just participation in all the decisions that affect and control our lives. (p. 83)

Critical literacy transcends conventional notions of reading and writing to incorporate critical thinking, questioning, and transformation of self and/or one's world. At the core of critical literacy is a focus on power—who has it? Who does not? How is power being used in hidden or invisible ways? Most importantly, am I contributing to inequity due to my ignorance?

It is important to point out that critical literacy is not appropriate for everyone because it involves a particular mind-set. Likewise, it cannot be considered a packaged method for parenting or teaching in which we select certain components because they feel comfortable. I cannot stress enough that critical literacy is a way of life and a way of thinking. More importantly, it is a way of questioning that can be uncomfortable. If we genuinely believe in critical literacy, we must be prepared to hear questions we might not like; questions that force us to think differently, to listen and hear other voices and opinions, including those of children. We must be willing to see the world in new ways and to honestly ask ourselves sometimes painful questions.

Such an approach can be risky and unpopular for a variety of reasons, especially in educational settings. However, I believe the alter-

---

[1] "Status quo" means the existing condition or state of affairs. To maintain the status quo means to keep things the way they are.

native is more unsettling—overly obedient children who are taught to believe everything they are told, everything they read, and not to question the voice of authority, are prone to grow up and become lemming-like adherents to the status quo.

Heins (2001) argued that efforts to shelter children from reality and protect their innocence are ultimately counterproductive:

> Intellectual protectionism frustrates rather than enhances young people's mental agility and capacity to deal with the world. It inhibits straightforward discussion about sex. Indeed, like TV violence, censorship may also have 'modeling effects,' teaching authoritarianism, intolerance for unpopular opinions, erotophobia, and sexual guilt. Censorship is an avoidance technique that addresses adult anxieties and satisfies symbolic concerns, but ultimately does nothing to resolve social problems or affirmatively help adolescents and children cope with their environments and impulses or navigate the dense and insistent media barrage that surrounds them. (p. 257)

As discussed later, genuine inquiry is crucial for a truly democratic society, and self-reflection is an essential habit toward becoming a thoughtful individual committed to personal growth as well as social justice. Self-reflection cannot be something we practice only when asked to submit a self-evaluation, nor should it occur when we happen to think about it. As thinking individuals and citizens, not to mention our roles as teachers and/or parents, it is imperative that we develop a habit of genuine reflection in order to understand ourselves and others, as well as to recognize ways in which we need to change.

Self-Reflection: Necessary and Ongoing #1

A student I'll call Gabriel once told me I care too much. He said this in front of the entire class when I was trying to figure out how we could modify group work to encourage more constructive feedback. This was a young man who submitted an essay with a photo of a mutilated man he took while serving as a soldier in Iraq. The essay was about death. And life. He explained that it was about why people kill (the assignment was a definition essay). Somehow he modified the assignment (others wrote about the usual stuff, such as "What is a hero?"). He was a very deep thinker—at least through his written responses—which is not always the case in freshman English. He told me after class one day that he loved Russian literature and asked me to recommend some titles to expand his reading experiences. A dream come true for an English teacher! I loaned him Steinbeck,

Chekhov, Kafka, and some others. This young man was craving to learn, craving to expand himself intellectually, and craving to discuss important issues with someone who was genuinely interested.

Was Gabriel's desire natural for him or was it a result of experiences—witnessing life, death, and everything in between—in Iraq? Regardless, he demonstrated an insatiable hunger for finding out "truth," whatever that might be at this point in his life.

Returning to the comment that I "care too much," I think Gabriel intended to point out that I shouldn't bother modifying anything just to please the students, or perhaps that I was babying them. I probably should have asked him for clarification, but I believe he did not want to waste time with issues related to classroom structure. He wanted to proceed with the content of the course because it was working *for him*. And maybe I "care too much" because I want the course to work for *everyone*.

Self-Reflection: Necessary and Ongoing #2

Every once in a while as I am teaching one of my college classes—perhaps once or twice per semester—I am momentarily paralyzed. I don't think the students notice it, but it strikes me quite hard. *This is me* introducing controversial topics, asking students to stretch themselves and think about the other side of an argument. *This is me* answering questions, creating assignments, and striving to find ways to help students learn. *This is me* standing in front of the class talking with a certain amount of authority about how to create an effective argument. What's the point about *this is me*? I'm surprised that I'm here with a classroom of students in the role of a teacher. I'm stunned that I actually have something valuable to share with others.

I'd like to clarify the word "authority" as used in the previous paragraph. It's not really authority. It may seem that way at first— teachers have power—but it's truly a sense of being with the students and discovering as I go. Throughout the process, I continually ask myself, "How can I be a better teacher?" I challenge myself to find out what the students need, to push them to be their very best, to discover their strengths, their interests, and perhaps their latent skills— maybe rediscovering the skills, confidence or enthusiasm that has disappeared through years of schooling and/or in the name of conformity.

Returning to my student Gabriel, clearly he is not stifled by a need to conform or a lack of self-confidence. More importantly, he is actively engaged in a process of learning about himself and the world through questioning and reflection. When I was in my early twenties like Gabriel, I approached life in a completely different manner—the word that seems to describe my state is "passive." I floated through life without considering my own opinions, my own value, my own abilities to act instead of being passive. I was eager to please others, afraid people wouldn't like me, dismissive of my own thoughts, and certain of the unfulfilling path my life would follow.

The Purpose of This Book

This book is as much about me as it is about people of all types, including students, teachers, and parents. This book reveals how sometimes the "expected" or "normal" path is not the best way to go, especially when thinking in terms of traditional schooling. Most importantly, it strives to demonstrate the various ways that adopting a stance of critical literacy can infuse hope and possibility in all aspects of our lives.

I provide a comprehensive discussion of critical literacy, highlighting its importance, especially with the current focus in education on standards. Also, I incorporate the work of other scholars, as well as my research with future elementary school teachers, to explain the ways in which the educational system perpetuates the status quo. I encourage readers to keep in mind my intention to reveal an overall trend, and I believe there are some fantastic educational environments in the United States. Likewise, I recognize that parents have their children's best interests in mind when they make decisions, and this book is not intended to be a parenting guide. Rather, my hope is that readers will view my work as another possibility, a way of perceiving children and their worlds differently, especially with the current saturation of sometimes conflicting messages from media and other sources.

Although I present criticism and drawbacks to critical literacy, I am clearly an advocate of this theory and practice. As you navigate through this text, I suspect that some concepts (especially theory) may not make sense, but do not give up. Reflect on your own beliefs as you read; I have attempted to set up this book in a manner that invites dialogue. Think about how the information presented fits into your own life and work. And ask questions!

As mentioned earlier, my personal story is interwoven because I have experienced the power of critical literacy. Briefly, I entered adulthood with the goal of being a stay-at-home mother, completely ignorant of my closed-mindedness. I stepped into my first college classroom at the age of 30, and I recently received my doctorate in education. My learning process was transformative in many ways, especially in terms of how I began to view the educational system. I experienced parallel growth as a parent, since my daughter was five years old when I began college. Hence, I personalize the theoretical concepts by using my own experiences as examples, which include my development as a student and as an instructor at the university. The core of my research focuses on students I worked with, who were future elementary school teachers. As an educator, I try to practice and model critical literacy with students by serving as a guide, encouraging learners to question themselves and their worlds.

Overview of the Research

For the most part, contemporary educational environments, as well as popular opinion, do not generally encourage or tolerate overt questioning and criticism. Moreover, because the majority of teachers in the U.S. are white, middle-class, female, and heterosexual, there is a need to provide students entering the field of education with opportunities to examine their own beliefs and to gradually "see" other perspectives. Considering the propensity of educational institutions to perpetuate the status quo, we need to better understand how future teachers respond to and interpret children's literature. Specifically, whether they are potential practitioners of critical literacy or essentially unreflective readers, suggesting a predilection toward preserving existing dominant ideologies.

Therefore, I studied future elementary school teachers' written responses to children's literature (as well as individual interviews) in order to describe their current thinking about literature. The university is large, with a diverse student population, but the participants were mainly white, middle-class females, reflecting the general population of elementary school teachers nationwide. I used the following research questions: How do future teachers read and interpret children's literature? As evidenced in their writing, to what degree do future teachers recognize stereotypes and underlying images in children's literature? Do they think about children's literature in a critical way that might lead to self-reflection? To what degree do future teachers adopt a stance of critical literacy?

The results of the study suggested that these future teachers believed critical literacy was important—immediately after learning about it in class. However, the majority of participants' responses before and after in-class discussions and writings about critical literacy did not exhibit evidence of a questioning stance. Rather, participants tended to draw on two overlapping cultural models of a "healthy" family and "good" education, which are rooted in middle-class images of "normal." However, rather than push or try to shock future teachers into thinking about other possibilities, it is best to help them change gradually. There are many effective ways to do this—some methods involve service learning—other techniques engage students in materials and topics that aren't too close to home or personal, such as the examination of fairy tales and advertisements as a way of beginning a conversation about messages we receive but do not necessarily evaluate.

Self-Reflection and Curiosity Lead to Research

I would say that I have been engaged in research since I began teaching classes at the college level—mainly informal investigations involving the students, the curriculum, and my own teaching—with the purpose of discovering ways to improve. However, I have conducted some formal research and the most recent involved a writing class with future elementary school teachers that focused on children's literature. Previously I had collected anecdotal evidence (through written work as well as classroom discussions) that students generally read and responded to literature on a relatively superficial level, rather than thinking critically and making connections to their own lives and their future classroom environments.

In my teaching position, I have the opportunity to learn about students' previous experiences with and current reactions to children's literature, including fairy tales. Many are "surprised" and "shocked" when they read earlier versions of fairy tales for the first time, often commenting on the graphic descriptions of violence and sexuality. Most people in American culture are more familiar with the Disney versions of fairy tales such as "Sleeping Beauty," "Snow White,"

"Cinderella," and "Beauty and the Beast," and do not realize that popular fairy tales have evolved through many variations, due to factors such as cultural transmission, authorial intention, and sometimes mistranslation. It is interesting to trace the transformation of stories as they change, because various renditions reveal much about the cultural norms of the time and place in which they were written.

For example, Perrault's version, "The Sleeping Beauty in the Wood" (1697), contained the stock characters typically found in fairy tales—a passive young beauty, a dashing prince, and an evil middle-aged woman (in this case the prince's mother), as well as the motif of cannibalism; but the sexual elements are more subtle than Basile's earlier rendition.[2] More than a century later, Jacob and Wilhelm Grimm presented a shorter version of "Sleeping Beauty," "Briar Rose," in the second edition of their *Children's and Household Tales* (1819), a collection of stories that was clearly intended for a child audience (Tatar, 1998). Additionally, according to Nodelman (1996), "in the process of adding to and deleting from the tales they heard, the Grimms gave preference to events and characterizations that suited their own middle-class, Christian values" (p. 249). Likewise, Tatar (1998) reported that "when it came to passages colored by sexual details or to plots based on Oedipal conflicts, Wilhelm Grimm exhibited extraordinary editorial zeal" (p. 369). Consequently, they edited the stories considerably, most notably excising or sanitizing any sexual references, in order to make the tales more acceptable (and marketable) to middle-class readers, who undoubtedly disapproved of children being exposed to such topics.

Similar to the Grimms, Disney modifies fairy tales to satisfy the demands of its perceived audience, usually updating the story somewhat, but paying careful attention to mainstream, middle-class expectations and sensibilities.[3] Giroux (1997) pointed out the ways in which contemporary Disney movies continue to present racial and gender stereotypes. For example, Ariel, the heroine of *The Little Mermaid*, might be perceived as independent and headstrong due to her rebellious behavior. Nevertheless, her ultimate goal is to become the wife

---

[2] In Basile's version (1634), a (married) king rapes the young sleeping beauty and returns nine months later to discover she has given birth to a boy and a girl.

[3] According to Zipes (1999), "In all forms and shapes, the classical fairy tales continue to be moneymakers and thrive on basic sexist messages and conservative notions of social behavior" (p. 26).

of a handsome prince—even at the cost of losing her voice. "Woman-hood offers Ariel the reward of marrying the right man and renouncing her former life under the sea—a telling cultural model for the nature of female choice and decision-making in Disney's worldview" (Giroux, 1997, p. 59). Likewise, Disney's version of "Sleeping Beauty" perpetuates images of female passivity, depicting the heroine lying on her back until she is rescued and chosen as a wife. Like Snow White, she is comatose when the prince approaches. Hourihan (1997) observed that "refusal is not an option for the bride. She is chosen, and to be chosen is all that she can ask" (p. 198). Girls continue to grow up waiting for a knight in shining Armani who will complete their personal fairy tale, which includes visions of lavish storybook weddings in which they can be princess for a day.

When I ask students to reflect more carefully and generate four- to five-page formal essays in response to fairy tales, many choose to focus on the pleasurable aspects in a fairly non-critical manner. For instance, one student fondly recalled her own experiences dressing up and feeling like a princess. She wrote:

> Young girls that maybe aren't very attractive, popular, and are unhappy can look at Cinderella or Snow White and hold out hope that maybe one day their lives too will change and *their prince will come*. It might not always sound like the most realistic scenario, but if we don't have dreams...what are we living for, right?" [ellipses in original; italics added]

"Some day my prince will come," lyrics from Disney's *Snow White*, contribute to what Holland (personal communication, January 26, 2004) calls the cultural model of romance, which entails a simplified conception of cross-gender relationships (Holland, 1992). Such models, which are internalized through social reproduction, serve as guides toward expected and appropriate behavior, and they tend to be taken for granted as the norm or status quo—"this is the way we do it in our culture."

By contrast, a few students exhibit a critical, questioning stance. For example, another young woman concluded her essay:

> What a girl wants should be respect for herself and a strong foundation of who she is. Fairy tales show common misconceptions of gender roles and stereotypes. They lead girls to believe that men can and will control their lives, and that the pretty girls always get the prince. Where is the fairy tale that emphasizes, once upon a time there lived a woman who stuck up for what she believed in and did not settle for cheap tricks? Women and girls

today need realistic gender roles, roles that show how beautiful and strong
every girl can be.

This student (Penny), as will be discussed in future chapters, had personal experiences that seemed to influence her to adopt a critical stance when reading and making meaning of fairy tales as an adult. During a private conversation, she discussed her relatively sheltered upbringing and subsequent move toward self-education once she became aware of her ignorance. I understood the sense of urgency she felt—a desire to make up for lost time—and the tangible need to share her newfound knowledge with others.

Self-Reflection: Necessary and Ongoing #3

As a nontraditional college student, perhaps I arrived in the classroom with a more "mature" perspective than many of my younger peers. However, I clung to my passive stance, but I found myself deeply disturbed and sad. Why was I sad when I was embarking on the dream of a lifetime? I thought about it a lot and finally realized that I was losing my innocence. Or ignorance. Perhaps both. My old life was dying and a new, uncomfortable perspective was replacing it. I was becoming a "scholar" and recognizing my lack of knowledge, my inability to think critically, and my overall naiveté. I began to understand the meaning behind the adage, "ignorance is bliss."

For example, during my first semester in American history, students were required to write a book report, choosing from one of the texts on a reading list. I chose Dee Brown's *Bury My Heart at Wounded Knee*. I approached the book with a certain amount of prior knowledge (in my case, unquestioned assumptions)—the Indians in history were savages who viciously attacked white settlers and present-day Indians lived on reservations, not doing much of anything except receiving handouts from the government (this was before the Indian casino boom). As I reflect on these beliefs now, I realize that my ideas were formed through visual media (television and movies) and my home environment, which included outdoor games such as Cowboys and Indians. Everyone wanted to be a cowboy; nobody wanted to be an Indian.

From the beginning, *Bury My Heart at Wounded Knee* was truly heartbreaking for me. I read about massacre after massacre of Indians by whites with shame, disbelief, and genuine sorrow. Why didn't I know about this? Was I absent when this was discussed in elementary, middle, or high school? Did we have to wait until college to find out the truth?

It didn't occur to me to question Brown's book, because at the time I believed everything I read. But it did prompt me to find out more on my own, leading me to a rudimentary practice of evaluating different sources of information. Gradually, however, I began to question myself and my world. Knowledge is painful. Ignorance is comfortable and safe. The desire to find "truth" is a personal decision we make—at least when we are old enough to make such decisions. Young readers are rarely in a position to make decisions because adults typically choose the material they read or view.

Books Are Dangerous

"My Mommy and Daddy got a divorce last year." So begins the children's picture book *Daddy's Roommate* (Willhoite, 1990). The young narrator continues by explaining that his father now has a "roommate": the two men "live together, work together, eat together, sleep together, shave together and sometimes even fight together, but they always make up" (pp. 7-13). The boy's mother explains that the men are gay, and the narrator tells his readers that "being gay is just one more kind of love." I would argue that *Daddy's Roommate* is overly didactic in its effort to present gay families in an understated manner and lacks literary qualities that would engage young readers. However, Willhoite's expressed intention was "to provide a simple, fun book for a previously ignored audience: the children of gay parents" (Willhoite, 1990, Afterword).

Controversy surrounds *Daddy's Roommate*, which is consistently cited as one of the most frequently challenged books (see ALA[4] or the Freedom Forum) by critics who claim it promotes homosexuality. Some scholars provide a counterargument, explaining that "multicultural" literature presents a variety of perspectives regarding race, class, and gender, but fails to include sexual orientation. Hermann-

---

[4] Other frequently challenged books include Maurice Sendak's *In the Night Kitchen* for "nudity and offensive language," Maya Angelou's *I Know Why the Caged Bird Sings* for "racism, homosexuality, sexual content, offensive language, and unsuited to age group," and Dav Pilkey's Captain Underpants series for "offensive language and modeling bad behavior" (www.ala.org). Also, the popular Harry Potter books are often challenged for anti-Christian content, including the promotion of learning witchcraft.

Wilmarth (2003) discussed the silence around the issue of sexual orientation, claiming homophobia among preservice teachers. Additionally, Carl Tomlinson (1995) asked, "should we wait until young people are in high school and already have firmly ingrained attitudes to teach them the truth?" (p. 45). He pointed out that "there are those who persist in their efforts to provide an illusory 'protected' childhood for young people by trying to censor, ban, or rewrite anything controversial in children's books" (Tomlinson, 1995, p. 47). Judy Blume (1999), one of the most frequently challenged authors, extended the argument:

> What I worry about most is the loss to young people. If no one speaks out for them, if they don't speak out for themselves, all they'll get for required reading will be the most bland books available. And instead of finding the information they need at the library, instead of finding the novels that illuminate life, they will find only those materials to which nobody could possibly object. (p.66)

In "The Students' Right to Read," the National Council of Teachers of English (NCTE, 2001) affirmed that "Some books have been attacked merely for being 'controversial,' suggesting that for some people the purpose of education is not the investigation of ideas but rather the indoctrination of certain set beliefs and standards" (p. 1). Consequently, when censorship occurs, students' learning environments do not promote free inquiry, and they are not provided with an accurate, realistic understanding of their culture.

Nonetheless, one of the most valuable qualities of literature is that readers can benefit when they identify with characters (Rosenblatt, 1995). For instance, Katherine Paterson's *Bridge to Terabithia* (1977) provides a realistic account of the grieving process, which could help children to understand and learn to deal with death. Yet, like *Daddy's Roommate*, *Bridge to Terabithia* has been the target of censorship efforts, ostensibly due to inappropriate language and promotion of New Age religion. Paterson (1997) believed that "what might be behind a lot of these attacks is a fear of death, or perhaps a fear of talking about death to children" (p. 5). She explained,

> Often the people who want to censor my books argue that all the characters in a children's book should be exemplary or else children will copy the bad behavior of the characters and will be lead [sic] astray. I disagree. I think that children recognize what stories are about. When they read a story, they don't feel compelled to run out and do whatever the character does in the book" (1997, p. 7).

Some would disagree with Paterson, citing recent incidents of school violence as evidence to support their assumptions that children are undeniably influenced by events in books or other media. Responding to this line of logic, Frank Zappa commented at a Congressional hearing (9/19/85) on explicit lyrics: "I wrote a song about dental floss but did anyone's teeth get cleaner?" Zappa's facetious remark may have mocked the seriousness of the hearing, but he made an important point, insinuating that audiences are intelligent enough to make decisions about whether or not to act upon messages in texts. According to Reichman (1988), "would-be censors share one belief: that they can recognize 'evil'; and that other people should be protected from it" (p. 11).

Referring back to *Daddy's Roommate*, some individuals and organizations (such as PABBIS: Parents Against Bad Books in Schools) advocate banning the book because they believe it encourages homosexuality, whereas others praise the book's straightforward depiction of a gay family, claiming that readers will become more open minded.[5] Who is right? Perhaps we should ask and truly listen to what the intended audience—young children—think about *Daddy's Roommate*, which is precisely the goal of critical literacy. Perhaps we should keep in mind a chilling passage in Ray Bradbury's *Fahreinheit 451*: "You don't have to burn books to destroy a culture. Just get people to stop reading them."

---

[5] Two examples from reviewers of *Daddy's Roommate* on Amazon.com: "A good motto to go by: God made Adam and Eve, not Adam and Steve; let's let it stay that way, by encouraging our kids to stick to the morals of the Bible!" and "Informing our children that there are millions of people who are gay and that they are not bad people (unlike what many hypocritical religious freaks would say), is not promoting it. Being a heterosexual is not an excuse for being ignorant."

◆◆ CHAPTER 2
Theory and Research

We are often tempted to dismiss theory and research as unnecessary because we do not have the time or inclination. "Give me the methods and practical stuff that I can actually use. Besides, all that theory and research is way over my head." It's true that such texts are often difficult to understand, and the main reason is because there is a particular language used in theoretical discussions and research studies. We can compare it to the specialized language of other fields such as computer science, anthropology, or any other area of study that involves a vocabulary with specific definitions for terms. For instance, most of us know that a "cookie" is something good to eat. However, in the world of computers, "cookies" have a different meaning; they are messages sent by web servers. (Even the word "web" has a specific meaning.) Making a complex text understandable does not mean we are "dumbing down" the theory or research. We are simply translating it, using concepts that are familiar to help make associations.

On a side note, when we encounter difficult texts, we can relate our experience to students (of all ages) who do not have the background experience or skills to decipher what we may perceive as simple. My point is that lessons in reflecting on our unquestioned assumptions are *everywhere*.

Theory

What is theory and why should we care about it? Just as fields of study have specialized languages, they also draw on particular theories. However, there are theories that tend to cross disciplines, such as Feminist Theory, which is often used in humanities-based studies. There are various offshoots, but the major concern is the role of women. For example, a classical music scholar might investigate whether there were gifted women organists during Bach's lifetime. A literature professor might analyze Shel Silverstein's book *The Giving Tree* and argue that the tree is female, and the male character ungratefully uses her to the point of total destruction.

There are various definitions of theory: (1) a mental scheme of something to be done, or a way of doing something; a systematic statement of rules or principles to be followed; (2) the knowledge or exposition of the general principles or methods of an art or science, especially as distinguished from the practice of it; (3) a system of ideas or statements explaining something; and (4) the formulation of abstract knowledge or speculative thought; systematic conception of something (Brown, 1993, p. 3274).

Such dictionary definitions may not be completely understandable, so we can look for some common factors, which I would translate as basically: a way of making sense of things. We do this in real life all the time; after experiencing particular events, we come up with a theory to explain or make sense of the situation. If a student arrives late to class every day, we might theorize that her parents are irresponsible. Of course, we are making inferences—making connections that may or may not be accurate; there are a variety of other possible explanations for the student's tardiness. Some theories are more accurate or useful than others, and we look for valid evidence to support theories.

Why care about theory? Because it gives us a conceptual framework and a way to organize our thinking. It also provides a common vocabulary, can help unify phenomena that may not seem related, and often leads to new discoveries.

Research

True research involves curiosity; we have a question and we want to find out more. We do this all the time in our real lives. For example, if we are looking for the perfect cheesecake recipe, we will probably access the Internet and search until we are satisfied with our discovery. This is a form of research, although in scholarly settings, we are expected to meet specific standards and use systematic methods.

Definitions of research are straightforward: (1) the action or instance of searching carefully for a specified thing or person; (2) a search or investigation undertaken to discover facts and reach new conclusions by the critical study of a subject or by a course of scientific inquiry; and (3) systematic investigation into and study of materials, sources, etc., to establish facts, collate information, etc. (Brown, 1993, p. 2558). The key terms here are "searching carefully" and "discover facts and reach new conclusions."

Research is important because we are creating something new. Through the process of examining information related to our topic, reading about prior research, and then conducting our own studies, we synthesize what is already known with new information. Subsequently, it is our responsibility to share our discoveries with others who are interested in our field of study. Our research often leads to new questions, which can be frustrating, but also interesting and exciting.

The sections below discuss theories and research related to my interests in critical literacy. As mentioned earlier, some of the concepts might be unfamiliar and complicated. Once you have a general sense of the material, you might go back and reread for better understanding.

Critical Literacy

The notion of "critical" when applied to theory can be traced to the Frankfurt School (Kincheloe & McLaren, 2000), a group of scholars who included Theodor Adorno, Walter Benjamin, Jurgen Habermas, Max Horkheimer, and Herbert Marcuse, founders of the Institute for Social Research in Frankfurt, Germany, in the mid-1920s (Arato & Gebhardt, 1978). Drawing on Kant's critical philosophy and Marx's critique of ideology, the Frankfurt School sought to uncover and explain fundamental inequalities and hypocrisy within society. They utilized two techniques: (1) immanent critique, which involves questioning a view from within, exposing contradictions between our claims (what we say we do; image or concept) as individuals or a society, and our conditions (the "truth" of how we live; reality or object)—exposing the discontinuity between the ideal and the real; and (2) dialectical thought, which "attempted to trace out the historical formation of facts and their mediation by social forces" (Siegel & Fernandez, 2000, p. 145). Kincheloe and McLaren (2000) emphasized the nebulous quality of critical theory, explaining that there are many critical theories, they are always changing and evolving, and they purposely avoid too much specificity.

Also influenced by Marxist theory, Paulo Freire (1921-1997) called for radical pedagogical change, advocating for a sweeping transformation in ways of thinking rather than specific teaching strategies or techniques.[6] Freire was born into a middle-class family in Brazil, but he experienced poverty and hunger during the Great Depression. He studied law, but became interested in education as a young man, soon helping poor adults to become literate. However, at that time, adults could only vote if they were functionally literate, and Freire was exiled from Brazil in 1964 due to his "subversive" teaching.

In the seminal *Pedagogy of the Oppressed* (1970/2000), Freire explained that exploited people do not necessarily recognize their own oppression. He wrote, "as long as the oppressed remain unaware of the causes of their condition, they fatalistically 'accept' their exploitation" (p. 64). Additionally, the oppressed "prefer the security of conformity with their state of unfreedom to the creative communion produced by freedom and even the very pursuit of freedom" (p. 48). It is important to note that critical theory "refuses the propaganda model's assumption that people are passive, easily manipulated victims. Researchers operating with an awareness of this hegemonic[7] ideology understand that dominant ideological practices and discourses shape our vision of reality" (Kincheloe & McLaren, 2000, p. 283).

The solution, according to Freire, was a liberating education implemented by the oppressed in which the roles of teacher and student are redefined—teachers learn and learners teach. Contrary to conventional models, students' ideas and experiences would be respected as valuable knowledge. Instead of treating students as passive receptacles of information,[8] teachers would encourage students to question their worlds, focusing on the use of authentic dialogue, in which educators speak *with* not *for* the students.

Freire advocated for a praxis (informed, committed action) entailing "reflection and action upon the world in order to transform it" (p.

---

[6] Because we tend to associate the word "radical" with images of rebellious extremists, it is worthwhile to consider a key definition, which is "of or from the root or roots; going to the foundation or source of something; fundamental; basic."

[7] Hegemony in this context specifically refers to Gramsci's theory that cultural institutions effectively "win people's consent to domination."

[8] Freire used the term "banking," in which the educator made deposits in the student. He abhorred such practices, explaining that "The more students work at storing the deposits entrusted to them, the less they develop the critical consciousness which would result from their intervention in the world as transformers of that world" (1970/2000, p. 73).

51). Additionally, Freire emphasized the need for hope—an optimistic attitude rooted in a sense of possibility that would stimulate and support work toward improvement and transformation.

It is extremely important to recognize that Freire's theories should be viewed in terms of a philosophy rather than a set of methods or techniques; he believed that these ideas would need to be "reinvented" for each person's or group's particular context (Graff, 2000; Macedo & Freire, 2001). "Unfortunately, in the United States," wrote Donaldo Macedo, "many educators who claim to be Freirean in their pedagogical orientation mistakenly transform Freire's notion of diaglogue into a method" (Macedo, 2000, p. 17). The term "critical literacy" is becoming more prevalent in educational environments, but a watered-down or packaged version with a prescribed set of activities is not true critical literacy. Of course, these texts may offer useful methods, but by their very nature, they are uncontextualized. In other words, the activities should emerge from the needs of the students, the particular situations and settings, the educational goals, and the possibilities inherent in the educational context.

Current theorists sometimes clarify critical literacy on a continuum in terms of other literacy movements. For instance Cadiero-Kaplan (2002) explained that functional literacy refers to the basic ability to read and write well enough to understand signs, ads, and newspaper headlines, to make shopping lists, to write checks, and to fill out job applications. Cultural literacy denotes knowledge of the canon or "great books," with emphasis on the teaching of morals and values, without regard for individual and community experiences. Progressive literacy, a liberal ideology focused on the student, "fails to examine questions of cultural and political context. Such practices, while designed to empower, are not transformative because they ignore students' cultural capital" (p. 376-377). Similarly, Luke and Freebody (1997) pointed out that "traditional, skills-based, psychological, and progressivist approaches to reading have more in common with one another than might first appear and certainly than is evident from the perennial debates among their advocates" (p. 222).

Regarding empowerment, Freire would argue that it does not come *from* the educator *to* the student, or *from* the adult *to* the child. Rather, the educator or adult provides the skills that will hopefully lead to the development of a sense of agency, self-sufficiency, and confident decision-making. Donaldo Macedo, who worked closely with Freire and translated many of his writings, vehemently argued against the notion of empowerment and "giving voice," explaining that if you have the power to give someone voice, then you have the power to take it away. Voice is prepackaged as a "gift" that is being given or loaned, and the recipients are supposed to be grateful and behave (conform) because the gift can be taken away. This delimits possibilities and there is an inherent censorship. Rather, the op- pressed must "come to voice," which involves: (1) political clarity; (2) the pain that is natural with change,[9] and (3) hope. Macedo stressed that voice is not a gift; it is a democratic and human right. We—well- meaning educators—cannot give voice; instead, we must create de- mocratic structures so voice can emerge (Macedo, 2003). The risk and the pain, of course, come from the possibility that we will not like what we hear. As Macedo emphasized, true democracy is a common theme found in discussions of critical literacy, as are the concepts of social justice, possibility, and questioning.

Perhaps the most unique element of critical literacy is social action stemming from readers' increasing understanding that literacy and who gets to be literate are related to issues of equity and power. Once we become aware of injustice, it is our duty as citizens to work to- ward change. Freire believed that non-elite people needed to master the dominant language. Students needed to gain fluency in the domi- nant discourse but they should also understand the underlying ethi- cal and historical context of Standard English and academic discourse (Shor, 1999). According to Shor (1999), "By themselves, taught in a curriculum that emphasizes isolated skills and rhetorical forms, aca- demic discourse and Standard English are certainly not democratic roads to critical consciousness or oppositional politics" (p. 22).

Regarding language and texts, definitions of critical literacy usu- ally adopt an expanded definition of "text" to be anything that can be "read" or interpreted. For example, Morgan (1997) described "texts" as "whatever in our social environment can be read as a text: what- ever constructs a meaning through shared codes and conventions, signs and icons" (p. 28). This broad definition of "text" necessarily includes the inextricable aspect of social influences, binding interpre- tation of texts with making meaning of one's world. The "shared

---

[9] Macedo (2003) asserted that the dominant culture avoids the pain of change, espe- cially involving hearing the voices of the oppressed. They have the privilege to with- draw from the conversation and regulate the dialogue.

codes and conventions, signs and icons" represent discourse communities (Gee, 1996), and critical literacy typically seeks to examine the mainstream discourse—the language utilized by the dominant culture. The ability to negotiate various aspects of this discourse represents (often unexamined) power and privilege. Moreover, language is not neutral (also Fairclough, 1995; Gee, 1997; Gee, 1999; Jaworski & Coupland, 1999); rather, "linguistic forms are paramount, for they filter and organize information from the physical and cultural realms and transform it into the meanings that make up human knowledge and experiences" (Polkinghorne, 1988, p. 158).

Language is social and political. Giroux (1993) explained that critical literacy "points to pedagogical practices which offer students the knowledge, skills, and values they will need to critically negotiate and transform the world in which they find themselves. The politics of critical literacy and cultural difference engages rather than retreats from those problems that make democracy messy, vibrant, and noisy" (p. 376). "Messy, vibrant, and noisy" classrooms are perceived by many as out of control and undesirable.

Problems with Critical Literacy

As Cossett and Pipkin pointed out in *Silent No More: Voices of Courage in American Schools* (2003), teachers in the United States "are generally perceived—and often perceive themselves—as agents of the state, paid to do its bidding and transfer state-sanctioned facts and skills to their charges" (p. ix). Active implementation of critical literacy, or any "unorthodox" approach to teaching, can be dangerous—the constraints are real and they can be costly. For instance, fifth- and sixth-grade teacher Hadden (2000) explained how she was inspired by critical literacy in her master's program, describing an exercise in which "my students and I analyzed the overt curricula regulated through the Utah State Core Curriculum Guide" (p. 527). Hadden also sought to investigate the "hidden" curriculum and "null" curriculum, the latter of which she explained to be "what is deliberately made absent from overt curricula" (p. 528). She claimed to notice a positive change in the children, asserting that "once young students acquire the ability and tools to analyze, they become extremely reluctant to discard them" (p. 528). However, Hadden was essentially forced to resign due to charges of insubordination, consequently losing her home and uprooting her family.

How does one simultaneously challenge and work within the "system"? I would argue that Hadden, despite her well-intended desire to enlighten her students, could have taught critical literacy just as effectively through a more balanced approach. Returning to Freire's insistence that his theories should not be considered techniques but should be adapted to specific situations, Hadden might have enjoyed more success by using other types of texts rather than the state's policies. Clearly, it is important that readers be exposed to relevant texts, and I can understand Hadden's belief that the Core Curriculum Guide directly influenced her students, but the material should also be engaging, which may not have been the case in this instance. Likewise, the notion of investigating the hidden and null curriculum seems extraordinarily abstract, especially considering the classroom population of eleven- and twelve-year-olds. I also believe that it is common for a teacher to refer to her pupils as "my students," but I would expect an attitude of collaboration to be evident when discussing a joint endeavor, and Hadden's comment "my students and I also investigated and sought to identify the hidden curriculum in *my* classroom" (p. 527; emphasis added) seems very telling. The reference to "*my* classroom" instead of "*our* classroom" suggests a power imbalance, or at the very least, an unquestioned perception of educator as authority.

Additionally, critical literacy certainly has the component of transformation, which is very important. However, inherent in the theory is the notion that an individual's consciousness must change before he or she can effect any apparent transformation upon the world. A gradual shifting of perspective and adoption of a questioning stance does represent tremendous change—the way in which a person thinks and acts will necessarily have an influence on his or her surroundings. Therefore, it would be unwise to speed up the process by insisting on immediate, tangible results without sufficient time for reflection. Such haste and dogmatism[10] explain some of the objections to using critical literacy: that it is political, it engenders despair, and it

---

[10] By "dogmatism," I mean insistence rather than guidance, suggesting that the teacher is setting up students to arrive at particular conclusions and perspectives expected by the teacher. Students must be free to develop their own ideas. Of course, this is where risk and pain become possibilities: teachers (and other facilitators of critical literacy) may not like what we hear.

is idealistic (Alvermann, Moon, & Hagood, 1999; see also McKinnon 1997; Murrell, 1997; and Scapp, 1997).

In an effort to practice critical literacy, I struggled to look at the various objections to this theory, asking myself if I am simply idealistic and naïve, especially in light of the fact that I am not in the trenches[11] struggling with official policies like so many K-12 public school teachers. I continue to weigh my own experiences, arguments from other perspectives, and the possible alternatives. I must admit that giving up has occurred to me. But as an individual who was encouraged not to think, certainly not to question, not to trust my own instincts, and to have my "reality" denied (that is, being told *"that* didn't happen to you" when in fact *it* did happen), giving up is not acceptable. Hadden's comment resonates: "I could never go back to the uncritical, complacent elementary teacher I had been before my graduate education" (p. 532).[12] I believe that implementation of critical literacy is possible, but it is crucial for practitioners to be aware of the consequences, thereby formulating their approaches appropriately. As Alvermann, Moon and Hagood (1999) explained, "researchers who use critical theory to frame their work argue that while it may be idealistic to think it is possible to change the world, doing nothing is not an acceptable alternative" (p. 137). (Also, see Meyerson, 2001, for an excellent discussion about the various *realistic* ways people can inspire change through their work.)

Educational Environments in the United States

Just as language is not neutral, education is political, contrary to many people's, especially the general public's, assumptions (Beyer, 2001; Gee, 1997; Graff, 2000; Graff, 2001; Shannon, 1995). In many ways, educational institutions perpetuate the status quo by not adopting a truly critical perspective (Baez, 2000; Breault, 2003; Broadfoot, 2000; Cook-Sather, 2002; Garrison, 2003; and Tappan & Brown, 1996). Giroux (1993) pointed out the socializing aspects of education, asserting that teachers "produce knowledge and they provide students with a sense of place, worth, and identity. In doing so, they offer students selected representations, skills, social relations, and values that

---

[11] See "Notes from the Trenches" by Galen Leonhardy in Cossett and Pipkin (2003).

[12] See also Marriott's "Ending the Silence" (2003) for a discussion of choosing action over inaction.

presuppose particular histories and ways of being in the world. The moral and political dimension at work here is revealed in the question: Whose history, story, and experience prevails in the school setting?" (p. 372-373). Likewise, Villanueva (1997) asserted that contemporary schools encourage individual achievement rather than genuinely fostering collective accomplishments. Additionally, Graff (2001) expressed the "need to make classrooms more democratic and less hierarchical, and the need to bring political issues out of hiding and explicitly before students' view" (p. 26).[13] By neglecting to expose students to political topics in the "real world," and by avoiding opportunities for vigorous, authentic debate, educators fail to effectively teach children to question, contemplate, and make up their own minds about important issues.

However, in contrast to educational practice in the United States, teachers in Australia generally present texts to students with an emphasis on their underlying power-laden qualities, encouraging critical reading and analysis in the classroom (Comber, 2001; Johnson, 2002; Morgan, 1997; Longfellow, 2002; Luke, 2000; Wilson, 1994). Nevertheless, Luke (2000) suggested that this widespread practice may be "just a watered down version of educational progressivism" rather than true critical literacy, mainly because it has become institutionalized (p. 449). The danger of institutionalization lies in the "packaging" of a concept, neglecting to consider individual context and assuming that "one size fits all." More importantly, the transformational component is lacking, and Morgan asserted that "It would be naïve to expect that the state would endorse a pedagogy which proclaims its intention to undermine the economic status quo and the legitimacy of the present practice of government" (1997, p. 24).

Official policies mandated by various levels of government greatly determine the overall educational climate, and the current emphasis on raising student achievement, combined with drastic budget cuts, has created an atmosphere in which experimentation with new philosophies and approaches to teaching is dangerous and difficult. In addition to escalating commercialization of schools and

---

[13] As mentioned below, critical literacy tends to be more prevalent and accepted in Australia, and journals such as *Australian Journal of Language and Literacy* and *Practically Primary* regularly report on successful implementation. For example, in "Critical Moves with the Wiggles" (2002), Longfellow introduced critical literacy to very young children.

encroaching corporate power that models a message of consumerism for children (Giroux, 1999), the current educational environment focusing on reform efforts increasingly deemphasizes social justice and equity (Berlak, 2002; Necochea & Cline, 2002). Equally disturbing is the shift of focus away from crucial issues such as "overall funding for schools, racism in expectations for learning, cultural mismatches between teachers and students, [and] the reduction of curriculum to test preparation" (Sleeter, 2003, p. 27), thereby diverting attention from entrenched structural and contextual policies and practices.

There is a definite tension between the everyday realities faced by a classroom teacher and his or her mind-set toward promoting social justice (Kohl, 2002). Weighing the costs and benefits, educators most likely consider the preparation of obedient, persuadable students as preferable to the unconventional goal of creating environments in which children are encouraged to question prevailing ideologies—especially if teachers are members of the dominant culture. Nevertheless, children can be guided toward respectful questioning in which they learn to value others' ideas as well as their own (e.g. Shannon, 1995; Wink, 1999).

Sleeter (2001) claimed that the "cultural gap between children in the schools and teachers is large and growing" (p. 94), explaining that most White preservice teachers have "stereotypic beliefs about urban children" and they "interpret social change as meaning almost any kind of change except changing structural inequalities, and many regard programs to remedy racial discrimination as discriminatory against Whites" (p. 95). Sleeter also claimed an "overwhelming presence of Whiteness in teacher education" (p. 102), an assertion echoed by Banks and Banks (2001) and Bennett, Cole and Thompson (2000), despite the fact that the student population in the United States is becoming increasingly diverse.

Preservice Teachers

Studies support the claim that preservice teachers have a propensity to reinforce the status quo (Edmundson, 1990; Ginsburg & Newman, 1985; Lortie, 1975; Pajares, 1992) and to avoid controversy (Lowery, 2002; Saul & Wallace, 2002; and Williams, 2002). Ginsburg and Newman (1985) wrote, "Indeed, if preservice teachers enter programs treating political and economic inequalities as natural or unproblematic (and if they are not successfully encouraged to critically examine these issues during their program), we may have part of the explanation for the tendency among teachers to function as professional ideologists, i.e., apologists or at least preservers of the status quo" (p. 49). Pajares (1992) also discussed the notion that such "familiarity plays in the political process of reproducing society. Most students who choose education as a career have had a positive identification with teaching, and this leads to continuity of conventional practice and reaffirmation, rather than challenge, of the past" (p. 323). However, the intention of this discussion is not to set up a dichotomy between conformity and revolution; the point is to draw attention to areas that could benefit from the incorporation of new ideas.

Future educators enter teacher preparation programs as "insiders" because their beliefs about teaching and learning are entrenched by the time they reach college (Pajares, 1992; Whitbeck, 2000). Therefore, future teachers "have commitments to prior beliefs, and efforts to accommodate new information and adjust existing beliefs can be nearly impossible" (Pajares, 1992, p. 323). Reinforcing the notion that preservice teachers are not particularly reflective, Pajares (1992) asserted,

> Most preservice teachers have an unrealistic optimism and a self-serving bias that account for their believing that the attributes most important for successful teaching are the ones they perceive as their own. They believe that problems faced by classroom teachers will not be faced by them, and the vast majority predicts they will be better teachers than their peers. Entering teacher candidates view teaching as a process of transmitting knowledge and of dispensing information. (p. 323)

Without explicit guidance and modeling, unreflective future teachers are not likely to recognize their lack of awareness regarding social issues, such as "white privilege."

However, some studies have demonstrated that when provided with guidance and the opportunity to reflect on their attitudes and expectations, future teachers often hold differing beliefs and attitudes about education and literacy instruction through both their perspectives as teachers and as learners (Many, Howard, & Hoge, 2002; Whitbeck, 2000; Doyle, 1997), and their teaching philosophies are often "loosely formulated" (Richardson, 1996, p. 108). Pajares (1992) explained, "Recent findings also suggest that educational beliefs of preservice teachers play a pivotal role in their acquisition and interpretation of knowledge and subsequent teaching behavior and that unexplored entering beliefs may be responsible for the perpetuation of antiquated and ineffectual teaching practices" (p. 328). According to Maxson and Sindelar (1998), "more research needs to be done to determine how clear entering images are for the majority of teacher education students" (1998, p. 23), because students will not receive the maximum benefits from teacher preparation until they have a coherent understanding of the relationship between their own beliefs and future classroom practices.

Furthermore, Otis-Wilborn, Marshall, and Sears (1988) delineated several reasons high-ability individuals choose not enter the teaching profession: (1) they are "encouraged by others to pursue high status, financially rewarding careers in areas such as medicine, law, engineering, or business;" (2) there is a "perceived lack of 'rigor' in teacher education;[14]" and (3) the intrinsic and extrinsic rewards may not be satisfying enough (p. 108). Additionally, many future teachers' images and expectations regarding their future careers may be simplistic and unrealistic (Richardson, 1996; Whitbeck, 2000), partly due to their limited background experiences, especially with diverse populations. Moreover, future teachers' concepts of themselves as readers and writers greatly influence their expectations for classroom practices as well as the likelihood of explicitly nurturing a love of reading and writing (Draper, 2000).

Reading

Since the participants in the study read children's books and engaged in meaning making activities, it is important to consider the process of reading as well as various associated factors. Traditionally, children's literature has been viewed as a less important genre in the field of "serious" literary study for a variety of reasons, especially due to the belief that it is less complex than "adult" literature. Nevertheless, it has been considered valuable in providing pleasure and important learning opportunities for children (e.g., Bottigheimer, 1998; Galda, Ash, & Cullinan, 2000; Hoewisch, 2000; Kohl, 1995; Rosenblatt, 1995).

Hade (1997) asserted that "Reading is inherently social and is dominated by culture. And the meanings we hold about race, class, and gender (many of which may be stereotypes) mediate how we interpret text" (p. 235). Similarly, Luke and Freebody (1997) explained that "Reading is a social practice using written text as a means for the

---

[14] See Berliner (2000) for a discussion of (mis)conceptions about teacher education.

construction and reconstruction of statements, messages, and meanings," and it is "tied up in the politics and power relations of everyday life in literate cultures" (p. 185).

Apple (1992) claimed that reality is socially constructed, writing that "Texts are not simply 'delivery systems' of 'facts.' They are the simultaneous results of political, economic, and cultural activities, battles, and compromises." (p. 4). "What counts as legitimate knowledge is the result of complex power relations and struggles among identifiable class, race, gender, and religious groups" (p. 4). "For it is not a 'society' that has created such texts, but specific groups of people" (p. 5). Hence, both the process of reading and the materials being interpreted are power-laden; moreover, when considering children's reading materials, it is important to keep in mind the notion of availability—adults typically choose books for children, thereby adding another layer to the concept of power in literacy.

In addition to the sociocultural aspects of reading, attention to the ways in which individual readers respond to texts is significant for this study, which was informed by Rosenblatt's Transactional Theory of reading, which suggests a "reciprocal, mutually defining relationship" (Rosenblatt, 1986, p. 122) between the reader and the literary text. She was influenced by Dewey, who believed that the experiences of the learner were important and advocated for rich, democratic processes and interactions. Rosenblatt believed that literature plays both an aesthetic role by emphasizing personal response and an instrumental role by bringing readers the experience of others, and she emphasized the contribution of literature to a democratic society, making explicit the broad social role of literature.

Rosenblatt used the terms "aesthetic stance" and "efferent stance" when describing her Transactional Theory, and these terms can be useful for students when we want to demonstrate how we read (texts and our worlds) for different purposes. I like to use the example of watching a sunset to explain the response we have to purely aesthetic material. Although the response may not always be positive, it is highly emotional. Another example is the way we can become enveloped in music—it "speaks" to us on a deep level that seems to involve all of our senses. By contrast, purely efferent reading involves finding information, which can be exemplified by texts such as the dictionary or a telephone directory. Rosenblatt's reading stances can be understood on a continuum:

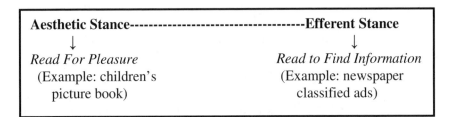

Clearly there is much opportunity with such a continuum to develop a balanced stance, in which we read for both pleasure and information. This may involve two readings, such as reading a humorous essay first for pleasure and then to analyze the author's writing techniques. However, it can also be a simultaneous process in which a particular text is both informative and enjoyable the first time we read it.

Rosenblatt's Transactional Theory can be viewed as a reaction to New Criticism, the predominant literary theory from the 1930s to the late 1960s, which viewed the work of art as an object in itself, subjecting it to close analysis, believing in a single "correct" answer or meaning to a particular text (which the teacher knows and expects the students to "find"). However, transactional theory should not be considered simply Reader Response, which focuses mainly on the reader, because a text scarcely exists until somebody reads it. The following diagram indicates the place of Transactional Theory on a continuum:

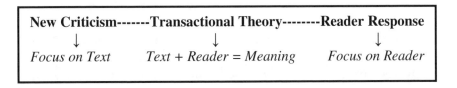

Rosenblatt argued for a redefinition of terms, suggesting that it is misleading to speak of the text as "poem" (which served as a general term for any literary work). The text is simply ink on paper until a reader comes along. The "poem," on the other hand, is what happens when the text is brought into the reader's mind and the words begin to function symbolically, evoking, in the transaction, images, emotions, and concepts. That symbolic functioning can happen only in the reader's mind. It does not take place on the page, in the text, but in the act of reading. The text in the absence of a reader is simply print—it does not become a poem until the act of reading makes it one.

Transactional Theory insists that the reader's individuality must be respected and considered and that readers initially understand a work only on the basis of prior experience. They cannot make sense of a text except by seeing it in the light of other experiences, other texts. The reader's background, the feelings, memories, and associations called forth by the reading are not only relevant, they are the foundation upon which understanding of a text is built. And so transactional theory invites the reader to reflect upon what he or she brings to any reading, and to acknowledge and examine the responses it evokes. Clearly, the larger social context shapes meaning.

Rosenblatt (1995) believed that literature should be personally experienced because it "may result in increased social sensitivity" (p. 175), encouraging individuals to become more empathetic toward others and to develop a greater sense of responsibility for their own behaviors.

> This increased ability to imagine the human implications of any situation is just as important for the individual in his broader political and social relationships. Many political blunders or social injustices seem to be the result not so much of maliciousness or conscious cruelty as of the inability of citizens to translate into human terms the laws or political platforms they support. . . . A democratic society, whose institutions and political and economic procedures are constantly being developed and remolded, needs citizens with the imagination to see what political doctrines mean for human beings. (Rosenblatt, 1995, p. 176)

Hence, Rosenblatt's work corresponds to the theory of critical literacy, with its emphasis on the importance of democracy and social justice.

Unfortunately, as with Freire's theories, Rosenblatt's ideas are sometimes misinterpreted. Some common misconceptions appear to be the belief that Rosenblatt advocated more strongly for aesthetic reading, that one must "choose" to read either efferently or aesthetically rather than somewhere on the contiuum (see Harris, 1999), and that the Transactional Theory somehow precludes simultaneous incorporation of alternate "lenses." For instance, Yenika-Agbaw (1997) wrote about children's texts, "Efferent and aesthetic reading must be reinforced with readings that propagate social change—readings that enable readers to ask questions about situations and ideas they encounter within texts. Such reading stances attempt to make connections between real life experiences and print" (p. 447).

I would certainly agree with part of her statement, especially when hoping to promote critical literacy with texts "that propagate social change." However, Yenika-Agbaw also suggested employing postcolonial and multicultural readings as *"possible alternatives* to Rosenblatt's efferent and aesthetic stances" (p. 452; emphasis added). Rosenblatt's terms (efferent and aesthetic) described the ways we read—for information and/or for pleasure. Therefore, it seems that Yenika-Agbaw confused *how* we read with *what* we read. Moreover, Kincheloe and McLaren (2000) explained that "oppression has many faces and that focusing on only one at the expense of others (e.g., class oppression versus racism) often elides the interconnections among them" (p. 291). In other words, it may be dangerous to select texts, especially for children, that isolates a particular problem from the context of the whole, thereby compartmentalizing the issue as separate and unrelated to other issues.

Additionally, Freire encouraged taking a broader view of reading, going beyond "reading the word" to posit the notion of "reading the world" (See Freire & Macedo, 1987). Reading the word is essentially decoding, practicing literacy in the narrowest sense, whereas reading the world involves investigation of power structures as well as our roles within these processes. Wink (1999) defined Freire's concept of reading the world as: (1) to decode/encode the people around us; (2) to decode/encode the community that surrounds us; and (3) to decode/encode the visible and invisible messages of the world. I would add a fourth point that entails "reading" oneself; that is, examining one's role within the larger social, cultural, and historical context. (The influences of social, cultural, and historical contexts are discussed below.)

This broader view of reading is important for the study because many of us do not consciously question texts in order to discover our tacit perspectives. For instance, the popular picture book *Olivia* (2000) by Ian Falconer depicts an energetic pig and her various activities. Students say they enjoy *Olivia* because "she's so cute" and "she's like a normal kid." How can a pig be like a "normal kid"? Certainly, as white middle-class readers, we accept anthropomorphism (attributing human-like qualities to non-human beings or objects) as a convention of children's literature, which explains the ease with which we equate a pig with a child. However, Olivia is clearly a representative of a white, middle- or upper-middle class lifestyle. She is shown with her nuclear family (mother in a dress and father in a tie), she has her own bedroom and lots of clothes to choose from, her mother takes Olivia and her brother on outings to the beach and the museum, and she gets to read books at bedtime. Unquestionably, *Olivia* is an aesthetically pleasing picture book, and the goal in reading should not be to deconstruct and disparage the text so completely that we ruin it. The goal should be to help readers who view Olivia's lifestyle as "normal" to understand that this text represents a particular perspective.

However, when dealing with literature, I believe it is important to consider Rosenblatt's continuum of aesthetic and efferent reading. A practice I have adopted with students is "the first time for free" suggestion. Fu and Lamme (2002) recommended that "The most important consideration in using a book for any purpose in a classroom is that the children first appreciate and enjoy the book. If books are 'used' without first being read for enjoyment, the teacher is 'basalizing the literature,' a practice that is likely to negatively impact the writing curriculum, as well as contributing to children's dislike of reading" (p. 66). Regardless of the reader's age or development or the intended "use" of the text, I believe that the initial reading should focus on the individual's aesthetic response, followed by reflection. Then, subsequent readings can concentrate on specific purposes. Moreover, instead of prescribing the use of particular interpretative stances, readers can be guided and encouraged to make meaning based on their own concerns, questions, and purposes. Interestingly, Lewis (2000) argued for a broader view of aesthetic reading, inviting "students to take pleasure in both the personal and the critical" by addressing social and political dimensions of texts (p. 264).[15]

Drawing on literary theory, Apol (1998) recommended the negotiation of a "tricky balance between theory and practice," which integrates the content and methods of English departments with the concepts and strategies of colleges of education. Literary theory, which Apol defined as a questioning critical stance, can help readers (of all ages) to determine the ideology—the cultural assumptions and unexamined messages—contained in a text. She wrote, "Contemporary theories, I believe, allow us to imagine more—to consider the reader's response as a starting point, the *beginning* of a conversation

---

[15] Similarly, Sloan (2002) claimed, "Above all, children need to know that the unexamined response [to literature] is not worth having" (p. 29).

between reader and text rather than the end" (p. 33). Moreover, it is not necessary to teach readers the specific theories (such as deconstruction, structuralism, feminist theory, Marxist criticism, etc.); rather, questions can be developed that encourage multiple readings and careful examination of texts (Apol, 1998).

Overall, children's literature scholars tend to apply literary theory in the same ways as "regular" scholars of literature, although Thacker (2000) argued that "The transformation of critical theory over the last few decades has meant that theory *needs* children's literature" (p. 1 [emphasis in original]), explaining that literary theory essentially neglects children's ways of reading. In addition to Thacker's (2000) call for the application of children's literature to theory, she offered a valuable observation about reading, pointing out that adults and children read differently for many reasons, due to factors such as development and life experiences. This brings up the concept of nostalgia and how an adult's "reading" of children's literature might be influenced by his or her childhood experiences with literature—an important consideration for this study.

Well-known scholars employing various types of literary criticism include Perry Nodelman (*The Pleasures of Children's Literature*, 1996), John Stephens (*Language and Ideology in Children's Fiction*, 1992), Peter Hunt (*Criticism, Theory and Children's Literature*, 1991), and Roderick McGillis (*The Nimble Reader: Literary Theory and Children's Literature*, 1996). Likewise, Kay E. Vandergrift of Rutgers University maintains an extensive website of information about children's literature, and the Children's Literature Association provides a comprehensive list of resources, including criticism. Explicit application of critical theory can be found in Jill May's *Children's Literature and Critical Theory: Reading and Writing for Understanding* (1995). A survey of children's literature criticism does not seem to indicate a trend toward rejection of critical theory. Rather, much of the focus in the field is directed toward "legitimizing" children's literature through rigorous scholarship.

Regarding criticism, Apol (1998) maintained that "Literary theory is a tool we can use to help us determine the ideology—the cultural assumptions and unexamined messages—contained in a text" (p. 35) "Because ideology—whether intended or unintended—is an inherent force in a text, and because writers, writing from within their own ideological positions, assume that their perspectives are 'natural' or 'neutral,' texts act as a subtle kind of propaganda and tend to manipulate unwary readers into an unconscious acceptance of their values" (p. 36). Through purposeful, meaningful interpretation of texts, readers can simultaneously appreciate the writer's craft and learn more about their worlds and themselves.

Writing

Just as we learn (gain information and new perspectives) from reading, many would argue intuitively that we also learn from writing. That is, we learn more about the craft as we go through the process of writing, and we often learn what we think about a particular topic. According to Sperling and Freedman (2001), the writing to learn connection is more complex, and studies have "often ignored the diverse ways of knowing and doing that are associated with different academic disciplines and fields" (p. 386). Sperling & Freedman (2001) also argued that "Writing practices (e.g., personal writing, writing that challenges authority, and writing that explores new ideas) carry cultural values, and writing cannot in and of itself lead to learning without some congruity of values between the writer and the writing task" (p. 386). Hence, one of my assumptions in this study was that participants would not modify their current practices without scaffolding and direct instruction.

For many college students and instructors, the goal of writing courses is to reinforce academic discourse—the language of power and privilege (Gee, 1996) that facilitates entry into high-paying careers and a comfortable lifestyle. The gap between the privileged and the oppressed widens as we consider the fact that many "disadvantaged" students' ways of knowing are not valued (Moll, 1994), they are not proficient in academic discourse, and they may not be as adept at "doing school" as their white, middle-class counterparts. By contrast, the privileged students have experience with the dominant discourse and they are not encouraged, nor do they seem to be prompted by their own volition, to question the institutionalized preference for form over substance. Privileged groups, as Kincheloe and McLaren (2000) pointed out, "often have an interest in supporting the status quo to protect their advantages" (p. 281). Smith (1997) underscored this point in his discussion of gatekeeping, explaining that most writing teachers perpetuate the problem by avoiding the issue of power and academic discourse, encouraging students to concentrate on improving their skills in order to mimic the accepted model of "good writing."

In terms of future teachers' attitudes about writing, Briggs and Paillotet (1997) conducted a study with disturbing results involving fifty participants who wrote short-essay responses to an exam in which they were required to respond to writing errors. These preservice elementary teachers "wrote as if they viewed errors as deeply rooted in individuals, and as if they themselves were the ones with the answers the writers needed, but expressed few doubts about their own abilities or knowledge. They expressed many doubts about the abilities and knowledge of the writer" (p. 51). The researchers described these future teachers' responses as "hierarchical," "monologic," "haughty," and "negative." Briggs and Paillotet believed such attitudes were evidence that the future teachers "were very good students of the educational system" (p. 57), and suggested that an attitude of helpfulness and charity would be more productive and beneficial. Regardless, their study illustrated how "grammar can be used to exercise power over people of lower status" (p. 46), with each group (university administration, faculty, and students) imposing rules on the next lower level of the hierarchy. Such a practice reinforces the idea that "written discourse is not just 'situated' but is also 'situating'...helping to shape and maintain roles and relationships that are ratified in the broader social and cultural world" (Sperling & Freedman, 2001, p. 377).

Nevertheless, Briggs and Paillotet's research also reinforces my belief in nurturing writers' strengths in order to provide an encouraging context in which to address their weaknesses. I do not advocate undeserved praise or avoidance of writing problems. Students need to be challenged, but their work should be purposeful, their ideas should be respected, and they should be provided with a supportive environment. Along these lines, Pajares and Johnson (1994) noted the value of self-confidence in their study of thirty preservice teachers' written texts. Additional research specifically addressing preservice teachers' beliefs about writing includes Chambless and Bass (1995), who utilized pre- and post-tests with seven female participants, discovering that discussion, modeling, and practice of the process approach to writing in an elementary student teacher seminar resulted in more positive attitudes toward writing. Similarly, Florio-Ruane and Lensmire's (1990) study used a combination of nontraditional field assignments and course content to gradually help future teachers modify their ingrained assumptions about writing instruction. However, their study focused on helping preservice teachers transform their notions about teaching children.

Regarding the relationship between writing and reading, current research indicates that "Because writing and reading involve the development of meaning, both are conceptualized as composing activities in the sense that both involve planning, generating, and revising meaning—which occur recursively throughout the meaning-building process as a person's text world or envisionment grows" (Langer & Flihan, 2000, p. 118). Additionally, both forms of literacy are viewed as "embedded in social and cultural contexts" (Langer & Flihan, 2000, p. 115).

Sociocultural Theory

A common theme emerging from the information presented above is the influence of social, historical, and cultural contexts. The theory and practice of critical literacy, current educational environments, the beliefs and characteristics of preservice teachers, and approaches to reading and writing are all informed by Vygotsky's theoretical framework, which entailed the interrelated concepts of social learning, mediation (semiotic; signs and symbols), and genetic analysis. John-Steiner and Mahn (1996) explained that these ideas are "based on the concept that human activities take place in cultural contexts, are mediated by language and other symbol systems, and can be best understood when investigated in their historical development" (p. 191). Vygotsky demonstrated the ways in which individual and social processes were not only connected, but interdependent, greatly influencing our understanding of how knowledge is constructed.

Although critical literacy was foregrounded in the research, sociocultural theory definitely informed every aspect of my investigation. Moll (1990) argued that Vygotsky's ideas "represent a theory of possibilities," reminding us that "there is nothing 'natural' about educational settings" (they are social creations), and "point to the use of social and cultural resources that represent our primary tools, as human beings, for mediating and promoting change" (p. 15). Regarding the idea of tools (or artifacts), which are created/constructed by human culture, Vygotsky posited two types: (1) physical or material and (2) symbolic or psychological, which incorporates language. Consequently, our relationship to the world is mediated through language;

words and thoughts interact through a dialectical relationship as we make meaning and express ourselves.

Cultural Models

The concept of cultural models is informed by sociocultural theory. Holland (1992) explained, "In the context of social interaction, the individual comes to internalize cultural resources, such as cultural models, language, and symbols, as means to organize and control her thoughts and emotions" (1992, p. 63). She also described cultural models in terms of "simplified worlds, taken-for-granted worlds" that are "stereotypical distillates, generalizations from past experience that people make" (Holland, 1998, p. 55). Gee (1999; 2001) emphasized the inextricability of reading, writing, and social influences, through his explanation of cultural models and situated meanings. Cultural models are our tacit understandings of what is "appropriate" or "normal" and situated meanings are the ways in which we "*recognize* certain patterns in our experience of the world" (Gee, 1999; emphasis in original). Hence, we tend to interpret texts through unquestioned perspectives, automatically making meaning based on our individual experiences and entrenched understandings. Gee (1996) compared cultural models to "movies or videotapes in the mind" (p. 78).

An example may help to illustrate cultural models, which involve our unquestioned assumptions. A simple explanation would involve describing the attributes of a "bachelor," who is often viewed as charming, fun-loving, and perhaps tall, dark, and handsome. However, a "bachelor" is simply an unmarried man. The words traditionally used to describe an unmarried woman have negative connotations, such as "spinster" and "old maid." A more complex cultural model involves the courtship-engagement-wedding pattern in our society. There are certain "narratives" that we typically accept without question: the man should ask the woman to marry her in a romantic way, he should buy a diamond engagement ring, they will set a date, plans will be made, and the marriage ceremony will take place, followed by a reception. There are other expected rituals or "traditions" involved and we tend to react or question only if components of this cultural model deviate ("the bride wore neon yellow!")

Most of us view this cultural model as the norm, and there is nothing wrong with it. Many young women dream of being princess for a day in her own fairy tale wedding. Problems arise when we fail to be aware of automatic beliefs and actions, when we do not see other possibilities because we unquestionably accept what is and always has been as viewed as right or "the only way." The difficulty lies not in noticing unusual events, but in recognizing our own lack of thinking and reflecting about that which we consider ordinary.

For example, a phrase my mother sometimes used with my brother and me was, "Get your cotton pickin' hands off..." to mean "don't touch." I knew that we did not pick cotton, so her comment was confusing; however, I understood that I was not supposed to touch something. As an adult, I realized that her comment was racist, although I doubt that it ever occurred to my mom. It was simply something that her mother used to say, and perhaps her mother before. However, the matter became more serious in my mind when, as an adult, I found out that my mother's father was born in Louisville, Kentucky, and the "old family house" is Oxmoor, a former slave plantation.[16] I made a conscious effort to avoid using the offensive phrase, but at the same time, I realized that I may have "blind spots"—areas of my life that need to be examined carefully for automatic, unquestioned thoughts and behaviors. And so, "necessary and ongoing reflection" is another form of research.

Research Related to the Study

The following studies are presented because they are similar in content and/or design to my research. Although more detail is provided in the Research Design and Methodology section (Chapter 5), the study analyzed preservice teachers' responses to children's literature through qualitative methods, relying heavily on discourse analysis to generate a theory of the participants' perspectives. Unlike my teaching situation, the research involving responses to literature discussed below occurred in university classrooms that highlighted issues of social justice and equity, and emphasized the participants' future roles as teachers.

Lowery (2002) conducted research in her children's literature course with 32 predominantly white female preservice teachers who composed journals and engaged in small group discussions. Explicitly focusing on issues such as social justice, cultural diversity, and gender when presenting books, Lowery prompted students to reflect

---

[16] One of my great aunts proudly described Oxmoor to me, adding that the former slaves' quarters are now changing rooms for the swimming pool.

on their own thinking about gender prior to critical discussions of the texts. Regarding data analysis, Lowery simply stated that she began to see three developmental stages from "reading students' responses to children's literature in their journals" (p. 27). In other words, a particular theoretical lens or method of data analysis was not utilized (or, at least, not reported). One finding relevant to my research was that "preservice teachers shared initial warm reactions and sentiments to the books" (p. 28). Lowery stated that at first they "felt uncomfortable going beyond the pleasurable read" (p. 28; see also Grisham, 2001), and her students were apathetic to gender issues until prompted to think more critically.

Similarly, using the controversial picture book *Daddy's Roommate* by Michael Willhoite, Williams (2002) collected data from 31 preservice teachers who wrote down their initial responses after hearing the book read aloud in class, focusing on whether or not they would use the book in their future classrooms. Students' follow-up responses contradicted their original reactions, demonstrating that the "majority of preservice teachers are willing to conform to the prevailing viewpoints of parents and community groups."

In a children's literature class comprised of all white, female preservice teachers, Saul and Wallace (2002) prompted participants to compose "dialogue papers" in response to reading Mildred Taylor's *Roll of Thunder, Hear My Cry*. Students were asked to "choose any two characters, perhaps two teachers or two people of varying political persuasions, who would discuss the book. Then write out what each might say" (p. 43). Analysis of the responses (although not specifically stated, the method of interpretation was apparently a type of textual analysis) revealed that 65 of the 71 participants created "characters who worried about what it means for a white reader to be engaged in a text in which white is not the norm, not the dominant perspective, and not what one would wish to be" (p. 44). As with my study, the goal of Saul and Wallace's research was mainly to describe preservice teachers' responses to literature, although I explicitly utilized a critical literacy framework.

I found many studies that utilized discourse analysis (which will be discussed later), and particularly relevant to my research included:

- *Lewis, Ketter, and Fabos's (2001)* examination of multicultural young adult literature with white, rural teachers and researchers. This was an ethnographic case study, investigating influences of the larger context (society and educational institution) as well as the smaller, more immediate setting (professional status and identities), and utilizing discourse analysis to reveal participants' ideological stances.

- *Bean and Stevens' (2002)* investigation of preservice and inservice teachers' use of scaffolded reflection through online and written responses was also significant. Using constant comparative and critical discourse analyses, the researchers explored the ways in which participants' "responses dealt with local, institutional, and societal dimensions" (p. 211). Their research was grounded in the work of Fairclough, "who posited that social structures position people in ways that tend to reproduce societal conventions and norms" (Bean & Stevens, 2002, p. 211), a fundamental assumption of my own study.

- *Young (2000; 2001)* also utilized critical discourse analysis to investigate "four young adolescent boys' awareness of how masculinity constructs and is constructed by texts, both written and spoken" (2000, p. 313) through a framework of critical literacy. Similar to my study, Young introduced the concept of critical literacy through activities with her participants, although she did not specifically "name" the approach for her students—the focus was on the activities rather than an explicit awareness of a "new" way of reading one's world.

- *Rogers (2002)* described her efforts to implement critical literacy with African-American adolescents. Drawing on discourse analysis, Rogers engaged in literature discussions with her participants, focusing on critical social issues that demonstrate that the process of critical literacy—both the learning and the teaching—is an interactive process dependent on the (local) interactions between the teacher and the student and the texts and curriculum (institutional), as well as on the discourses that are being discussed and critiqued (societal) (p. 784).

The above-mentioned studies helped to serve as models for the design of my study and interpretation of the data, and they also revealed the need for further research.

Galda, Ash, and Cullinan (2000) explained how children's literature is present—although often "invisible"—in current research focusing on reading comprehension or literature-based classrooms, and they called for more studies that "explore particular readers and particular texts in particular contexts" (p. 374). Specifically, they suggested:

> We need more studies that are grounded in theory, whether it be sociocultural, transactional, narrative, or critical, and that use articulated strategies for a close and careful analysis. We need more studies that cross the boundaries among us, that allow us to speak to one another across schools of library science, colleges of education, and departments of English. Today we have many ways of looking at the complex issues that surround children's literature. Scholarship can benefit from hearing from multiple, informed voices. (Galda, Ash, & Cullinan, 2000, p. 375)

In keeping with the above recommendation, my study utilized sociocultural, transactional, and critical theories, as well as bridging the fields of English and education.

Based on my research, I noticed a lack of studies describing how future teachers read and react to children's literature. As mentioned earlier, research indicated that future teachers are neither practitioners of critical literacy due to their own experiences in the educational system, nor do they exhibit behaviors indicating a propensity toward adopting such a stance. Therefore, I studied a group of future elementary school teachers, describing their written responses to children's literature through a framework of critical literacy. I also conducted open-ended interviews with seven students to investigate possible antecedents as to why they might adopt a critical literacy stance. Rather than attempting to predict how future teachers will present children's literature to their students, I focused on *describing* their current thinking about children's literature. The study will be discussed in-depth in Chapters 4 and 5.

CHAPTER 3
Background Information

I always tell students on the first day of class that I did not attend college until I was 30 years old. Their reactions are varied: some seem to be calculating in their minds to figure out how old I am; others appear to be amused, surprised, and some even look impressed. I share this information because I believe it sends the message that anything is possible, and students have told me later that my story inspired them. For others, I think they are able to see me as approachable because I am willing to share an important personal information with them and I obviously had some "real-life" experiences (outside of the ivory tower) before becoming a professor.

Self-Reflection: Necessary and Ongoing #4

In the back of my mind, I knew I always wanted to be a teacher. But how could a mousy, unconfident person even dream of such a career? I actually surprised myself by making some of the choices I did, such as entering the sexual abuse program and quitting my full-time job to go to college. I have noticed that older students tend to be more engaged, and I was no different. Every new subject was fascinating: anthropology, art history, geography, philosophy, women's studies, history, and so on. Near the end of my first year, it occurred to me that the field of English could satisfy my desire to study a variety of subjects because I was able to read about different ideas, people, time periods, and cultures—from a multitude of perspectives.

After earning an associate's and a bachelor's degree in English, I began teaching writing and literature at the local state university, where I also pursued a master's degree in English. A condensed version of my master's thesis, *Prevention of Child Sexual Abuse through Literature*, was published in the journal *Children's Literature in Education* (McDaniel, 2001). This study focused on current and suggested literature related to sexual abuse for children ages four through eight years old, since the average sexual abuse victim is eight years old.[17] Following a survey of thirteen children's books that deal with child sexual abuse, I suggested ideal characteristics of prevention and proposed some literary models, calling for more entertaining and engaging (aesthetic) literature instead of books that are predominately didactic (efferent). I also argued, "Improvements in the increasingly disturbing statistics connected with problems such as child sexual abuse will only occur if we change our attitudes and approaches to the issues" (McDaniel, 2001, p. 221).

We seem to naturally want to protect our children from losing their "innocence," but in the long run, it is detrimental to shelter them, and thereby create a false sense of security. As a parent, I had adopted a similar stance with my daughter from the beginning, and I was pleased by the ways in which she was able to question her world while maintaining a respectful attitude toward adults (see McDaniel, 2004). Moreover, teachers often commented on how "well adjusted" she was, surprised to find out that I was a single parent. Change is difficult, often painful, but I consciously rejected my own upbringing and willingly discussed any issue my daughter brought up, taking cues from her responses regarding the appropriate amount of information to provide. Likewise, instead of censoring many of the images she was exposed to through television, movies, and other media, I used the opportunities to begin ongoing conversations about stereotypes, materialism, inequality, and misrepresentation of reality. Despite my daughter's knowledge of real-life issues, she was not depressed or frightened—she was (and still is) confident, curious, and compassionate. Most importantly, I have never perceived my daughter as a "special case"; rather, I believe she exemplifies the ways in which individuals can be guided toward genuine reflection, respectful questioning, and thoughtful action.

Based on my experiences and ongoing research, I began to realize that there was an alternative to censorship of materials for young children: showing them how to question and think critically. With help from adults, children can learn to become critical readers of the multiple texts that inundate their daily lives, including music, television, videos, advertisements, and other media (Giroux, 1999; Semali, 1999; Shannon, 1995). While working to assimilate these ideas, I wrote a

---

[17] For example, see the websites for the National Call to Action, Silent No More, or Voices in Action.

paper on censorship and selection, which I presented at the Children's Literature Association Conference in Pennsylvania (June 2002). I had tacked on a conclusion suggesting a solution, a theory I had just discovered called "critical literacy." After presenting my paper, I attended a conference session called "Children's Literature and Trauma," and I was stunned when one of the presenters said, "According to Cynthia McDaniel…" I honestly did not hear the rest of her comment, although I did speak with her afterward. This event was a turning point for me because I realized that my work mattered and my voice was heard.

However, I am learning to come to terms with the hard reality that not everyone will agree with my work. For instance, I was delighted to discover a reference to my article (McDaniel, 2001) on Perry Nodelman's (a respected scholar) website of children's literature resources. Under the heading of Psychoanalytic Approaches (I did not know my work fell into this category), and the subheading of Bibliotherapeutic Approaches, Nodelman wrote: "Discussions of children's literature that recommend bibliotherapy—the use of fictional texts in helping children understand and deal with their problems—have a psychological focus, but tend to make shallow assumptions both about psychology and about the ways in which we read and respond to texts. Among texts with such an approach are…" (Nodelman, 2002) and he cited publications by Masha Kabakow Rudman, Ellen Handler Spitz, and Cynthia McDaniel. I was disheartened by the term "shallow assumptions," but perhaps this criticism is valid information I need to accept or at least consider in order to improve my work. And so it was with a spirit of confidence, curiosity, and compassion that I embarked on my research into critical literacy.

Background of the Study

In addition to my increased awareness regarding the importance of critical literacy and its apparent deficiency in practice, a variety of researchers and/or practitioners advocate adopting a critical, questioning stance toward reading texts of all kinds, which includes interpretations of one's world (Bean & Moni, 2003; Boutte, 2002; Cadiero-Kaplan & Smith, 2002; Comber & Simpson, 2001; Falk-Ross, 2001; Flint, 2000; Giroux, 1993; Harste, 2000; Kohl, 1995; Langford, 2001; Luke, 2000; Muise, 2001; Philion, 1998; Shannon, 1995; Shor &

Pari, 1999; Villanueva, 1997; Whitin & Whitin, 1998; Wink, 1999). Critical literacy is necessary for effective participation in democracy as well as the development of a truly thoughtful, reflective individual (Giroux, 1993; Shannon, 1995). Rooted in the work of the Frankfurt School and Paulo Freire, critical literacy transcends conventional notions of reading and writing—encouraging readers to adopt a questioning stance and to work toward changing themselves and their worlds. It also has foundations in the sociocultural theory of language, challenging readers to think about the relationship between language and power (Gee, 1996). Readers are encouraged to question the underlying ideologies of discourses and everyday life, asking questions such as "why are things the way they are?" and "who benefits from the status quo?" Shannon (1995) suggested that social injustices persist in our society because people do not "ask why things are the way they are, who benefits from these conditions, and how can we make them more equitable" (p. 123).

There are many reasons that critical literacy is seldom taught or modeled in the United States (e.g., Apple, 1992; Evans, Avery, & Pederson, 1999; Giroux, 1993; Kohl, 1995). It is safer to follow the status quo, especially in current educational environments. Also, such a critical stance is dangerous—for educators and children (Graff, 2001; Wollman-Bonilla, 1998). Understandably, educators may be intimidated by official policies (Westheimer & Kahne, 1998) or feel paralyzed by imagined constraints (Meyerson, 2001) despite their desires to promote social change. Teachers often face rejection and ostracism when they criticize the "system," as well as disapproval from parents for "subversive" teaching that utilizes "inappropriate" texts or undermines adult authority (Wollman-Bonilla, 1998), despite the fact that children can be taught to question and to engage in dialogue in a respectful manner. Likewise, educational institutions tend to reproduce the dominant ideology (Shannon, 1995; Giroux, 1993). Shannon pointed out that "schools in general and literacy programs in particular are often organized to promote a specific set of values—normal American values" (1995, p. 15). For the most part, children in the United States are taught not to question the status quo and to accept and obey the voice of authority (Boutte, 2002).

Moreover, studies consistently reveal that preservice teachers are not particularly reflective (e.g., Pajares, 1992; Richardson, 1996; Whitbeck, 2000). Studies have supported the need for all educators to adopt a reflective stance toward themselves and their profession, emphasizing the importance for future teachers to reflect on their beliefs and attitudes about education (Boyd, Boll, & Brawner, 1998; Ginsburg & Newman, 1985; Loughran, 1997; Mallette, Kile, & Smith, 2000; Risko, Roskos, & Vukelich, 2002), especially as a method to improve current and future instructional approaches and practices toward literacy (Draper, Ladd & Radencich, 2000; Richardson, 1996). Likewise, due to their own experiences with education, they often perceive teachers as knowledgeable authorities who provide information to students, and students as receptacles for this knowledge.[18] Consequently, without the opportunity for thoughtful consideration and articulation of one's beliefs and attitudes, it is difficult to truly understand one's overall educational philosophy.

In a previous study, I used in-depth interviews to examine pre-service teachers' perceptions of themselves as future educators. The participants clearly drew on their own experiences as pupils when envisioning their roles as teachers, and they were leaning toward status-quo teaching, exhibiting definite comfort in conceptualizing school similarly to their own experiences. Furthermore, research shows that future teachers have a tendency to reproduce the status quo rather than work toward change (Pajares, 1992; Lortie, 1975; Edmundson, 1990; Ginsburg & Newman, 1985).

There are many drawbacks to replicating educational environments informed by the idea of "that's how it's always been done." Without question, change involves discomfort, uncertainty, and the possibility of mistakes. However, it is not necessary to set up a rigid dichotomy between maintenance of the status-quo and radical revolution (see, for example, Breault, 2003). We can strive for a balance that incorporates children's needs and perspectives (Cook-Sather, 2002), but does not require us to adopt blatant, insubordinate attitudes toward educational institutions. It begins when we revise (as in re-vision and re-see) the ways we interpret our own worlds—an internal revolution—permeating our consciousness as we gradually re-think our teaching and parenting approaches.

We can start by paying more attention to the bigger picture and our role within the "system." For instance, most people intuitively believe that children are socialized by stereotypical images, although we often ignore these messages competing for children's attention in our media-rich culture, assuming "that's the way it is." Research has

---

[18] Freire referred to this as the "banking concept" of education.

suggested that these messages influence young children (Creighton, 1997; D'Andrade and Strauss, 1992; Eisenberg, 2002), shaping the ways in which children perceive themselves and their world (McGinley, et al., 1997; Kohl, 1995), and much popular and widely used children's literature reinforces mainstream ideologies (McDaniel, 2002). However, many children learn at an early age that certain subjects, such as sex or homelessness, are uncomfortable for adults and therefore off-limits. Evans, Avery and Pederson (1999) investigated the topics considered suitable for social studies courses and discovered that there is "a system of taboo and *noa* [safe] topics" that guides text selection (p. 222). They argued that the "closer to students' lives, the more meaningful, the more likely the topic is to be taboo" (p. 221).

Hence, ideas that adults deem disturbing or forbidden are often avoided, despite children's possible desire to learn more about them. Ironically, such taboo topics pervade mainstream media. Rather than examining underlying ideologies and social structures from which these messages arise, we frequently strive to maintain children's "innocence" by filtering out what we consider to be overly realistic or disturbing texts. Kohl claimed,

> There is no way to avoid having your children exposed to many objectionable or problematic aspects of our culture. Guns and Barbies, and *Babar*[19] too, are part of cultural life in the United States, and children have to develop critical attitudes toward them. These attitudes will not develop through prohibition. (1995, p. 15)

In a discussion of the colonialism, stereotypes, and potentially negative images, Kohl (1995) asked, "Should we burn *Babar*?" Just the opposite is true. We can use texts as resources to help children discover and learn about underlying ideologies. "The intent should not be to avoid books because of their ideological stances," wrote Boutte (2002), "but rather to become aware of the ideologies, be critical consumers of books, and teach children to think about what they are reading and hearing" (p. 151). By developing critical perspectives toward texts, students can transfer these skills to the larger society, thereby "reading" their worlds through a critical stance that leads to empower-

---

[19] *The Story of Babar*, by Jean de Brunhoff, was originally published in 1931 and it has been criticized for glorifying colonialism. When the young elephant Babar's mother is killed by a hunter, Babar is educated and taught to be a "gentleman" in Paris.

ment. Critical literacy can be an effective alternative to censorship and an essential tool for truly understanding oneself and the world.

Purpose of the Study

Considering the propensity of educational institutions to perpetuate the status quo (Baez, 2000; Breault, 2003; Broadfoot, 2000; Cook-Sather, 2002; Edmundson, 1990; Garrison; 2003; Ginsburg & Newman, 1985; Giroux, 1993; Lortie, 1975; Pajares, 1995; Shannon, 1995; Tappan & Brown, 1996), we need to better understand how future teachers respond to and interpret children's literature. Specifically, whether they are potential practitioners of critical literacy or essentially unreflective readers, suggesting a predilection toward preserving existing dominant ideologies.

Critical literacy seeks to unmask and explain contradictions, hypocrisy, and unexamined beliefs, within ourselves and society, and we have ample evidence to show that critical literacy is effective in transforming teachers and students. There are excellent examples of teachers and parents successfully engaging in critical literacy with children (e.g., Bean & Moni, 2003; Comber & Simpson, 2001; Falk-Ross, 2001; Freedom Writers, 1999; Morgan, 1997; Shannon, 1995; Wink, 1999). However, contemporary educational environments, as well as popular opinion, do not generally encourage or tolerate overt questioning and criticism, especially when practiced by children (Boutte, 2002; Graff, 2001; Wollman-Bonilla, 1998).

There are studies that present examples of successful implementation of critical literacy in elementary school classrooms, as well as research discussing future teachers' responses to children's literature through discussions and informal writing assignments. However, I found no studies explicitly describing preservice teachers' propensity toward critical literacy, especially through written responses—formal essay assignments as well as informal responses. Additionally, as indicated in the Research Design and Methodology section (Chapter 5), the context of my study was unique because it transpired in a setting that did not explicitly promote active questioning of the status quo or present children's literature with overt consideration to the participants' future roles as teachers. Therefore, I investigated future elementary school teachers' responses to children's literature in order to *describe* their current thinking about literature. I sought to understand their responses through a framework of critical literacy rather than attempt to predict how future teachers will present children's literature to their students.

Research Questions

The following questions guided my research:

1. How do future teachers read and interpret children's literature?

2. What do future teachers choose to focus on when they respond in writing to children's literature?

3. As evidenced in their writing, to what degree do future teachers recognize stereotypes and underlying images in children's literature? (Do they just add it to their repertoire and repeat it as "fact"? Do they read it against other texts?)

4. Do they think about children's literature in a critical way that might lead to self-reflection? Does this exercise lead to inquiry about themselves and/or action?

5. To what degree do future teachers adopt a stance of critical literacy?

Assumptions and Limitations
Related to the Study

Despite my trust in critical literacy as a necessary educational philosophy, it would be naïve to expect sudden or massive change (Evans, et al., 1999). Also, some people have claimed that critical literacy is negative or counterproductive (e.g., Ellsworth, 1989; Kimbal, 1990; Soles, 1998). For example, Graff (2000) claims that practitioners of critical literacy attempt to indoctrinate students into their own political viewpoints. However, such practices are not representative of true implementation of a critical literacy philosophy—rather, they represent variations on the "banking" education model, in which students are simply passive depositories for information provided by the authority figure(s). The biggest limitation related to critical literacy would be avoidance of its possibilities, which include fostering children's potential to become truly thoughtful, active citizens in a democracy who can work toward transformation of themselves and/or their worlds (Giroux, 1993; Shannon 1995). Kincheloe and McLaren

(2000) argued that "qualitative research that frames its purpose in the context of critical theoretical concerns still produces, in our view, undeniably dangerous knowledge, the kind of information and insight that upsets institutions and threatens to overturn sovereign regimes of truth" (p. 279). People may resist critical literacy because it disrupts the status quo—especially when adults speak *with* instead of *for* children. It involves relinquishing power as a knowledgeable authority and adopting a sense of openness and possibility—an uncomfortable situation for many. I was driven in my research by a statement attributed to Clarence Darrow (1857-1938): "Just think of the tragedy of teaching children not to doubt."

Definition of Terms

Below are definitions of particular terms with clarification regarding how they are used specifically in this research:

Childhood

The concept of childhood is not static through time and place; rather it is a socially constructed idea, reflecting the norms and values of a particular culture (James and Prout, 1997). The prevailing notion of childhood within Western culture emphasizes the innate quality of innocence—as a biological characteristic—mainly through the influence of Locke's and Rousseau's writings in the seventeenth and eighteenth centuries. Prior to that time, children were predominately viewed as miniature adults, because of economical situations as well as high infant mortality rates. By continuing to project the notion of innocence on children, we set up a contradiction due to the pervasiveness of adult information available to children through various forms of media. Steinberg and Kincheloe (1997) discussed a contemporary crisis of childhood, asserting that "the traditional childhood genie is out of the bottle and is unable to return" (p. 3). It is important to take into consideration the influence of "cultural pedagogy," which is "the idea that education takes place in a variety of social sites including but not limited to schooling. Pedagogical sites are those places where power is organized and deployed, including libraries, TV, movies, newspapers, magazines, toys, advertisements, video games, books, sports, and so on" (Steinberg & Kincheloe, 1997, pp. 3-4).

Children's Literature

As this study adopts the stance that language is not neutral, children's literature presents a dilemma regarding power relationships between the author and the reader—the author's ideology is an important consideration (Boutte, 2002). Likewise, as Stephens (1992) explained, "Every book has an implicit ideology, nevertheless, usually in the form of assumed social structures and habits of thought" (p. 9). Also, it is important to keep in mind that children's literature is typically written by adults. "Indeed, something called 'children's literature' exists only because people are convinced that children are different from adults—different enough to need their own special texts" (Nodelman, 1996, p. 15).

Cultural Models

Strauss (1992) explained that motivation is inherently tied to cultural messages and social interaction. Cultural models are described as "culturally formed cognitive schemas" that have *"motivational force* because these models not only label and describe the world but also set forth goals (both conscious and unconscious) and elicit or include desires" (Strauss, 1992, p. 3). Gee (1996) referred to cultural models as "tacit theories" (p. 17) that "shape the way they see other people and the world around them" (p. 6). Social groups and whole societies tend to share basic assumptions ("master myths," according to Gee) that are viewed as normal and natural, thereby unquestioned—the dominant cultural models tend to be accepted as "that's just the way things are."

Culture

According to Geertz (1973), culture is "an historically transmitted pattern of meanings embodied in symbols, a system of inherited conceptions expressed in symbolic form by means of which men communicate, perpetuate, and develop their knowledge about and attitudes towards life" (p. 89). As participants within and products of our own cultures, we are socialized into particular ways of seeing and being in the world. As insiders, it is difficult to question a view from within (see "immanent critique," above, p. 19).

Democracy

We tend to associate "democracy" with freedom of the individual or a particular form of government. Dewey (1916) described democracy as

> Primarily a mode of associated living, of conjoint communicated experience. The extension in space of the number of individuals who participate in an interest so that each has to refer his own action to that of others, and to consider the action of others to give point and direction to his own, is equivalent to breaking down barriers of class, race, and national territory which kept men from perceiving the full import of their activity. (Dewey, 1980a, p. 87)

Although Dewey believed that individuals should be educated to develop a continued capacity for growth, he envisioned an environment of respectful interaction leading to equity.

Freedom

According to Petruzzi (1998), "Both Dewey and Freire argue that authentic educative situations create a context in which the process of inquiry becomes the practice of freedom." This is a key concept in critical literacy because freedom or "emancipation" does not mean that the "oppressed" should turn the tables on their oppressors. Rather, freedom comes from discovering the truth, which sometimes involves unmasking hidden sources of oppression or inequity within the larger system.

School

Giroux (1993) wrote that public schools and institutions of higher learning are more than just "instructional sites." Rather, "they produce knowledge and they provide students with a sense of place, worth, and identity. In doing so, they offer students selected representations, skills, social relations, and values that presuppose particular histories and ways of being in the world" (p. 372). Particularly important for this study is the reproduction of culture through school.

Students are dependent on adults, especially in the school environment, and the choices teachers make regarding the material they present shapes children's perceptions of the world. When censorship occurs, students' learning environments do not promote free inquiry, and they are not provided with an accurate, realistic understanding of their culture. Lois Lowry, the author of *The Giver*, received a letter from three boys in Kansas who asked her two questions: "How did the world of Jonas come about? and "How do you feel about censorship?" They also told her that *The Giver* had been removed from their school. Lowry responded to their letter:

> *The Giver* describes a world in which leaders strive to abolish war and crime and poverty—and…in Jonas' world, as soon as one is removed, another evil becomes the focus. She continued explaining that all of this is accomplished by groups of people with *good intentions* [emphasis added]. Lowry told the boys that she finds censorship and all the issues surrounding it frightening. Censorship closes the door on the future by allowing others to make decisions the readers themselves should be allowed to make—the decision to read or not to read certain books. (Pavonetti, 2002, p. 12)

In our well-intended efforts to try to prepare our children, making sure they can cope with new experiences, we frequently strain to predict all possibilities in order to protect them from harm or undue loss of innocence.

Certainly, children exhibit a delightful sense of wonder, optimism, and curiosity, but they are acutely aware of their surroundings, often comprehending more than we realize. Nevertheless, we typically scrutinize materials that might adversely affect our children–often defining negative influences through our personal ideologies. We (adults) tend to decide what is *right* for children because we believe that they are not able to make intelligent, informed choices. And for many of us, the decisions we make are based on our own experiences as we refer to the actions of our parents, former teachers, and other adults as models. The choices we make may indeed be the most appropriate; nevertheless it is important to consider whether we are acting out of habit, drawing on ingrained cultural models, or if we are truly engaging in a process of critical thinking and questioning, especially when considering the degree to which we introduce "reality" and "sensitive issues" to children.

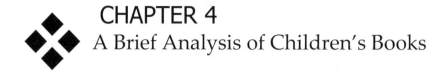

CHAPTER 4
A Brief Analysis of Children's Books

I believe in telling children the truth, even when the truth is unpleasant. I believe that children have a right to know about their world. I believe they cannot learn to recognize and rise above evil if they are not taught it exists. (Howard, 1988, p. 9)

Many parents and educators would disagree with children's literature author Ellen Howard's perspective, and there is certainly debate regarding the degree to which children's books should present the real world (for example, see Blume, 1999; Howard, 1988; Paterson, 1997; and Sendak, 1997). Literature is powerful, affecting readers in many ways (for example, see Grindler, Stratton, & McKennam, 1995; Hoewisch, 2000; Rosenblatt, 1994; and Rudman, 1995), and research indicates that texts can greatly influence young readers (Creighton, 1997). This appears be a widespread notion, since parents and educators often feel compelled to scrutinize children's reading material.

Some educators suggest that children need to see themselves—their cultures, experiences, and ways of knowing—represented in literature (Altieri, 1996; Nichols, Rupley, & Webb-Johnson, 2000). Moreover, it is important for children to encounter new ideas and situations (Athanases, 1998), and the educational community has increasingly provided multicultural and nontraditional reading material in classrooms.

However, Apol (1998) explained that "adults mediate most, if not all, of a child's reading, and that mediation is not disinterested; it is a way for adults to shape children, to promote for children a certain version of reality" (p. 45). In addition to prescribing *how* children should read, adults decide *what* should (and should not) be read. Despite heightened sensitivity toward diversity, contemporary books are not neutral. Furthermore, acceptable children's literature presents "appropriate behavior" (Boutte, 2002), and most published authors depict the world as they think it *should* be (Bottigheimer, 1998).

I was intrigued by Kohl's (1995) statement that "there is still an almost total absence of books, fiction or nonfiction, that question the economic and social structure of our society and the values of capitalism" (p. 59). Kohl's assertion provoked my curiosity because I realized that most of the children's literature I had encountered as a parent and educator does not encourage readers to question their worlds. Consequently, I designed a study, using a framework of critical literacy, to investigate whether contemporary literature tends to promote and reinforce the status quo.

I compared two sets of children's books: the first set represented popular and widely-used literature, and the second set was comprised of texts that offered a variety of perspectives and actually depicted characters engaging in critical literacy—characters "reading" their worlds critically and questioning reality, transforming themselves, or embarking on social action. My research questions were: (1) to what extent do the popular and widely-read texts promote critical literacy? (2) to what extent does the literature identified as promoting critical literacy actually succeed?

The study was a comparative literary analysis in which the data were children's picture books. Since many proponents of critical literacy believe that even very young children can be taught to read texts and their worlds critically (Apol, 1998; Boutte, 2002; Creighton, 1997; Shannon, 1995), I focused on picture books because their intended audience is typically younger children. Regarding the definition of a picture book for this study, I selected texts that contained words (some children's books are wordless, such as Briggs, 2000; Carle, 1987; and Wiesner, 1999), and were clearly intended for three- to eight-year-old readers. I assembled two sets: (1) a representative sample of the most popular and widely read picture books, and (2) a collection of texts that I perceived to be conducive to critical literacy. I analyzed each text through a framework of critical literacy, and then evaluated the two sets in terms of availability and literary quality.

Text Selection (First Set N=22)

In an effort to compile a book list comprising the most popular and widely-used picture books, I sought texts from the following sources: children's choices, contemporary bestsellers, university-level elementary education and/or English department curricula (specifically introduction to children's literature courses clearly intended for future teachers), all-time bestsellers still being used, and librarians' choices. I devised a coding system to indicate the list from which each text was found and then separated the books alphabetically to determine how many lists each book appeared on. I selected books that represented a wide range of lists as often as possible, although I paid particular attention to children's choices, which are not always reflected on bestselling lists and/or university curricula. Table 4-1 shows the selected texts and corresponding codes.

Table 4-1: Book Selection (First Set N=22)

Title	Codes
The Cat in the Hat	C2, D1
Chicka Chicka Boom Boom	C2, D3
Corduroy	C2, D3
Click Clack Moo: Cows that Type	A1, A2, B3
Curious George	C5, D3
David Gets in Trouble	B1, B2
Goodnight Moon	B3, C2, D1, D2
I Will Never Not Ever Eat a Tomato	A1
If You Take a Mouse to School	B1, B2, B3
The Little Engine that Could	C2, D1
Love You Forever	B3, D1
The Napping House	C6, D3
Olivia	A2, B1, B2, B3
The Polar Express	C6, D1, D3
The Soccer Mom from Outer Space	A1
Stone Soup[20]	C6, D3
The Tale of Peter Rabbit	C4, C5, D1, D3
There Was an Old Lady Who Swallowed a Fly	A3, D3

---

[20] *Stone Soup* is the retelling of a folk tale. Some versions include: "Stone Soup" from Belgium, which has only one soldier (Courlander, 1955), "The Clever Pilgrim" from Switzerland/Germany, and "The Old Woman and the Tramp" from Sweden (Ashliman, 1987).

Title	Codes
The True Story of the Three Little Pigs	C3, C5, D3
Ugly Vegetables	A1
The Very Hungry Caterpillar	B3, D1, D3
Where the Wild Things Are	B3, C1, C2, C4, C7, D1, D2, D3

Categories:
  A = Children's Choices (7 titles)
  B = Contemporary Bestsellers (13 titles)
  C = Elementary Education and/or English Department Curriculum (specifically an introduction to children's literature clearly intended for future teachers (undergraduates) (17 titles)
  D = Other (All-time best sellers still being used, librarians' choices) (21 titles)

Text Selection (Second Set N=12)

I compiled a second set of books that I theorized would promote critical literacy (see Table 4-2), which I discovered through my research projects, teaching, and discussions with colleagues. Although as Boutte (2002) pointed out, "no one book will provide a complete view or comprehensive coverage of an issue" (p. 151), I believed each text addressed a topic or presented a situation that could promote critical literacy.

Table 4-2: Book Selection (Second Set N=12)

Title	Code
Daddy's Roommate	0
Fly Away Home	0
Heather Has Two Mommies	0
The House that Crack Built	0
Seven Blind Mice[21]	D3
Sister Anne's Hands	0
Sitti's Secrets	0

[21] *Seven Blind Mice* (Young, 1992) retells an old Indian story in which seven blind men encounter an elephant for the first time.

Title	Code
Smoky Night	C3, C7
Tar Beach	C3
Voices in the Park	0
We Are All in the Dumps with Jack & Guy	0
Whitewash	0

The only texts from the second set on the selection list were *Seven Blind Mice* (D3; Young, 1992), *Smoky Night* (C3, C7; Bunting, 1994), and *Tar Beach* (C3; Ringgold, 1991). The remaining nine texts were not on any of the book lists I consulted.

Data Collection

Research on children's literature as text typically involves content analyses, which tend to be quantitative (Denzin & Lincoln, 2000), or literary analyses, in which researchers often delve more deeply into a book than would average readers, using close reading and explication. According to Galda, Ash, and Cullinan (2000), "Unfortunately, many studies do not acknowledge, much less account for, the importance of the reader in the creation of meaning, assuming, instead, that meaning resides in the text alone. Thus the researcher's reading becomes the reading, and the transactional nature of the literary experience is ignored" (p. 365). Throughout the data collection process, I sought to read the selected texts on the most straightforward, literal, and obvious level. In other words, I avoided searching for underlying meanings or hidden messages, concentrating instead on the actual words and illustrations.

Crosschecking of the results was achieved through published information from children's literature scholars, as well as discussions with colleagues and undergraduate students. For example, according to Lurie (1998), in *The Tale of Peter Rabbit* (Potter, 1902/2000), "Potter at first seems to be recommending restraint and obedience," but "the concealed moral of the story [is] that disobedience and exploration are more fun than good behavior, and not really all that dangerous, whatever Mother may say" (Lurie, p. 95). As with Lurie's mention of "the concealed moral of the story," literary analyses of children's books often reveal deeper interpretations than those of ordinary readers, especially children. Hence, the texts were considered to meet the criteria for critical literacy only when it was apparent that the text and illustrations would be interpreted unambiguously by a majority of readers.

Although this study was based on literary analysis, I consulted research about children's books involving content analysis (Bishop & Van Orden, 1998; Marciano, 2001) for comparative models of data collection. The unit of measurement for this study was an entire text. In other words, each picture book was analyzed holistically through a framework of critical literacy, using seven categories on a coding sheet. Therefore, the first set of books (N=22) contained 154 elements and the second set of books (N=12) contained 84 elements.

Data Analysis

I analyzed each text in terms of the words, illustrations, and their interaction (see Bang, 1991, and Nodelman, 1988, for explanations of picture book interpretation; also, refer to Kiefer, 1995), using the following seven criteria for books that promote critical literacy. (Note that the examples to illustrate each point are from the second set of books.)

1. "They don't make difference invisible, but rather explore what differences make a difference" (Harste, 2000; Leland & Harste, 1999). In other words, the text calls attention to disparities or imbalances that are traditionally depicted as "the norm," such as differences in social class or race. For instance, *Whitewash* (Shange, 1997), based on a series of true incidents, portrays a young African American girl being attacked by a gang of racist youths who paint her face white and call her a "mud" person.

2. They enrich our understanding of history and life by giving voice to those who traditionally have been silenced or marginalized (Leland & Harste, 1999), "those we call 'the indignant ones'" (Harste, 2000). Hence, the reader has the opportunity to "hear" the voice of someone who has typically been positioned as "other" in terms of ethnicity, social class, gender, etc. *Smoky Night* (Bunting, 1994), for example, depicts the 1992 Los Angeles riots from the perspective of an African American boy who recounts his fear as well as the ways in which he became more open-minded due to the experience.

3. "They show how people can begin to take action on important social issues. (Harste, 2000; Leland & Harste, 1999). Social action, a

key component of critical literacy, is modeled in such a way that readers can "see" individuals working to effect change. In *Sitti's Secrets* (Nye, 1994), a young American girl describes a visit to her grandmother in a Palestinian village on the West Bank. Upon her return home, the girl writes a letter to the president of the United States communicating concern for her grandmother and the people "on the other side of the world" and expressing her hope for peace.

4. "They explore dominant systems of meaning that operate in our society to position people and groups of people" (Harste, 2000; Leland & Harste, 1999). Some of the assumptions and ideologies upon which many aspects of our society function are exposed, encouraging readers to question the "status quo" and the meaning of "normal." The young narrator in *Tar Beach* (Ringgold, 1991) questions prejudice and poverty, comparing her own situation to the lifestyles of more privileged and affluent people.

5. "They help us question why certain groups are positioned as 'others.'" (Harste, 2000). This takes the second point further by encouraging the reader to think about why some people's voices typically are not heard. For example, *Daddy's Roommate* (Willhoite, 1990) and *Heather Has Two Mommies* (Newman, 1989) present gay parenting as a natural situation, which may prompt readers from traditional families to reconsider others' lifestyles.

6. "They don't provide 'happily ever after' endings for complex social problems" (Leland & Harste, 1999). Although the conclusion may be upbeat, some problems may be depicted as too entrenched for immediate transformation, and difficult issues are not resolved unrealistically with quick fixes. In *Fly Away Home* (Bunting, 1991), a homeless boy describes how he and his father live in an airport. Although the narrator desperately wants to have a real home, the author avoids a contrived resolution by concluding the book with the boy's hope that someday his life will improve.

7. They depict multiple (sometimes contradictory) perspectives (Boutte, 2002), through techniques such as providing more than one narrator or offering the voices of many characters. For instance, *Seven Blind Mice* (Young, 1992) portrays multiple viewpoints as each mouse inspects one aspect of the elephant and

reports to the rest what he has found. Finally, the seventh mouse takes her time to investigate and discovers that the Something is an elephant. The last page states: "The Mouse Moral: Knowing in part may make a fine tale, but wisdom comes from seeing the whole."

Results

First Set of Picture Books

Five of the 22 texts met at least one of the requirements. *Click Clack Moo* (Cronin, 2000), *The True Story of the Three Little Pigs* (Scieszka, 1989), and *Ugly Vegetables* (Lin, 1999) each satisfied three criteria, although none of these books gives voice to those who traditionally have been silenced or marginalized, unless the reader were to consider the cows in *Click Clack Moo* (Cronin, 2000) or the wolf in *The True Story of the Three Little Pigs* (Scieszka, 1989) as traditionally "silenced or marginalized." *The Cat in the Hat* (Seuss, 1957/1985) offers multiple viewpoints through the dialogue of the narrator, the fish, and the Cat. Likewise, *The Tale of Peter Rabbit* (Potter, 1902/2000) depicts the perspectives of Peter, his mother, and Mr. McGregor. Of the 22 texts, 11 of a possible 154 requirements were met (7%), averaging .5 criteria per book.

Meeting the criteria at an average of only .5 per text, the popular and widely-used children's books as a whole are not conducive to critical literacy. However, when the five texts that fulfilled at least one requirement were separated from the rest of the books, the average reached 31%. Finally, when considering the three books that each met three of the criteria, the average jumped to 52%, which is the same as the average for the second book list. These three texts can be considered appropriate for critical literacy:

- ♦ *Click Clack Moo* (Cronin, 2000) presents animals taking action on a social issue, exploring the labor/economics of society and offering the perspective of the animals as well as the farmer. The cows use a typewriter (hence, "click, clack, moo") to protest their poor working environment, and the farmer eventually concedes to their demands.

- ♦ *The True Story of the Three Little Pigs* (Scieszka, 1989) addresses sensationalism by the media, does not offer a "happily ever after" ending, and also provides alternate viewpoints.

♦ *Ugly Vegetables* (Lin, 1999) explores Asian lifestyles, questioning the differences between mainstream and Chinese culture, while offering multiple perspectives. (The book also provides a glossary of unfamiliar words and a recipe for "Ugly Vegetable Soup.")

Second Set of Picture Books

Using the same criteria mentioned above, I found that each book met at least two points. Of the 12 books, 44 of a possible 84 requirements were met (52%), averaging 3.67 criteria per text.

Both *Sitti's Secrets* (Nye, 1994) and *Whitewash* (Shange, 1997) met five of the criteria, and *Voices in the Park* (Browne, 1998), which has been cited as an exemplary critical literacy text and defined as a "multi-view social issues book" (Lewison, Leland, & Harste, 2000), satisfied six of the seven requirements. *Voices in the Park* presents four perspectives of the same incident through the narrations of a wealthy mother, her lonesome son Charles, an out-of-work father, and his bubbly daughter Smudge. Addressing issues such as gender, class, and prejudice, the book provides multiple perspectives and readers can decide for themselves which voices seem most credible. For instance, the mother explains she saw Charles "talking to a very rough-looking child [Smudge]," whereas Charles states that Smudge is "nice" but "my mother caught us talking together, and I had to go home." The mother perceives Smudge to be an inappropriate playmate for Charles based upon her working class appearance. By contrast, young Charles has not yet developed such an arrogant perspective and he judges Smudge by her personality.

Unlike the first set of books, all but two of the texts in the second collection (*Seven Blind Mice* (Young, 1992) and *We Are All in the Dumps with Jack and Guy* (Sendak, 1993) give voice to those who traditionally have been silenced or marginalized. Although *We Are All in the Dumps with Jack and Guy* does not actually give voice to the homeless, the book offers a detailed portrayal of the suffering and fear experienced by a neglected orphan. However, this book presents a relatively happy ending, with Jack and Guy adopting and caring for the orphan despite the squalid conditions of the dump. Likewise, the conclusion of *Sister Anne's Hands* (Lorbiecki, 1998) seems overly idealistic, as a seven-year-old white girl transcends racist attitudes toward her African American teacher during the course of one year. However, *The*

House that Crack Built (Taylor, 1992) offers no easy solutions from beginning to end; it simply presents a horrifying situation: "And these are the Tears we cry in our sleep / that fall for the Baby with nothing to eat, / born of the Girl who's killing her brain, / smoking the Crack that numbs the pain..." *The House that Crack Built* is certainly not an upbeat book, as it graphically describes the consequences of drug abuse but does not offer solutions.

Unfortunately, like many of the texts in both book sets, the authors do not show how people can begin to take action on important social issues. Nevertheless, *Sitti's Secrets* (Nye, 1994), *Smoky Night* (Bunting, 1994), and *Whitewash* (Shange, 1997) discuss social action, mainly in terms of racism. This finding reinforces Kohl's assertion (cited above) that children's literature rarely questions the economic and social structure of our society and the values of capitalism, although *Click Clack Moo* (Cronin, 2000), which deals with labor/economic issues, is a notable exception.

Discussion

The first research question was: to what extent do the popular and widely-read texts promote critical literacy? Since this first book set met the criteria at an average of only .5 per text, these books *as a whole* are not conducive to critical literacy. *Where the Wild Things Are* (Sendak, 1963/1984), which met none of the criteria for critical literacy, was located on the most lists (N=8), but was not in the children's choices categories (refer to Table 4-1). However, of the three books that met three criteria: (1) *Click Clack Moo* (Cronin, 2000) was on the children's choices and bestseller lists (A1, A2, B3); *The True Story of the Three Little Pigs* (Scieszka, 1989) was on English department and librarians' lists (C3, C5, D3); and *Ugly Vegetables* (Lin, 1999) was only on the children's choices list (A1). Although this data set is not large enough to make generalizations, there appears to be a trend of buying and using "classic" children's literature. Whereas 13 of the 22 texts in the first book set were published prior to 1990 (59%), only one of the 12 texts in the second book set was published prior to 1990 (8%). Based on this study, picture books that promote critical literacy tend to be relatively recent publications.

The second question was: to what extent does the literature identified as promoting critical literacy actually succeed? Meeting the criteria at an average of 3.67 per text, all of the books in the second set appear to be conducive to critical literacy. However, a bestselling rank-ordering of both book sets revealed that the texts identified as promoting critical literacy were located predominately on the bottom of the list. Several of the books were difficult to obtain and one (*White-wash*) was out of print. There are some possible reasons for the lower popularity of texts identified as promoting critical literacy as compared to the more popular and widely-used books. The bestseller lists probably represent adults' choices because they purchase the literature, and the children's choices lists may indirectly reflect adults' selections because the books must be made available to readers. That is, children usually receive their reading material from teachers, parents, and librarians. Likewise, the other two categories of book lists were compiled by librarians and university instructors, suggesting that the "classics" and texts considered acceptable by the majority of adults exemplify the reading material that is ultimately available to children.

Most importantly, the literary quality and aesthetic value of the books must be considered because a reader's level of engagement and degree of pleasure are significant factors (Rosenblatt, 1994; Sipe, 1999). Many of the texts in the first book set are "classics," such as *Goodnight Moon* (Brown, 1947/1975) and *The Cat in the Hat* (Seuss, 1957/1985) which adults may remember as children. However, much of the literature in the first set is aesthetically pleasing for a variety of reasons. For instance, *Olivia* (Falconer, 2000) presents a spunky pig with a lot of self-esteem who lives life to the fullest; *The True Story of the Three Little Pigs* (Scieszka, 1989) is witty and humorous: "If cheeseburgers were cute, folks would probably think you were Big and Bad, too," explains the wolf; and *The Polar Express* (Van Allsburg, 1985) contains magical, mesmerizing illustrations. By contrast, *Daddy's Roommate* (Wilhoite, 1990) and *Heather Has Two Mommies* (Newman, 1989) have an overly didactic tone (Heather's two mommies "waited and waited to see if the sperm and the egg had started to grow into a baby"); *The House that Crack Built* (Taylor, 1992) is simply depressing; and *We Are All in the Dumps with Jack and Guy* (Sendak, 1993) is fairly confusing and overly busy. Some of the books in the second set are commendable, such as *Sister Anne's Hands* (Lorbiecki, 1998), with gorgeous, detailed illustrations, although many have less literary quality in comparison to the books in the first set.

I would call for more children's book authors and publishers to create *engaging* texts that promote critical literacy. Authors such as

Eve Bunting[22] appear to be in the vanguard, but challenges from parents (see ALA, 2003) and a general attitude of resistance and revulsion toward providing young children with realistic fiction (see Blume, 1999; Howard, 1988; Paterson, 1997; and Sendak, 1997) ensures that the majority of young children will be exposed to "safe" reading materials.

Self-Reflection: Necessary and Ongoing #5

Toward the end of my master's program as I was working on my study related to children's literature and child sexual abuse, I was struggling to figure out how my work would make any tangible difference in the world. After all, for someone who loves to read, the study of English is much more akin to play than work. However, I was at a point in which I wanted to find a way to use the knowledge and experience I had gained in a positive manner. I discovered a new doctoral program in education, which seemed like a perfect fit with my goals (it was). Although I did not have a clear direction regarding my career path, I wanted to find a way to combine my passions for teaching and English.

I stayed focused on my interest in children's literature, and as an English instructor—mainly of undergraduate writing courses—at the local university, I was able to begin teaching writing to future elementary school teachers. At the same time, I became more involved with education, coordinating the university's America Reads program, which places undergraduates as reading tutors in struggling elementary schools.

Through the course of my doctoral studies, I stumbled on a name I had never heard before: Paulo Freire. As I began reading *Pedagogy of the Oppressed* (1970/2000), everything started to make sense to me. His theories were the thread that would weave together my various interests and beliefs. More importantly, I understood the concepts he presented as mirroring my gradual formation of a philosophy of life—permeating the intertwined realms of home, school, our culture, and the world. Freire challenged us to question all aspects, including our

---

[22] In addition to two texts designated as promoting critical literacy in this study, Bunting has published picture books dealing with topics such as the Holocaust (1980), the Vietnam War Memorial in Washington (1990), and migrant workers (1994a, 1996).

own roles, within our worlds. This can be painful, but truly enlightening if we are able to face the truth of a situation.

By this time, my daughter was in high school, but I thought back to the way in which I raised her and realized that I had made a conscious effort to be honest and to answer her questions in an age-appropriate but truthful manner. I had taught her to question her own world, including me, in a respectful way. Together we devised methods to deal with discomfort or angry initial reactions. And I learned a lot from her because I made a commitment to myself to see the world through her eyes as much as possible, to truly listen when she had concerns, and to make changes as necessary.

Freire's concepts of banking education and genuine dialogue provided an explanation for the philosophy I had been developing since becoming a parent. Of course, his ideas were popularized in the context of education, but I came to believe that a person must truly embrace this philosophy in all aspects of life in order to put it into practice. Therefore, I sought to investigate the role of critical literacy using the population I was currently educating—future elementary school teachers.

However, I was and still am continuously aware that critical literacy is a philosophy that one chooses whether to acquire. As such, we would expect a person to "walk the talk." In other words, we would be relativists[23] and/or hypocrites if we decided to change our core beliefs depending on the situation. My main point is that no one should be forced to practice critical literacy because it is a way of thinking; one cannot genuinely encourage questioning unless he or she is prepared to truly listen to possibly uncomfortable responses.

Likewise, we must be prepared to (create) change if we are adherents of critical literacy. Much earlier than Freire, Henry David Thoreau (1817-1862) wrote in "Civil Disobedience" (1849), "Even voting *for the right* is *doing* nothing for it" (p. 392, emphasis in original) and "What I have to do is to see, at any rate, that I do not lend myself to the wrong which I condemn" (p. 396). We may know on some level, consciously or not, what is "right," but simply thinking about it and not *doing* anything makes no difference.

In fact, inaction is the same as contributing to the problem. Eldridge Cleaver said during a speech in 1968, "You're either part of the

---

[23] A relativist believes that values or judgments are relative, differing according to circumstances, people, cultures, etc.

solution or you're part of the problem." According to this way of thinking, we need to constantly remind ourselves that "wishing does not make it so." The sometimes forgotten element of critical literacy is social action—making a positive difference, however small, in our world.

❖ CHAPTER 5
Research Design and Methodology

"What is it?" they cried.
The red mouse said, "it's a [red] pillar."
The green mouse said, "it's a [green] snake."
The yellow mouse said, "it's a [yellow] spear."
The purple mouse said, "it's a [purple] great cliff."
The orange mouse said, "it's a [orange] fan."
The blue mouse said, "it's a [blue] rope."

Finally, the white mouse spent more time investigating. She figured out that the strange Something was "as sturdy as a pillar, supple as a snake, wide as a cliff, sharp as a spear, breezy as a fan, stringy as a rope, but altogether the Something is…an elephant!"

The Mouse Moral of *Seven Blind Mice* is "Knowing in part may make a fine tale, but wisdom comes from seeing the whole" (Young, 1992).[24] Qualitative research encourages us to be like the white mouse, looking carefully at the whole "Something." Although we acknowledge our own subjectivity, we strive to represent the environments and participants of our research as accurately as possible, providing readers with a "complex, holistic picture" (Creswell, 1998, p. 15). Most importantly, the voices of participants are expressed, and readers have the opportunity to act as tools of validity, in a sense, as they "interpret" participants' words along with the researcher.

As mentioned earlier, research involves genuine curiosity; we have a question and we want to find out more. There are a variety of ways to conduct research, and some methods are considered more valid or useful than others. The two main types, especially in the field of education, are quantitative and qualitative. Quantitative research measures, counts, and/or classifies data (usually in the form of numbers), and uses statistical models to explain the findings. The design is preset and the researcher remains as objective as possible to avoiding

---

[24] At this time, APA does not have a style for unpaginated sources such as picture books.

tainting or skewing the study. By contrast, qualitative researchers seek to provide detailed and complete descriptions of data, which are usually in the form of words (such as interviews), pictures (such as videotapes), and/or artifacts. The design often changes during the course of the study, as the research discovers new information. In fact, the researcher is the instrument and he or she is necessarily subjective and immersed in the study. Researchers' questions determine the designs of their studies, and sometimes both qualitative and quantitative aspects are used in a study, which is called "mixed methods." Due to the nature of my questions, I chose to use qualitative research.

My study of future teachers' responses to children's literature through a framework of critical literacy can be categorized as "interpretive," according to Erickson's criteria for utilizing this term:

> (a) It is more inclusive than many of the others (e.g., ethnography, case study); (b) it avoids the connotation of defining these approaches as essentially nonquantitative (a connotation that is carried by the term *qualitative*), since quantification of particular sorts can often be employed in the work; and (c) it points to the key feature of family resemblance among the various approaches—central research interest in human meaning in social life and in its elucidation and exposition by the researcher. (Erickson, 1986, p. 119)

Erickson explained that one of the reasons for utilizing interpretive methods is due to the "invisibility of everyday life. 'What is happening here?'" (1986, p. 121). This focus parallels critical literacy's goal of problematizing the taken-for-granted, to "make the familiar strange" (Erickson, 1986, p. 121). Additionally, Erickson described the task of interpretive research as, "to discover the specific ways in which local and nonlocal forms of social organization and culture relate to the activities of specific persons in making choices and conducting social action together" (p. 129). Moreover, the "task of the analyst is to uncover the different layers of universality and particularity that are confronted in the specific case at hand—what is broadly universal, what generalizes to other similar situations, what is unique to the given instance" (p. 130).

Kincheloe and McLaren (2000) also provided a useful lens regarding critical theory and qualitative research: "The 'discourse of possibility' implicit within the constructed nature of social experience suggested to these scholars [the Frankfurt school] that a reconstruction of the social sciences could eventually lead to a more egalitarian and democratic social order" (p. 280). In an effort to assert my voice in the "discourse of possibility," I studied a group of future elementary school teachers (liberal studies majors at the local university). Rather than attempt to predict how future teachers would present children's literature to their students, I wanted to focus on *describing* their current thinking about children's literature. The following statement regarding critical research by Kincheloe and McLaren (2000) informed my overall approach to design and methodology:

> Inquiry that aspires to the name *critical* must be connected to an attempt to confront the injustice of a particular society or public sphere within the society. Research thus becomes a transformative endeavor unembarrassed by the label *political* and unafraid to consummate a relationship with emancipatory consciousness. (p. 291)

The study took place during the course of one semester within the "local" context of a writing classroom. I sought to understand the participants' responses to children's literature both as a group and as individuals, keeping in mind the influences of the local setting as well as the larger sociocultural environment. A breakdown of each research question details the purpose and assumptions:

1. How do future teachers read and interpret children's literature? The purpose of this question was to describe how future teachers think about and respond to children's literature. My assumption was that future teachers would respond to children's literature in different ways.

2. What do future teachers *choose* to focus on when they respond in writing to children's literature? The purpose of this question was to determine the topics that future teachers believe are most important to discuss. My assumption was that future teachers would have different ideas concerning what topics and elements of children's literature are important.

3. As evidenced in their writing, to what degree do future teachers recognize stereotypes and underlying images in children's literature? (Do they just add it to their repertoire and repeat it as "fact"? Do they read it against other texts?) The purpose of this question was to discover how future teachers seek out stereotypical images and the types of images they uncover.

My assumption was that some future teachers would pay more attention to stereotypes and underlying images than others.

4. Do they think about children's literature in a critical way that might lead to self-reflection? Does this exercise lead to inquiry about themselves and/or action? The purpose of this question was to detect how future teachers' transactions with various texts, combined with classroom information about critical literacy, influences their thinking and behavior. My assumption was the future teachers would practice self-reflection to varying degrees. Likewise, I believed that some would adopt new ways of reading (and responding) that would influence how they think about children's literature.

5. To what degree do future teachers adopt a stance of critical literacy? The purpose of this question was to describe the ways in which future teachers demonstrate a desire to practice critical literacy on some level. My assumption was that some future teachers would be interested in using critical literacy whereas others would disagree with it or perceive it to be impractical.

Context

The research took place at the local university, through a writing course in the English department during the fall 2003 semester. Unlike many universities, the majority of writing courses at the university are not offered by the English department, but a separate writing department that was formed in the early 1990s. The class I taught was part of a pair of courses that liberal studies majors take concurrently: English 306A (the children's literature portion) and English 306W (the writing portion). The description of English 306A from the university's general catalog simply states, "reading, analysis, and discussion of classic works of children's literature." However, the English 306A professor's syllabus description of the course objective was as follows:

> This class surveys various aspects of children's literature, with emphases on fairy tales, picture books, and novels. To help you develop an understanding of and appreciation for children's literature, this class will teach you to rec-

ognize its various features, to analyze it critically,[25] and to demonstrate your increased knowledge through writing and exams. In addition to learning basic literary terms, you will also learn about various genres of children's literature, including adventure, fantasy, and realism. Because this is **not** a methods or curriculum development course, we will not be concentrating on children's literature in the elementary or secondary school classroom; rather, we will focus on enhancing your adult literary understanding. Throughout the course, we will be especially concerned with how children's literature reflects—or creates—social attitudes toward children. [boldface in original]

Unfortunately, the English 306A course introduced literature to future teachers who "have yet to develop a framework that might help them reflect on the importance of literature in children's lives and in educational settings" (Hoewisch, 2000, p. 2). Prior to the study, I audited the course, attending every class period of this professor's class during the fall 2002 semester, and the format was strictly lecture with occasional opportunities for question and answer. During data collection in the study, I asked students regularly to report their experiences in English 306A. (This information was not formally part of a data set, but it was taken into consideration.) The general catalog's description for English 306W (the course I taught) is:

Advanced composition; improvement of student skills through writing assignments based upon reading and work in the lecture part. Primarily designed to meet Upper Division Writing and Literature requirements for Liberal Studies—Emphasis in Education, but also open to students with other majors.

Researcher's Role (aka Self-Reflection: Necessary and Ongoing #6)

As mentioned earlier, because of my unexamined beliefs and adherence to the status quo, which I have since observed to be a relatively common way of life, I eventually gravitated toward critical literacy as a way toward enlightenment, envisioning a modern-day scenario in which the people in Plato's "Allegory of the Cave" (Plato, trans. 1992) emerge from their shadow existence. In some ways, I think of myself

---

[25] This is a major problem because there are a multitude of critical lenses—this was not clearly discussed in the English 306A class. The texts were analyzed mainly through the instructor's perspective and the students were not explicitly informed that this is simply one viewpoint.

as being able to understand the lived experiences of many different types of people, but I have to be constantly aware of my privileged status, especially my outward appearance as a white middle-class woman. In the past, I have learned a lot from students and I make a conscious effort to change in ways that seem most productive. I fully expected to make valuable discoveries about myself through the research process—which I did—and I tried to maintain a sense of possibility and openness to transformation throughout the course of the study. Kincheloe and McLaren (2000) explained that

> Critical researchers enter into an investigation with their assumptions on the table, so no one is confused concerning the epistemological and political baggage they bring with them to the research site. Upon detailed analysis, these assumptions may change. Stimulus for change may come from the critical researchers' recognition that such assumptions are not leading to emancipatory actions. (p. 292)

Although "emancipation" is an element of critical literacy, I had to continually remind myself that my idea of emancipation—what would seem liberating to me—was and still is not necessarily right or true for others. Therefore, it was crucial for me to reflect on the ways in which I presented information about critical literacy and controversial materials, persistently seeking to be "with" students rather than trying to think or speak "for" the participants.

It is also important to explain that it is not my intent to disparage the English 306A instructor. Nevertheless, I believe it is essential to my research to clarify how she approached the course, which generally reflects the overall philosophy of the university's English department. Moreover, at the December 12, 2002, meeting discussed above, this particular professor complained that we (the university) are producing "morons." This comment was painful for me to hear, because I realized that it is a common belief, and it informs the attitudes of professors and other people in power toward teachers and future teachers—definitely a situation in which language was being used "to exercise power over people of lower status."

Concerning my teaching philosophy, I try to expose students to the expectations and contradictions of academic discourse. However, I felt very limited (oppressed?) in my position as an instructor because I was reminded to focus on writing (I was not supposed to "teach" literature), especially in terms of conventions, but I was bothered by the disturbing feeling that I was disserving students. Working within the constraints of the course "description," the expectations of the English Department, and the reality of keeping a job, my main goal was to concentrate on helping the students become better writers.

I "dared" to tell the English 306A teacher that I do not focus on grammar (she asked about it), and that I do not agree with teaching grammar out of context (based on research I offered to cite). I do point out errors, in the context of students' writing, especially errors that will "get them in trouble" in the academic world. The thrust of my teaching seeks to discover and highlight students' strengths as writers, expose them to a variety of writing (including that of their peers), foster the practice of reflection, and prompt them to improve in ways that are most meaningful to them.

Nevertheless, I was aware of my dual roles as teacher and researcher during the process of data collection, paying attention to the convergences and divergences of goals—hoping to fulfill the requirements of the study without manipulating students or sacrificing students' learning. Also, as an advocate of critical literacy, I tried to stay true to the philosophy of speaking and acting *with* not *for* students.

Setting and Participants

The research was conducted at the local university, a large public institution that had an undergraduate enrollment in fall 2003 of 27,345 students, 12,278 of whom were identified as white; 11,211 were men and 16,134 were women. The total number of undergraduate degrees for 2002-2003 was 5,816, with 2,422 degrees granted to men and 3,394 degrees granted to women (from the university's Analytic Studies and Institutional Research Department, 2003). Below is the breakdown of all bachelor's degrees granted in 2002-2003 by ethnicity and gender:

Bachelor's Degrees	Men	Women
American Indian	21	23
African American	72	141
Mexican American	344	589
Other Hispanic	92	134
Asian	79	82
SE Asian	56	90

Bachelor's Degrees	Men	Women
Pacific Islander	14	9
Filipino	159	212
White	1,159	1,560
Other/Not Stated	340	444
International	86	110
Total	**2,422**	**3,394**

Interestingly, a breakdown by major indicates that Liberal Studies (future teachers) degrees were granted to 57 men and 406 women, and this trend was evident among the students in a fall 2003 advanced composition course I taught, with 25 women and 1 man. Moreover, although I cannot make assumptions based solely on appearance (see Dutro, 2003), as in the past, the majority of preservice teachers in this course would seem to be white and middle-class (Brookhart & Freeman, 1992).

Three students indicated on the first day of class that English was not their native language.[26] This information, collected via questionnaire, was taken into consideration, but was not formally part of a data set. Other details I gathered, which were not formally part of a data set, included personal information revealed through class discussions, private conversations, and observations. This includes the facts that all participants were relatively the same age (early to mid-twenties), although two students were a few years older and had children.[27] None of the participants could be considered "nontraditional" students, in the sense that they were considerably older than the majority of their classmates. By the time preservice teachers reach the writing class I teach, they are usually within one to two semesters of graduating, and they have participated in an early field experience course in which they spend at least 30 hours in an elementary school classroom. After graduation, preservice teachers in California must complete a fifth year of teacher preparation. (Most teacher preparation in California is done post-baccalaureate.)

I provided a description of the research to the entire class, emphasizing the fact that students' course grades, liberal studies portfolios,

---

[26] These three students appear in the data set tables as #8, #9, and #21; they were not interviewed.

[27] Participant #1 had a second or third grade daughter, and participant #5 had a very young (pre-K) son and an infant daughter.

and future entry into the credential program would not be compromised in any way. I also provided each student with a recruitment handout that was approved by the university's institutional review board. Of the 26 students enrolled in the course, all but 1 (a female) agreed to participate in the overall research. To request volunteers for interviews, I explained the procedures during class and reminded students that participation was voluntary. I then passed around a sign-up sheet and 7 students (6 females and 1 male) agreed to be interviewed. Pseudonyms (chosen by the participants) were used to protect anonymity. The interview participants were as follows:

Number	Pseudonym	Gender	Class	Major	Language
2	Eloise	Female	Senior	Liberal	English
6	Dory	Female	Senior	Liberal	English
10	Penny	Female	Senior	Liberal	English
15	T.D.	Male	Senior	Liberal	English
17	Katie	Female	Junior	Liberal	English
23	Ella	Female	Junior	Liberal	English
24	Kiera	Female	Junior	Liberal	English

The numbers (first column) refer to the identifying number I assigned to each of the twenty-five participants. Based on information gathered from our conversations, all participants who agreed to be interviewed were white, middle-class, native English speakers.

All 25 participants in the study were concurrently enrolled in two courses—the children's literature course (English 306A) and my writing course (English 306W). Normally there are two writing sections (approximately 20 students) for each literature section (approximately 40 students). Due to budget constraints at the university, one literature section for fall 2003 was expanded to include six writing sections, making a total of about 120 students in one class, which was primarily a lecture format. The writing class met on Tuesdays and Thursdays from 8:00 a.m. to 9:15 a.m., then the students went directly to the large ampitheater for the literature class from 9:30 a.m. to 10:45 a.m. The other five writing courses met at various times and were taught by other instructors.

Data Collection: Written Responses

I collected three sets of formal essays, two sets of in-class essays, and two sets of informal responses, for a total of seven data sets—photocopying each data set on the day I received them in order to comment on the papers and return them to the students. I used the readings, divided into three basic sections (fairy tales, picture books, and novels), assigned by the 306A teacher as a basis for the three formal essays. I also kept a log of classroom activities and discussion. Rather than list every activity occurring during the semester, the chronology below indicates the pertinent information provided to students and key events related to data collection. Briefly, the data sets were as follows: (a) Data set #1: out-of-class essay regarding fairy tales, (b) Data set #2: response to reading about various approaches to literary criticism, (c) Data set #3: in-class essay regarding critical literacy, (d) Data set #4: out-of-class essay regarding picture books, (e) Data set #5: response to *Daddy's Roommate*, (f) Data set #6: in-class essay regarding controversial issues in children's books, and (g) Data set #7: out-of-class essay regarding children's/young adult novels.

September 2, 2003. This was the first day of class. I asked students to write a paragraph in response to the following question: "Do you consider yourself a writer? Why or why not?" I also asked them to generate a list in response to the question, "What is good writing?" I typed the list (condensing any repetitions), made copies, and distributed the list to the students on September 4, 2003, and we referred back to this list several times during the semester.

September 9, 2003. Students had been assigned to read "Writing Lessons with Gavin Curtis" by Danling Fu and Linda Lamme (2002), which discussed how to read like a writer, and I pointed out that the article applied to the students in our class as well as their future students. I described aesthetic and efferent reading, explaining how Rosenblatt would want readers to be somewhere in the middle of the continuum.

September 11, 2003. In order to generate the prompt for the first formal essay about fairy tales, I asked students to respond to the follow questions: "Consider the 306A readings so far; what are your reactions?" "Why do you think these readings were assigned?" "What is relevant in the readings to your life and/or experiences?" "Is anything particularly interesting and/or disturbing?" The students then discussed their responses in small groups, we came together as a class, and the following prompt was generated for the first formal essay (Data set #1: out-of-class essay regarding fairy tales):

> In class, we discussed some of the ways in which fairy tales influence us. We pondered the notion that stories reflect society—that fairy tales are created in response to contemporary life. We also considered the idea that stories shape us; in other words, fairy tales influence our expectations and standards of behavior. So, you need to decide which side of this debate you agree with, but you might believe that the relationship between fairy tales and society is reciprocal—a bit more complicated approach to the topic. Clarify your opinion. A secondary consideration will help you to narrow the focus: do you want to discuss versions of fairy tales from the past, the present, or past to present (tracking the changes over time). Then, select the fairy tale(s) that have led to your opinion. Your essay may be more manageable if you select particular elements of the tales as examples to illustrate your main idea. You might want to discuss gender roles, stereotypes, or common themes, etc.

All essay prompts included criteria for evaluation, as well as information about drafts and final revisions (see Appendix G for a sample handout).

September 25, 2003. First drafts of the essay regarding fairy tales were submitted and students participated in small group workshops to evaluate each other's papers.

October 7, 2003. Final versions of the essay regarding fairy tales were submitted. (Data set #1: out of class essay regarding fairy tales).

October 9, 2003. Students read "Critical Approaches Important to the Study of Literature" from Edgar V. Roberts's *Writing about Literature* (1995), which includes definitions and examples of the following approaches to literary criticism: Moral/Intellectual, Topical/Historical, New Critical/Formalist, Structuralist, Feminist, Economic Determinist/Marxist, Deconstructionist, Psychological/Psychoanalytic, Archetypal/Symbolic/Mythic, and Reader Response. I discussed the various approaches with the class and asked students to respond in writing. (Data set #2: brief written response to literary theory).

October 14, 2003. I began the class by setting up a display of more than 20 picture books from the California Department of Education's

(CDE) Recommended Reading List, and then I read *Olivia* (Falconer, 2000) to the class, which everyone seemed to enjoy. Afterward, I divided the class into five groups to discuss different parts of the article "Critical Literacy: A Questioning Stance and Possibility for Change" (McDaniel, 2004), focusing on the main ideas in each section.[28] We came back together as a class to report on the article, and the first group explained that teachers "always" choose books that are safe and not controversial. The second group expressed confusion, so I explained who Freire was and the key ideas of critical literacy theory. I tried to be careful throughout the entire discussion to let the students know that the article was someone's opinion and they did not have to agree. The remaining three groups reported a basic idea from each section, although group 4 seemed to enjoy their section, which applied the discussion to real children's books. (I had given this group the books used as examples so they were able to use them when they discussed their section.) One student, who was later an interviewee (Ella), particularly liked *Voices in the Park* (Browne, 1998), which presents four different perspectives of the same situation, and she decided to use the text for her essay regarding picture books. After the groups were finished reporting, I brought out *Olivia* again to show how we might read it through a framework of critical literacy, specifically stating that our purpose is not to ruin the enjoyment. Looking at the page depicting Olivia's nuclear family, I asked the students what they knew by the picture. They said there was an intact family ("two and a half kids"), "dad isn't around much" (he's busy at work), and "mom doesn't work." I asked the students to reflect on their experiences as observers in elementary school classrooms (a requirement of the Liberal Studies major). Most of the students agreed that there were not very many "Olivias" in the schools they had visited. However, one student had observed a classroom in La Jolla (an affluent community) and she said that a lot of those children probably lived that way. I asked the students what they thought children might think when reading *Olivia*, and some students said children might

---

[28] "Critical Literacy: A Questioning Stance and Possibility for Change" was in press at the time of the study. I provided students with photocopies of the article and I used my maiden name (Cynthia Blair) in order to avoid influencing participants' attitudes toward the content. This article explains critical literacy, offers examples of books that can be used to support critical literacy, and then discusses the need to enhance the availability of critical literacy models.

wish they could live like Olivia. I told them it is valuable to understand that some children might not see themselves in literature and we need to be aware—not that we should avoid using *Olivia*—but we should be **aware** so we can provide other books and/or discuss these issues with our students. Then I briefly introduced a few controversial books—*The House that Crack Built* (Taylor, 1992), which depicts the consequences of drug use in a sing-song manner (patterned after "The House that Jack Built"); *We Are All in the Dumps with Jack and Guy* (Sendak, 1993), which portrays the suffering and fear experienced by a neglected orphan; and *In the Night Kitchen* (Sendak, 1970), which reveals an anatomically correct young boy. (None of these books are on the CDE list.) I also mentioned *The Giving Tree* (Silverstein, 1964), which traces the life stages of a boy through old age, and the tree that willingly sacrifices everything for his happiness. Many students remembered reading this book as children, and I explained how *The Giving Tree* had been "ruined" for me when someone revealed the "real" meaning of the text—the tree is a female who sacrifices herself to please the selfish male.

October 16, 2003. Students wrote an in-class essay on critical literacy, based on the information from McDaniel (2004) and class discussions. The prompt was: "Write an essay in response to the following question: Do you agree or disagree with the critical literacy approach toward reading? Please explain." (Data set #3: in-class essay regarding critical literacy).

October 23, 2003. Students submitted draft versions of the second out-of-class essay regarding picture books (Data set #4). Similar to the first formal essay, students participated in a workshop to evaluate each other's papers, although the authors and evaluators were anonymous, based on class consensus from the first workshop. The assignment required students to select literature from the California Department of Education's (CDE's) Recommended Reading List (http://cde.ca.gov/literaturelist), unless they discussed alternate choices with me, and some students selected alternate books. The writing prompt asked students to identify an important theme (or message) in the book and then provide literary analysis to support their ideas. Final versions of the essays were submitted on November 13, 2003. (Data set #4: out-of-class essay regarding picture books.)

October 25, 2003. Nature intervened with the data collection process as wildfires raged in San Diego County. Schools were closed Monday through Wednesday, and assignments for both the English 306A and 306W courses were postponed.

November 13, 2003. Students submitted final versions of the out-of-class essay regarding picture books (Data set #4).

November 18, 2003. Students had been assigned to read handouts related to censorship, which represented a variety of viewpoints in preparation for the second in-class essay on November 20, 2003. These readings were:

1. American Library Association (ALA, 2003). A list of the ten most challenged books of the 1990s with rationale from the Freedom Forum (Freedom Forum, 2000).

2. Gish, K.W. (2000). "Hunting Down Harry Potter: An Exploration of Religious Concerns about Children's Literature" from *The Horn Book*, which provided an explanation by a librarian, who is also a conservative Christian, concerning religious objections to portraying the occult in a positive manner.

3. Herendeen, S. (2003). "District Removes Book after Parent's Objection" from the *Modesto Bee*, regarding *Always Running: La Vida Loca*, Luis Rodriguez's realistic young adult novel about gangs.

4. Solochek, J.S. (2003). "Parent Challenges Children's Library Book" from the *St. Petersburg Times*, concerning controversy over Judy Blume's *Deenie*, which revolves around a 14 year-old girl with scoliosis.

5. Stapinski, H. (2003). "The Battle Over Book Banning" from *FamilyFun.com*, which provides a synopsis of censorship and book challenges, offering examples from both sides of the debate.

At the beginning of the class period, prior to discussing the above readings, I modeled the exercise by Williams (2002) using *Daddy's Roommate*, a controversial children's book about gay families. I did not introduce the book, but I did ask if anyone had read the book and none of the students had, although some recalled the title of the book from two of the handouts (Stapinski, 2003; ALA, 2003). I asked the students to take out a piece of paper and if they wanted, they could write any reactions while they listened and looked at the pictures. I read very slowly and showed each picture for a while. Then I asked the students to spend about five minutes writing their reactions. (Data set #5: brief written response regarding *Daddy's Roommate*). After that, I asked, "would you use this book in your classroom?" We had a lively discussion, essentially the most passionate interaction to date in the semester. I adopted the role of facilitator—seeking to clarify and guide the discussion. One of the key points brought up was, "moral issues should be kept out of school," which returned our attention again to *Daddy's Roommate*. I asked the class to consider how we might draw the line regarding topics considered "moral issues," asking them to think about a situation in which a child was bullied at school because his father was gay. Although not all students spoke, there was certainly a vigorous discussion with a variety of viewpoints. I had also brought some other controversial books that were mentioned in the readings to share with the class: *Heather Has Two Mommies* (Newman, 1989), which is often challenged as promoting homosexuality and being inappropriate for the age group; *I Know Why the Caged Bird Sings* (Angelou, 1970), which is controversial due to the depiction of rape and other details of sexual abuse; *Bridge to Terabithia* (Paterson, 1977), which is denounced for offensive language and fantasy elements that are believed to be references to witchcraft, similar to objections about the *Harry Potter* series; and *What Is a Girl? What Is a Boy?* (Waxman, 1976), which has been labeled "pornographic." I did not own a copy of the anatomically-correct picture book *What Is a Girl? What Is a Boy?*, nor did the university library, so I requested the book via interlibrary loan from another university (CSU Hayward). I quickly previewed the book before class and it seemed somewhat disjointed. However, when I was sharing the book during class, I realized that some of the pages had been cut out—an interesting example of censorship. Subsequently, I ordered a used copy of the book from Amazon.com (it is out of print) and discovered that the missing pages contained photographs of a baby girl, a baby boy, a young girl, a young boy, a man, and a woman—all with no clothing. I brought the book to class for any students who were interested.

November 20, 2003. Students wrote an in-class essay regarding controversial issues in children's books. The prompt was: "There is debate about whether children should be exposed to books that deal with controversial issues such as homelessness, drug abuse, prejudice, and homosexuality. Some people think that even young children should be introduced to sensitive topics, whereas others believe that children's innocence should be protected. What is your opinion on this topic? Please explain." (Data set #6: in-class essay regarding controversial issues).

December 2, 2003. Students submitted draft versions of the third and final out-of-class essay regarding young adult novels, again participating in an anonymous peer writing workshop to evaluate each other's papers, based on class consensus. The novels assigned in the English 306A class, to be read in the following order were: *The Whipping Boy* by Sid Fleischman (originally published in 1986), *Harry Potter and the Sorcerer's Stone* by J.K. Rowling (1997), *Baseball in April and Other Stories* by Gary Soto (1990), *A Little Princess* by Frances Hodgson Burnett (originally published in 1905), and *The Watsons Go to Birmingham—1963* by Christopher Paul Curtis (1995). Students were offered three options for the writing prompt: (1) Analysis and interpretation of the main character's development, using the framework of the Hero Journey (which was discussed in class) or a more general discussion; (2) A literary analysis/interpretation of the novel in which they discuss a main theme(s) or important idea/message; and (3) Compare/contrast two novels. (Data set #7).

When responding to the participants' written work, I did not review their papers through a lens of critical literacy, asking them to look more deeply at the reading or to make connections to social issues. Rather, I focused on clarification of ideas and the criteria for evaluation explained on the assignment sheet because, as mentioned earlier in this chapter, I was extremely aware of my primary purpose in the classroom—helping students to become better writers. I highlighted important elements of academic discourse and conventions, while encouraging students to develop their own writing styles. At the same time, I tried to point out the ways in which our ingrained habits may be disservicing us, both as teachers and students.[29] In addition to the unreflective ways in which we teach writing, mainly due to our own educations, we may neglect to evaluate written work in a manner consistent with the assigned task. This is the reason I provide students with grading criteria whenever I distribute an assignment. Moreover, I realize I am a model for their future teaching and I believe it is important to demonstrate thoughtful planning and reflective practice.

Data Collection: Interviews

I announced in class the opportunity to participate in individual interviews and passed around a sign-up sheet during two class periods, once again emphasizing the voluntary nature of the interviews and providing each student with a handout. Seven individuals agreed to participate and they indicated on the sign-up sheet the most convenient times to meet. Interviews were conducted and audiotaped, with each participant's permission, in my office at the university during the period of December 11, 2003, through December 18, 2003.

I used a semi-structured format in which the same preestablished questions were asked in the same order, and I was careful to provide participants with time to think and to speak rather than intervening during their comments (Creswell, 1997). I sought to maintain the tone of a friendly conversation (Fontana & Frey, 2000), and I encouraged participants to expand on their ideas when they mentioned topics particularly relevant to my research questions (Warren, 2002).

I developed the list of open-ended interview questions (Patton, 2002) by referring to my research questions,[30] specifically the fourth and fifth: (4) "Do future teachers think about children's literature in a critical way that might lead to self-reflection? Does this exercise lead to inquiry about themselves and/or action?" and (5) "To what degree do future teachers adopt a stance of critical literacy?" Additionally, I was looking for antecedents as to whether they might or might not adopt a stance of critical literacy, so I constructed some questions to investigate the participants' experiences with and attitudes toward

---

[29] Schuster (2003) points out many of the ways in which teachers perpetuate misinformation and counterproductive writing habits.

[30] Warren (2002) explained: "From the 'research questions' generated by a possible review of the literature, the interviewer develops 10 to 12 specific questions" (p. 86).

education. Finally, I sought a logical order on which to build the conversation, starting with reflection of the participant's history, which led into literacy and book selection, anticipation of one's future classroom, consideration of controversial issues, and then into a general discussion regarding education. Below are the questions:

1. Why do you want to be an elementary school teacher?

2. What were your experiences as a student? Describe your education. Do you hope to provide similar and/or different experiences for your own students?

3. What kinds of books, if any, did you like to read in elementary school?

4. What is the role of the teacher in the classroom? What is the role of the student?

5. How would you describe a "good reader?"

6. What kinds of books do you hope to use in your future classroom?

7. How do you plan to use books in your classroom? What types of things would you like your students to focus on?

8. How realistic should books for children be? Are there certain topics that should be avoided?

9. Overall, what do you see as the purpose of education?

10. Is there anything you would change about the current educational system?

Data Analysis

Overall, the data were examined "working inductively from particulars to more general perspectives" (Creswell, 1998, p. 20). I concentrated on bringing the "concrete, the parts, the particular into focus, but in a manner that grounds them contextually in a larger understanding of the social forces, the whole, the abstract (the general)" (Kincheloe & McLaren, 2000, p. 287). The data were analyzed in stages, with the written responses analyzed based on type (formal essay, informal essay, or brief response). I developed a grid to record each student's main idea—what each participant chose to discuss—for each data set.

Out-of-Class Essays (Data Sets #1, #4, and #7)

Apol (1998) offered a series of questions to "help students explore the relationship between the text, the author, the reader and the world" (p. 38). I used Apol's questions (see Appendix A), which draw on a range of critical approaches to literature, as a guideline from which to generate specific categories of response. I simplified each of Apol's ten questions into a main concept, collapsed the overlapping concepts, and developed a set of questions from which to analyze each student's written response. The overarching question, which is a thread connecting each category, was "does the participant show evidence of questioning the text?" Appendix B delineates my process of developing the remaining questions, which were: Does the participant: (1) question power (dominance and submission)?; (2) address the text's unspoken, underlying message, such as influences of the author's values, contemporary culture and/or place?; (3) question the absences/gaps/ silences in the text (what is missing) or what is represented as normal?; (4) identify similarities with other texts ("texts" in a broad sense, including popular culture)?; and (5) consider the influence of his/her own experiences and/or culture when responding to the text?

In-Class Essays (Data Sets #3 and #6)

For data set #3, the in-class essay regarding critical literacy, as well as the remaining data sets (#6, #2, and #5), I developed a grid based on participants' responses: (1) they would use critical literacy, (2) they would use it with third grade and older, (3) they would not use it, and (4) they did not know (or did not indicate) whether or not they would use it. For data set #6, the in-class essay regarding controversial issues in children's books, the categories were: (1) they would expose children to all topics, (2) they would expose children to some topics, (3) they would not expose children to any controversial topics, and (4) they did not know (or did not indicate) whether or not they would expose children to controversial topics.

Brief Written Responses (Data Sets #2 and #5)

For data set #2, the response regarding various critical approaches to children's literature, the categories were: (1) literary criticism is valuable, (2) literary criticism is somewhat valuable, (3) literary criticism is not valuable, and (4) they did not know (or did not indicate) whether literary criticism is valuable. For data set #6, the response to *Daddy's Roommate* being read in class, the categories were: (1) they would use the book with children, (2) they would not use the book with children, and (3) they did not know (or did not indicate) whether they would use the book with children.

As mentioned above, the data were analyzed in stages, with each data set examined separately. The initial coding of each written response was the overall topic addressed—each piece of writing was coded according to what the participant chose to discuss (addressing research questions #2 and #3). This information is presented in Appendix C for the formal out-of-class essays: Data sets #1, #4, and #7; Appendix D for the in-class essays: Data sets #3 and #6; and Appendix E for the brief written responses: Data sets: #2 and #5). I then analyzed the written responses through the frameworks discussed above, identifying any instance in which participants' responses corresponded to a particular category. (I sought the opinions of my colleagues to verify my interpretations.) A third stage of analysis entailed identifying other ideas that were repeatedly evident in the participants' responses, which could be considered themes. I used the constant comparative method (Creswell, 1997), constantly comparing written concepts to emerging categories of themes. I utilized this process for all seven data sets.

Interviews

Seven individuals volunteered to be interviewed, and I transcribed each interview myself, including all utterances verbatim (such as "you know," "um," etc.) because I knew I needed a "narrow" record of speech (Gee, 1999) for my purposes of discourse analysis. The important point in this case, regarding transcription of the interviews, is the fact that I became quite familiar with the data—hearing it first during the interview, again as I transcribed, and once more when I coded the data. According to Gee (1999) "a transcript is a theoretical entity. It does not stand outside an analysis, but, rather, is part of it" (p. 88). Similar to the written responses (Data sets #1 through #7), I analyzed the interview transcripts in stages, first identifying specific answers to the questions asked. Then I examined the individual interviews for particular concepts that were repeatedly evident in the participants' responses, which could be considered themes.

Finally, I engaged in discourse analysis, focusing on "how 'minor' details can take on 'major' importance" (Gee, 1999, p. 89). For example, when discussing the importance of reading, Eloise said, "Yes, I love to read, and I think that reading opens doors for kids, 'cause I think that if you [the teacher] read different kinds of stories than maybe what their parents read to them or something then they're not so closed minded as to what they think the world is like." Eloise was pointing out the value of providing children with the opportunity to experience other perspectives. However, implicit in her statement is the assumption that middle-class parenting models are the norm, simply by taking for granted that parents will read to their children.

With all the data, I conducted in-depth analyses, concentrating on uncovering participants' cultural models—their "taken-for-granted assumptions about what is 'typical' or 'normal'" (Gee, 1999; p. 59) in order to discover their "theories" (addressing research questions #1, #4, #5). Jaworski and Coupland (1999) explained that "Discourse is implicated in expressing people's points of view and value systems, many of which are pre-structured in terms of what is 'normal' or 'appropriate' in particular social and institutional settings" (p. 7). Hence, I constantly kept in mind the sociocultural influences of the participants' responses—factors such as their use of academic discourse, their motivations for completing each assignment, their conceptions of audience, etc.—which Gee (1999) called giving consideration to the whole picture.

Kincheloe and McLaren (2000) asserted that the "moment(s) of interpretation" is the most crucial point in critical theory-informed research. Citing the hermeneutic tradition, they claimed that "in qualitative research there is only interpretation, no matter how vociferously many researchers may argue that the facts speak for themselves" (p. 285). Hence the methods employed must suit the data and the purpose of the research. Discourse analysis was appropriate because it is informed by sociology and linguistics, focusing on the explicit and implicit messages (both consciously and unconsciously produced) in written and verbal discourse.

Gee (1999) reinforced the fact that language simultaneously reflects and constructs reality, pointing out the importance of studying "reproduction," and he also explained that a discourse analysis should be based on the details that are "arguably deemed *relevant* in the situation *and* that are relevant to the arguments the analyst is attempting to make" (p. 88). Consequently, I focused on the elements that were most relevant to my research questions, which were the topics the participants chose to discuss, the social language(s) they used, and the assumptions they made—which stressed the need to also look at the absences in discourse in order to detect that which was not stated but implied (Fairclough, 1995). According to Jaworski and Coupland (1999), inferences are a primary source of meaning in most current approaches to discourse (p. 17). I continually reminded myself, however, that everyone has *good reasons* for his or her ways of thinking, writing, reading, and believing and that my conclusions were necessarily tentative (Gee, 1999).

Validity

Critical Discourse Analysis (CDA) informed analysis of the data, because CDA "sees itself as politically involved research with an emancipatory requirement: it seeks to have an effect on social practice and social relationships, for example in teacher development, in the elaboration of guidelines for non-sexist language use or in proposals to increase the intelligibility of news and legal texts" (Titscher, et al., 2000, p. 147). Nevertheless, as with critical theory, there are objections to CDA that I took into consideration, such as the problem of the "impossibility of there being a single interpretation of any text" (Hoey, 2001, p. 9) and that CDA "is an ideological interpretation and therefore not an analysis" (Titscher, et al., 2000, p. 163). To counter such criticism, I continually aspired toward rigor, especially by paying close attention to linguistic details in order to strengthen validity (Gee, 1999). Another objection is that "any form of ideological critique presupposes that the critic has privileged access to the truth" (Fairclough, 1995, p. 16), but the epistemological stance in this study assumed that "permanent, absolute truth is impossible." However, by "agreeing on criteria of evaluation of interpretation [in this case, discourse analysis], there can be warranted assertions, or alternative truths, with some more acceptable than others" (Cunningham & Fitzgerald, 1996, p. 51).

In order to validate my analyses, I engaged in the following verification procedures recommended by Creswell (1998). I clarified and continually reflected on my subjectivity from the outset of the study, and I used triangulation, specifically various forms of data (formal essays, informal essays, informal written responses, observation, and interviews). Additionally, I analyzed the data for strong findings, which were subsequently scrutinized for disconfirming evidence (negative case analysis), and I also consulted the work of literary scholars and solicited the opinions of my colleagues. Perhaps most importantly, my role as teacher and the context of the study allowed me to become familiar with the participants and to build trust.

I developed relationships with many students in the study, which proved to be both heartening and distressful, because when it came time to analyze the data and report my findings, I had to separate my feelings of friendship from my need to tell the "truth"—however unflattering that may be sometimes. Such is the paradox of qualitative study, as the researcher is the instrument. I was reminded of when writing students engage in peer workshops, and they are often afraid of being too critical and hurting their classmates' feelings. I always tell them (and try to show them) that there are ways of being critical but considerate—a mind-set I tried to maintain in the following chapters.

When reporting the findings of the study, I focused on problematizing the taken-for-granted and calling attention to participants' unquestioned cultural models. Interpretive research, as described by Erickson (1986), approaches a situation through a variety of lenses, or perhaps refocuses the same lens to various degrees in order to foreground particular phenomena at different times. Such a practice uncovers specifics but also allows for a holistic perspective, a process of maneuvering and meaning making in the hermeneutic tradition (Kincheloe & McLaren, 2000). Similar to the white mouse in *Seven Blind Mice* (Young, 1992), I gathered a variety of interpretations from the participants—each had a different viewpoint depending on his or her experiences—but I made a conscious effort to "see the whole" while acknowledging individual perspectives.

◆ CHAPTER 6
Findings

The picture book *Voices in the Park* (Browne, 1998) presents four perspectives of the same incident through the narrations of a wealthy mother, her lonesome son Charles, an out-of-work father, and his bubbly daughter Smudge. Addressing issues such as gender, class, and prejudice, the book provides multiple perspectives and readers can decide for themselves which voices seem most credible. For instance, the mother explains she saw Charles "talking to a very rough-looking child [Smudge]," whereas Charles states that Smudge is "nice" but "my mother caught us talking together, and I had to go home." The mother perceives Smudge to be an inappropriate playmate for Charles based upon her working-class appearance. The mother's judgment is signified by her description of Smudge as "very rough-looking," as well as the demand of her son, "'Charles, come here. At once!'" upon "catching" the two children playing together. By contrast, young Charles has not yet developed such an arrogant perspective and he judges Smudge by her individual qualities, explaining that "She was great on the slide—she went really fast. I was amazed" and "she's nice." This book illustrates how a person's experiences shape how he or she perceives the world, as four individuals reveal their world-building processes (Gee, 1999), that is, the ways in which they make sense of their surroundings and what is taken as "reality."

Similar to the various narrators in *Voices in the Park*, the participants in the study revealed different voices, different perspectives, and different approaches to thinking about children's literature and education. Gee (1999) explained that "meaning is multiple, flexible, and tied to culture" and described the "human mind as a 'pattern recognizing device'" (p. 40). "A situated meaning is an image or pattern that we assemble 'on the spot' as we communicate in a given context, based on our construal of that context and on our past experiences (Gee, 1999, p. 47). Discourse, whether oral or written, occurs in a social context, reflecting a person's situated meaning(s) and cultural models. However, according to Gee, "we are usually quite unaware we are using them [cultural models] and of their full implications, unless challenged by someone or by a new experience where our cultural models clearly don't 'fit'" (p. 60). Discourse analysis seeks to uncover tacit situated meanings and cultural models by interpreting spoken or written cues and clues, which guide us "as to how to move back and forth between language and context (situations)" (Gee, 1999, p. 85).

Gee identified six interrelated "building tasks" we use to make meaning from and through language:

1. *Semiotic building*: using cues or clues to assemble situated meanings about what semiotic (communicative) systems, systems of knowledge, and ways of knowing, are here and now relevant and activated.

2. *World building*: using cues or clues to assemble situated meanings about what is here and now (taken as) "reality," what is here and now (taken as) present and absent, concrete and abstract, "real" and "unreal," probable, possible, and impossible.

3. *Activity building*: using cues or clues to assemble situated meanings about what activity or activities are going on, composed of what specific actions.

4. *Socioculturally-situated identity and relationship building*: using cues or clues to assemble situated meanings about what identities and relationships are relevant to the interaction, with their concomitant attitudes, values, ways of feeling, ways of knowing and believing, as well as ways of acting and interacting.

5. *Political building*: using cues or clues to construct the nature and relevance of various "social goods," such as status and power, and anything else taken as a "social good" here and now (e.g., beauty, humor, verbalness, specialist knowledge, a fancy car, etc.).

6. *Connection building*: using cues or clues to make assumptions about how the past and future of an interaction, verbally and non-verbally, are connected to the present moment and to

each other—after all, interactions always have some degree of continuous coherence.

As mentioned in Chapter 3, discourse analysis should be based on the details that are most relevant in the situation, and in the case of this study, the building tasks most relevant to my research questions were world building, socioculturally-situated identity and relationship building, and political building.

Returning to the example from Chapter 1 of a student's written response to fairy tales (Data Set #1), it is apparent how the three building tasks (#2, #4, and #5) are relevant:

> What a girl wants should be respect for herself and a strong foundation of who she is. Fairy tales show common misconceptions of gender roles and stereotypes. They lead girls to believe that men can and will control their lives, and that the pretty girls always get the prince. Where is the fairy tale that emphasizes, once upon a time there lived a woman who stuck up for what she believed in and did not settle for cheap tricks? Women and girls today need realistic gender roles, roles that show how beautiful and strong every girl can be.

This student explicitly exhibited a questioning stance toward fairy tales. Looking through the lenses of building tasks, the student indicates that "reality" contains harmful stereotypes (world building), society values passive, marriageable (heterosexual) females (socioculturally-situated identity and relationship building), and men have power (political building).

Another student's response was quite different:

> Young girls that maybe aren't very attractive, popular, and are unhappy can look at Cinderella or Snow White and hold out hope that maybe one day their lives too will change and their prince will come. It might not always sound like the most realistic scenario, but if we don't have dreams...what are we living for, right?" [ellipses in original]

This student viewed waiting for one's prince to come as positive (world building), indicating that a woman's "dream" is to marry a man (socioculturally-situated identity and relationship building), and implying that men have power because women must wait and "hold out hope" until they are chosen, although this power is not perceived as negative (political building). Gee (1999) explained, "Cultural models are not just based on our experiences in the world, they 'project' onto the world, from where we 'stand' (where we are socially positioned), certain viewpoints about what is right and wrong, and what can or cannot be done to solve problems in the world" (p. 74). The above examples demonstrate participants' adherence to particular cultural models, which reveal these individuals' self-perceptions and viewpoints, thereby suggesting their roles in the social production of ideas.

Much of the data collected for this study "speaks for itself" in terms of revealing participants' assumptions about the world. The first section of findings presents a whole-class breakdown of responses to each writing prompt, reported here in the order in which the data were collected. The second section incorporates information gathered from the individual interviews, with data from the written responses interwoven as appropriate. The third section briefly organizes the whole-class and individual data into thematic categories. Hence, I begin with an overall interpretation, narrow the focus to particular individuals, assimilate the parts and whole, and then (in Chapter 7) present a "complex, holistic picture" (Creswell, 1998, p. 15), in an effort to "uncover the different layers of universality and particularity that are confronted in the specific case at hand—what is broadly universal, what generalizes to other similar situations, what is unique to the given instance" (Erickson, 1986, p. 130).

Whole Class Written Responses

As delineated in Chapter 5, the shaded entries in the tables below indicate participants who were interviewed; their responses are discussed in more detail in the second section.

Data Set #1

Out-of-class essay regarding fairy tales (N=25). The first stage of analysis, identifying the main idea of the essay, is represented in Appendix C. Two categories of main ideas adhered closely to the writing prompt. The first category was whether fairy tales reflect society or society shapes fairy tales (or perhaps a combination of both), which included the concept that traditional fairy tales present inappropriate stereotypes for today's readers. Implied in this category was the notion that since fairy tales influence readers, a particular lesson or moral is being conveyed and absorbed. Twenty participants focused on this main idea regarding the influence of fairy tales. The second category, how fairy tales have changed over time, included comparing various versions of the same tale, and three participants chose this topic. Finally, two participants discussed the predictable qualities of fairy tales versus the elements of surprise.

The table below represents the second stage of analysis, beginning with evidence of whether the participant exhibited any form of questioning the text, followed by the modified version of Apol's (1998) questions: Does the participant: question *power* (dominance and submission)?; address the text's unspoken, *underlying messages*, such as influences of the author's values, contemporary culture and/or place?; question the *absences*/gaps/silences in the text (what is missing) or what is represented as *normal*?; identify *similarities* with other texts ("texts" in a broad sense, including popular culture)?; and consider the influence of his/her own experiences (*self*) and/or culture when responding to the text? (More detailed responses are indicated in Appendix C.) An asterisk (*) indicates the participant was also interviewed.

Participant	Overall Questioning	Power	Underlying Messages	Absences/ Normal	Similarities	Self
1	✓		✓	✓	✓	
2*						
3	✓		✓	✓	✓	✓
4						
5	✓			✓	✓	
6*						
7	✓		✓	✓		
8	✓		✓			
9						
10*	✓	✓	✓	✓		
11						
12						✓
13						
14	✓		✓	✓		
15*	✓		✓			
16	✓		✓		✓	
17*	✓				✓	
18						
19	✓		✓	✓	✓	

Participant	Overall Questioning	Power	Underlying Messages	Absences/ Normal	Similarities	Self
20	✓			✓		✓
21	✓		✓			
22	✓		✓		✓	
23*	✓		✓	✓	✓	
24*	✓		✓			
25						
Totals	16	1	13	9	8	2

More than half of the participants exhibited some form of questioning the text (64%), with 13 pointing out underlying messages of fairy tales, mainly regarding gender roles. The English 306A (lecture portion) professor discussed underlying messages often, and some participants supported their main ideas with quotations from the professor. For example, one student cited the following statement by the English 306A professor: "'Each version reflects the culture of its time.'" Such methods of questioning the text seemed to parrot discussions from the lecture course, suggesting that the level of questioning was relatively superficial. Moreover, it would seem easier to find "problems," especially gender stereotypes, in fairy tales because they were clearly told and written long ago and have not been updated significantly for contemporary society. However, students' process of imitating the questions used by the English 306A process could also be the beginning level of understanding, in which participants learn to appropriate the use of questioning as a tool of inquiry (Wertsch, 1998). In their written responses, participants tended to highlight gender discrepancies when discussing the absences and presentations of what is considered normal in society (world building). One of the two participants with children of her own wrote, "Little girls need to hear stories about women getting ahead in society through hard work and determination." Another participant explained,

> Growing up in a society where a child's walls are adorned with Disney characters and having princess themed birthdays are the norm, it is no wonder that little girls grow up with certain ideals. When a young child travels to Disneyland for the first time, what is the main structure they see after walking down Main Street? Sleeping Beauty's Castle.

Regarding the similarities to other texts, most of the responses were related to comparing various versions of a fairy tale, such as

Disney movies or the film *Pretty Woman*, which depicts a prostitute in the role of Cinderella, and a wealthy businessman as Prince Charming. The cultural model of romance is apparent as "true love conquers all," a prevalent theme in cultural texts, especially media targeted toward women—"chick flicks," fashion magazines, and romance novels. The three comments mentioning one's own experiences essentially depicted childhood memories, such as,

> At one point in time, I felt that in order to achieve this state of bliss I was to marry, bear children, and live in a house surrounded by a white-picket fence. More specifically, I felt that I was to fall in "love at first sight," have an amazing "fairy tale" wedding, and live "happily ever after."

The one participant, Penny, who explicitly discussed power (political building) referred to "Snow White and the Seven Dwarfs," who required Snow White to "do the cooking, make our beds, do the washing, the sewing, and the knitting, and keep everything neat and clean" (Grimm, p. 57). Penny noted,

> The male characters take the poor girl in on one condition, no, six conditions. They control how the girl will be living. This male dominance may lead girls to believe it is okay to be controlled. Young girls need to have a strong sense of self to live in a male dominated society.

Penny rejected the cultural model of woman as servant, emphasizing her point with a list of duties that Snow White would cheerfully undertake.

While most participants questioned the texts to varying degrees, Katie clearly assumed that fairy tales were obviously not real—these stories exercised the imagination and could be valued for their elements of fantasy (world building). She wrote,

> No one really believes that they are going to bite into an apple, fall into a deep slumber, only to be awoken when the apple falls out of their mouth and have a prince say to them, "I love you more than anything else in the world." But it is fun to just think about it. People do not think that they are going to sleep for a hundred years like Sleeping Beauty and be woken up by a kiss from their true love, who assured the future princess that he "loved her more than himself." These ideas and stories allow for so much creative thought and enjoyment.

Katie claimed that "no one" would believe these far-fetched tales, although her opinion was definitely atypical. The concept that fairy tales influence us was a taken-for-granted idea in nearly all of the essays, with the following response as typical: "Fairy tales have long been a part of our society, for they influence and shape our expectations and standards of behavior." Moreover, participants offered numerous generalizations, including assumptions about parents, such as one participant's comment regarding the Grimms' version of "Snow White," "Parents today would never read a story like this to their children. Instead they can watch Disney versions that are softened up to protect children." Another student wrote, "Parents want their children to learn lessons and manners from the movies and books they are interested in, not how to kill an evil babysitter or hurt their brother" (neither participant was a parent). These responses revealed participants' assumptions regarding the cultural model of a "good" family, as well as beliefs in the innocence of childhood—examples of world building.

Many participants expressed a belief that the lessons and morals in fairy tales were important: "Although these stories were written several centuries ago, we continue to use their morals and values for direction in everyday life." Some of the qualities that were pointed out as stereotypical and negative for females (for example, passivity and sacrifice), were also considered positive attributes for children:

> Fairy tales mold our expectations at a very young age and we are taught what is expected of us. As little girls we are taught that if we are good and pure, and wait patiently one day we too will be rescued by our prince like Cinderella.

There was an assumption that readers absorb explicit and implicit "lessons" in texts, incorporating messages of "right" and "wrong" into their consciousness. The implication of this view of reality (world building) suggests a belief in the inherent influence of texts, but more importantly, it also indicates an expectation of didacticism privileging enjoyment with regard to books and movies directed expressly toward children. Consequently, other cultural texts (for example, the adult movie *Pretty Woman*) were not necessarily identified as didactic, pointing toward an assumption that only children's texts "teach." This belief invokes the cultural model of childhood innocence, in which adults select appropriate materials for children, who in turn, will learn the proposed lessons.

A corresponding trend was participants' assumption of knowing what is "right" for children, clearly using oneself as the standard. Discussing a version of "Little Red Riding Hood" in which the wolf tells the girl to undress, one participant wrote,

> This passage has explicit sexual connotations; therefore, the modern day version omitted this incident completely. It is inappropriate for children to be exposed to any type of sexual content within books; hence, the recent version reflects this belief by excluding that scene in the 1983 version. It is society's duty to protect a child's innocence. Those sections which could hinder a child's innocence have been omitted from the oral version.

Likewise, another participant revealed her beliefs about what constitutes a "healthy" family environment when discussing the characters Cinderella and Snow White,

> Neither girl is raised with a loving family who treats them with love and respect. This story is too often seen in families of today's society. Young children are brought up without both biological parents and many children are neglected. Fairy tales are a way for these children to escape their reality and enter a world of fantasy. A world filled with less pain and more happiness.

This comment reflects an assumption that children in single-parent families experience pain and unhappiness, thereby reinforcing the "normal" family as a preferable model for the health and happiness of children. Once again, responses revealed participants' assumptions regarding the cultural model of a "good" family, as well as beliefs in the innocence of childhood—examples of world building.

Data Set #2

Brief response to reading about various approaches to literary criticism (N=20). I developed a grid based on participants' responses; the categories were: literary criticism is valuable, literary criticism is somewhat valuable, literary criticism is not valuable, and the participant did not know (or did not indicate) whether literary criticism is valuable. (More detailed responses are indicated in Appendix E.) An asterisk (*) indicates the participant was also interviewed. A strikethrough (=) the number indicates the participant was absent.

Participant	Valuable	Somewhat Valuable	Not Valuable	Don't Know
1		✓		
2*				✓
3		✓		
4				✓
5	✓			
6*		✓		
7		✓		
8			✓	
9		✓		
10*			✓	
11		✓		
12		✓		
~~13~~				
14		✓		
15*	✓			
~~16~~				
~~17*~~				
18		✓		
~~19~~				
20		✓		
21		✓		
22		✓		
23*		✓		
~~24*~~				
25		✓		
Total	**2**	**14**	**2**	**2**

Five students were absent when these data were collected, and 14 of 20 participants (70%) indicated that literary criticism was somewhat valuable. However, their responses were relatively vague, probably because this was a fairly new concept. One participant wrote, "I enjoy reading for the simple fact that I am able to imagine the goings on in the story. Taking a critical approach to literature is obviously new to me." According to another student,

> I do not really agree totally with the interpretations we have gone over. I feel that we should interpret what we read on our own. I feel very disappointed when I have interpreted a fairy tale on my own and then get to the class and find out that I was wrong.

Ella believed that most interpretations were "workable, if one is able to back up the idea. Some, for me, really push the envelope or really stretch for an interpretation. And some are just downright knee slappers." Ella's comment seemed to capture the overall reaction of the students; they viewed literary criticism as a new concept that might be useful to people who have a more "sophisticated" relationship with literature.

Data Set #3

In-class essay regarding critical literacy (N=25). I developed a grid based on participants' responses: when in the classroom, the participant would use critical literacy, would use critical literacy with third grade and older, would not use critical literacy, and did not know (or did not indicate) whether or not he or she would use critical literacy. (More detailed responses are indicated in Appendix D.) An asterisk (*) indicates the participant was also interviewed.

Participant	Would Use	Would Use with 3rd Grade & Older	Would Not Use	Don't Know
1		✓		
2*	✓			
3	✓			
4	✓			
5	✓			
6*				✓
7	✓			
8		✓		
9		✓		
10*				✓
11	✓			
12			✓	
13	✓			
14				✓
15*	✓			
16	✓			
17*	✓			
18	✓			
19	✓			

Participant	Would Use	Would Use with 3rd Grade & Older	Would Not Use	Don't Know
20	✓			
21	✓			
22	✓			
23*	✓			
24*	✓			
25			✓	
Total	17	3	2	3

The majority of participants (68%) indicated they would use critical literacy once they became teachers, with 12% stating they would wait until students were in third grade, and another 12% did not know or did not indicate whether they would use critical literacy. Two students (8%) were adamant about not using critical literacy. One participant stated that children should learn to read for enjoyment first, explaining:

> While I understand we don't need to shelter children from the real world, I believe there's no need to shove it in their face either. Reading stories such as "Cinderella" and "Snow White" isn't a bad thing just because they stereotype genders and give the belief that everyone should strive to live "happily ever after." At least these stories allow children to use their imaginations. To me, that's more important than "saving the world" at this time in their lives.

Another student asserted that children's innocence must be protected:

> Innocence allows an individual to think freely without preconceived notions. It allows people to conjure their own ideas without the burden of others implementing specific models to follow.

This response revealed adherence to the cultural model of childhood innocence.

However, most participants conjectured they would be willing to use critical literacy in their future classrooms, although some responses were certainly more reflective than others. For instance, one participant's essay essentially repeated many of the concepts in the article (McDaniel, 2004), without introducing any of her own ideas or examples. Another student wrote,

> Critical literacy is an approach that all teachers should follow. It is an excellent way of learning and one that will better the students' life. I know that I

will be using this approach in my classroom and I hope that other teachers
will have the same good sense.

Aside from being written in such a general way that it could address
virtually any topic, it should also be pointed out that Freire would
argue that people should not adopt such a stance unless they truly
believe in it, so in the case of this participant's response, she appeared
to be speaking "for" rather than "with" others by hoping that other
teachers would have the same "good sense."

Many participants exhibited a more balanced approach, such as
the following:

> The question is whether or not only one method should be used: reading for
> entertainment or critical analysis. I believe that teachers can and should in-
> corporate both aspects into their lesson, where the lesson's goal determines
> which method will be used.

This student recognized the need for thoughtful, purposeful planning, and many responses indicated future teachers' desires to foster
students' imaginations and to encourage reading for pleasure. For
instance, one of the three participants who explicitly stated that critical literacy should be used only with older children wrote, "This approach, unfortunately, can ruin text for younger learners who want to
read for pleasure, not for critiquing literature."

As with most of the essays in this data set, the participant did not
provide evidence for her assertion; she merely assumed that critical
literacy would ruin enjoyment. Interestingly, participants discussed
the idea of reading for pleasure or entertainment only in this essay
regarding critical literacy. Previous and subsequent responses indicated an overall belief in the importance of children learning from
books, as well as the assumption that texts influence readers. Perhaps
reflection about the concept of critical literacy temporarily disrupted
participants' expectations of texts.

A few participants offered examples from personal experience,
such as Katie, who explained:

> Often when I read articles like this [McDaniel, 2004] I wonder who doesn't
> do this kind of thing? As a little kid my mom and I (my dad also!) always

had discussions about books like Emma[31] and her mom. Also, growing up and always volunteering in my mom's classroom, I have been exposed to many of the approaches suggested in a critical literacy approach. So whether or not my teachers used this approach towards reading I got it from another end at home.

Another participant wrote, "I personally wish that my parents would have taught me to take a story for more than its face value." Clearly, the participants' responses reflected their own experiences, which in turn influenced their thoughts about teaching future students (world building). Nevertheless, it would be a mistake to assume that a desire to use critical literacy on some level will transfer into practice—either in their roles as educators or students. In fact, for many participants, critical literacy seemed like a nice idea at the time, but it did not make a lasting impression.

Data Set #4

Out-of-class essay regarding picture books (N=24; participant #21 did not submit an essay). The first stage of analysis, identifying the main idea of the essay, is represented in Appendix C. The main ideas predominantly corresponded to two categories: the book's message or lesson, and synopsis of the text. Fourteen participants chose to discuss the didactic qualities of the picture book, pointing out the "valuable message" or "important lesson" inherent in the text. A crucial assumption underlying these essays was a belief that the message was obvious to readers, implying children would be influenced and that they would "learn" from the picture books. The second category, with nine essays, entailed varying degrees of summary, ranging from essentially a book review ("I love *Eloise*!") to more in-depth discussions of the interaction between words and illustrations. However, the focus in these essays was on talking about rather than questioning the text. One essay could be categorized as exhibiting intense questioning, as the participant analyzed the *David* series of picture books by David Shannon. She wrote, "it is quite obvious that Shannon feels that the majority of children today receive little attention from paren-

---

[31] Emma was the pseudonym I used for my daughter Megan in the participants' copy of the article (McDaniel, 2004). I used my daughter's real name (with her permission) in the published version.

tal figures and are forced to depend upon public schools to give them the structure they need." This participant used scenes of David depicted alone as evidence to support her claims, although one could refute her argument with examples of other illustrations, such as the final page of *No, David!* (Shannon, 1998), in which David's mother hugs him and says, "Yes, David...I love you!" Additionally, all of the words in the text are clearly coming from the mother, so one could also counter the claim that "there is little to no adult supervision in David's life." Nevertheless, this essay represents a clear attempt at questioning the text—looking for underlying messages and pointing out instances that are presented as normal. By contrast, another participant argued that *No, David!* is useful to "initiate a discussion about appropriate and inappropriate activities, as well as listening to your parents," and she referred to the book as an "effective tool for children."

The table below represents the second stage of analysis, beginning with evidence of whether the participant exhibited any form of questioning the text, followed by the modified version of Apol's (1998) questions: Does the participant: question *power* (dominance and submission)?; address the text's unspoken, *underlying messages*, such as influences of the author's values, contemporary culture and/or place?; question the *absences*/gaps/silences in the text (what is missing) or what is represented as *normal*?; identify *similarities* with other texts ("texts" in a broad sense, including popular culture)?; and consider the influence of his/her own experiences (*self*) and/or culture when responding to the text? (More detailed responses are indicated in Appendix C.) An asterisk (*) indicates the participant was also interviewed. A strikethrough (=) the number indicates the participant did not submit an essay.

Participant	Overall Questioning	Power	Underlying Messages	Absences/ Normal	Similarities	Self
1						
2*						
3						
4						
5	✓			✓	✓	
6*						
7	✓		✓			
8	✓		✓	✓		

Participant	Overall Questioning	Power	Underlying Messages	Absences/ Normal	Similarities	Self
9						
10*						
11	✓		✓	✓		✓
12						
13						
14						
15*						
16						
17*						
18	✓		✓			
19						
20						
~~21~~						
22	✓		✓	✓		
23*						
24*						
25						✓
Total	**6**	**1**	**5**	**5**	**1**	**2**

In contrast to the first out-of-class essay regarding fairy tales, in which 16 (64%) participants questioned the texts in some manner, only 6 participants (25%) questioned the picture books they chose to discuss. Moreover, the level of questioning was relatively superficial—tending to focus on particular elements of the texts rather than the overall works. For example, one participant pointed out the ways in which the bilingual picture book *The Three Pigs (Los Tres Cerdos: Nacho, Tito, and Miguel)* (Salinas, 1998) differs from the traditional tale. This essay celebrated the use of "Spanglish" and intertextual references to Chicano culture. Another participant wrote about *The True Story of the Three Little Pigs* (Scieszka, 1989), which presents the wolf's version of the tale—Alexander T. Wolf claims he was "framed," and insists the *real* story involves a cup of sugar and a sneeze. This essay focused on the wolf's persistence, claiming the "the book has a message of not giving up," rather than paying attention to the unreliable narrator's perspective.

Two of the participants who questioned texts used books that were discussed in class: *Olivia* (Falconer, 2000) and *The Giving Tree* (Silverstein, 1964). The essay about *Olivia* reiterated the concept of idealized childhood setting, as I had pointed out in class. By contrast, *The Giving Tree* essay highlighted the prevalence of materialism in our culture, questioning what is considered valuable within our society. The concept of prejudice was emphasized by two other participants, although not without some problems. One essay discussed discrimination in *Miss Spider's Tea Party* (Kirk, 1994), explaining

> This story as a whole conveys the feelings of the time period in which it was written. This book was written in 1955. This was the time of the Civil Rights Movement's strongest strength. This book has a significant purpose in conveying the belief of the author that things are not always as they seem. David Kirk has a lot of hidden meanings in this book that will continually be shared through his readers.

This student's claim was unwarranted because the book was actually published in 1994 (Kirk was born in 1955). Nevertheless, she detected a "message" of discrimination, which indicates an attempt at questioning the text. The second essay about prejudice used *Clifford and the Grouchy Neighbors* (Bridwell, 1989), asserting that the neighbors' dislike of the big red dog "is a direct implication to the racism that bombards our world still today." Similar to the essay about the *David* series, the evidence used to support this argument was weak. Moreover, as with 13 other participants, this student explicitly assumed readers will "learn" from the text: "*Clifford and the Grouchy Neighbors* is a didactic story with the purpose of teaching tolerance." Another participant claimed that readers of Carle's *The Very Hungry Caterpillar* would learn about "the seven days of the week, the numbers one through five, and the life cycle of a butterfly." She devoted the majority of the essay to discussing the important message of nutrition in the text: "giving children an example of how eating too much junk food can make them sick to their stomach."

Three participants selected picture books that overtly address social issues[32]: *The House that Crack Built* (Clark, 1992), which deals with drug abuse; *Voices in the Park* (Browne, 1998), which offers four different perspectives of the same scenario; and *The Big Box* (Morrison, 1999), about three children who are locked in a box because they "can't handle their freedom." Nevertheless, the first essay emphasized the lesson of the text, and the other two essays essentially sum-

---

[32] These were picture books I brought into class on October 14, 2003, which the students asked to borrow.

marized the books, pointing out the interactions between the words and pictures.

Similar to the responses for the out-of-class essay regarding fairy tales (Data Set #1), participants exhibited a trend toward assuming they knew what was "right" for children, once again using themselves as the standard. One participant discussed her childhood relationship with an elderly babysitter, and she used *Wilfrid Gordon McDonald Partridge* (Fox, 1991) to claim, "Children are the key to the future and it is important for them to have relationships with older, wiser people" (world building). She also asserted, "there are no hidden messages or meanings in the illustrations that the text does not mention." Certainly, this student's "transaction" with the book is based on her own experiences and beliefs. Regardless, it would not be absurd to offer another interpretation: the protagonist is a white, English-speaking male; there is obvious acceptance that old people should be separated from their families (institutionalized); and the cultural model of a "real" or "normal" family with one mother and one father is evident. Interestingly, this explication of the "apparently innocent" *Wilfrid Gordon McDonald Partridge* was published by the author of the book—Mem Fox (2001)—in an effort to point out that "there's no such thing as a politically innocent picture book." The participant also asserted, "the story *wants* children to see how easy it is for them to have something in common with an older person" (emphasis added). I believe Fox would argue otherwise. Certainly, there is a delightfully positive depiction of old age; however, it is inappropriate to presume to know an author's intention. Readers can cite evidence from a text to support their own interpretations, but without explicit information, such as personal correspondence or an interview, it is unreasonable to claim knowledge of a writer's thinking process.

In addition to some participants' assumptions about authorial intent, the cultural model of a "healthy" family—based on the white, middle-class model (perhaps best exemplified by *Olivia*)—was evident to varying degrees. An essay about *And the Dish Ran Away with the Spoon* contains references to a map, which "not only provides humor with silly expressions…and illustrations to go along with it, mainly for the parent reading the book as a bedtime story…." The participant clearly envisioned a scenario in which a parent and child engage in reading prior to the child going to sleep, an assumption which is likely based on the participant's own upbringing. Similarly, another participant commented, "I think Eloise looks up to her nanny to be her mother. I also find this a little sad that she sees a nanny as her mother since her biological mother is gone working so much."[33] This adult reader perceived the situation as "sad," although Eloise is not depicted as upset about her circumstances. Implicit in this participant's response was the belief that a "happy" family consists of a stay-at-home mother, a scenario that would depend upon a hard-working father.

Data Set #5

Brief response to *Daddy's Roommate* (N=22). I developed a grid based on participants' responses; the categories were: when in the class-room, the participant would use *Daddy's Roommate* with students, would not use *Daddy's Roommate* with students, did not know (or did not indicate) whether he or she would use *Daddy's Roommate* with students. (More detailed responses are indicated in Appendix E.) An asterisk (*) indicates the participant was also interviewed. A strike-through (=) the number indicates the participant was absent.

Participant	Would Use	Would Not Use	Don't Know
~~1~~			
2*			✓
3			✓
4			✓
5		✓	
6*			✓
7	✓		
8		✓	
9		✓	
10*	✓		
11		✓	
12			✓

---

[33] *Eloise,* by Kay Thompson, was originally published in 1955 with the subtitle *"a book for precocious grownups."* Initially a book for adults, the text was changed over time to appeal to younger audiences.

Participant	Would Use	Would Not Use	Don't Know
13		✓	
14			✓
15*	✓		
16	✓		
17*			✓
18	✓		
19		✓	
20	✓		
~~21~~			
22	✓		
23*			✓
~~24*~~			
25		✓	
Total	**7**	**7**	**8**

Seven participants (32%) stated that they would use *Daddy's Roommate* in a classroom setting, seven (32%) would not use it, and eight (36%) did not know whether they would use the book. *Daddy's Roommate* disrupted many participants' concept of a "normal" family, as well as their beliefs about the "innocence" of children's literature. The more violent and sexual versions of fairy tales were presented to the participants as not intended for children, but *Daddy's Roommate* was clearly a children's book—a disturbing thought for many. The following comments were typical among those who would not use the book in their classroom or did not know whether they would use it:

- "My first reactions were in shock because I did not think that a children's book would focus on that issue."

- "In no way am I opposed to homosexuality, it's just that I've never heard it being discussed so bluntly in a children's picture book before."

- "If I had kids, I wouldn't want them to be reading this book....This is a moral issue and parents are responsible for teaching morals and values to their children."

♦ "I'm not saying it's [homosexuality] bad but it's very important that parents discuss these kinds of subjects with their children."

Another student wrote,

> Many people, including myself, feel uncomfortable discussing this topic with their students because it is so controversial. I personally was shocked because I did not expect the book to be about a gay couple. I thought it was going to be about his new girlfriend moving in.

This comment revealed the participant's value system, as she seemed to oppose homosexuality, but believed unmarried heterosexual cohabitation was acceptable. Such responses suggest that participants are willing to present ideas that correspond to their own beliefs, and they expect parents (within the cultural model of family) to fill in any gaps. The participants who indicated they would like to use *Daddy's Roommate* in their future classrooms tended to be somewhat hesitant, responding with comments such as, "This book is something I would want to read to my classroom but would have to research it more so that I wouldn't get into trouble."

I collected the above data on November 18, 2003, and the participants' responses were fresh in my memory when I attended a session of the National Reading Conference entitled "Capitalism, Christianity, and Sexual Orientation: Issues of Power and Ideology in Children's Literature" on December 3, 2003. One of the presenters, Jill Hermann-Wilmarth, discussed using books about homosexuality with her children's literature undergraduates (future teachers), and reported similar results to my study. Her students strongly resisted using books with gay and lesbian themes with elementary school students. Hermann-Wilmarth claimed,

> If preservice teachers have never had the opportunities to explore their own homophobia, or the ways that homophobia affects students, the likelihood that they will successfully interrupt the ideological heterosexism of schools seems slim. (2003, December)

Despite "moral" issues such as potential violence targeted toward gay students or the children of gay parents occurring in school settings, many preservice teachers firmly believe that sensitive topics are off-limits in the classroom.

Data Set #6

In-class essay regarding controversial issues in children's books (N=25). I developed a grid based on participants' responses; the categories were, when in the classroom, the participant would expose students to all topics, would expose students to some topics, would not expose students to any controversial topics, and did not know (or did not indicate) whether or not he or she would expose students to controversial topics. (More detailed responses are indicated in Appendix D.) An asterisk (*) indicates the participant was also interviewed.

Participant	Expose to All Topics	Expose to Some Topics	No Controversial Topics	Don't Know
1			✓	
2*		✓		
3	✓			
4	✓			
5	✓			
6*	✓			
7			✓	
8			✓	
9			✓	
10*	✓			
11		✓		
12	✓			
13	✓			
14		✓		
15*	✓			
16	✓			
17*				✓
18				✓
19	✓			
20	✓			
21	✓			
22	✓			
23*				✓
24*	✓			
25			✓	
Total	**14**	**3**	**5**	**3**

Fourteen participants (56%) indicated that they would expose students to controversial children's books, but by this stage in the data collection process, it was becoming apparent that for the most part, participants had not thought much about controversial topics and whether they would discuss sensitive issues with their future students. Some participants seemed to contradict themselves by expressing shock at *Daddy's Roommate*, while two days later, one such participant insisted that

> Book banning is a severe form of action in which books that are deemed "inappropriate" for children are abolished from book shelves. As each day passes, more and more books are put on this list and soon library shelves in schools will be bare. The censorship and the banning of books in children's literature is a destructive aspect of society in that it goes against the first amendment, shelters the youth from issues in society, and decreases the need for parent participation in the lives of their children.

Similarly, another participant began her essay by stating, "I think that book banning is wrong" and commented on the ways in which *Daddy's Roommate* teaches tolerance. However, several pages later she wrote, "I have to agree with the mother who found the book *Boys and Sex* in her 10 year old son's school library that it probably should not have been available to him."[34]

The same participant who was surprised that *Daddy's Roommate* (Data Set #5) was not about a new girlfriend moving in stated, "In my opinion, certain books, depending upon age appropriateness and the content, are not meant for the classroom" (world building). She did not provide specific examples of books to illustrate her point, but she wrote,

> I do not believe young children should be exposed to topics such as religion, homosexuality, or sex inside the classroom. I would hope their parents discuss these topics when the time was right at home.

This response suggests that the participant knows what is "right" for children. Likewise, another student wrote,

> Introducing topics such as homosexuality and prejudice in the classroom may cause more harm than good because of differing views of teachers, parents, and students.

---

[34] The participant was referring to the article "Off the Shelves: The Battle Over Book Banning" (Stapinski, 2003).

Several participants were very clear about their opinions regarding controversial issues. One student claimed, "our children are innocent and should be kept out of harm's way." Another participant wrote, "I was quite surprised in my English class when about 50% of the class would allow extremely controversial books in their classroom." This participant was referring to our class discussion about *Daddy's Roommate*, and apparently she estimated the percentage of students who indicated by raising their hands that they would use the book. However, the participants' written responses about *Daddy's Roommate* did not support the claim of 50% (see Data Set #5). Nevertheless, many participants expressed belief in the cultural models of childhood innocence and a "normal" family.

Data Set #7

Out-of-class essay regarding children's/young adult novels (N=24; participant #21 did not submit an essay). Participants could write about any of the following novels *The Whipping Boy* (Fleischman, 1986), *Harry Potter and the Sorcerer's Stone* (Rowling, 1997), *Baseball in April and Other Stories* (Soto, 1990), *A Little Princess* (Burnett, 1905), and *The Watsons Go to Birmingham—1963* (Curtis, 1995). No participant wrote about *Baseball in April*. The first stage of analysis, identifying the main idea of the essay, is represented in Appendix C. The main ideas adhered to the writing prompt and were categorized as follows: analysis of the main character's (or characters') development (including the Hero Journey); highlighting an important message or lesson; and comparisons between two texts.

The table below represents the second stage of analysis, beginning with evidence of whether the participant exhibited any form of questioning the text, followed by the modified version of Apol's (1998) questions: Does the participant: question *power* (dominance and submission)?; address the text's unspoken, *underlying messages*, such as influences of the author's values, contemporary culture and/or place?; question the *absences*/gaps/silences in the text (what is missing) or what is represented as *normal*?; identify *similarities* with other texts ("texts" in a broad sense, including popular culture)?; and consider the influence of his/her own experiences (*self*) and/or culture when responding to the text? (More detailed responses are indicated in Appendix C.) An asterisk (*) indicates the participant was also interviewed. A strikethrough (=) the number indicates the participant did not submit an essay.

Participant	Overall Questioning	Power	Underlying Messages	Absences/ Normal	Similarities	Self
1						
2*						
3					✓	
4						
5						
6*						
7						
8						
9	✓		✓			
10*						
11						
12						
13						
14					✓	
15*						
16						
17*	✓	✓	✓	✓		✓
18						
19					✓	
20					✓	
~~21~~						
22						
23*						
24*						
25	✓		✓		✓	
Total	**3**	**1**	**3**	**1**	**5**	**1**

Three participants (13%) showed evidence of questioning the texts. One wrote about *The Whipping Boy,* pointing out how the main character develops in a positive way because he breaks the social barriers between himself and his lower class counterpart (political building). She stated,

> The ability for Prince Brat and Jemmy to break down the constrictions holding them to their classes provides an excellent theme in the book, and also may be utilized as an idea that discourages discrimination.

The second essay demonstrating a questioning stance was about *The Watsons Go to Birmingham*, which is an overtly political text because it addresses various forms of prejudice and dramatizes the 1963 bombing of the Sixteenth Avenue Baptist Church, in which four little girls were killed during Sunday school. This participant highlighted the message of discrimination, explaining that, "as a reader one can deduce that discrimination is dangerous because it can injure others emotionally and physically." This student's response indicates socioculturally-situated identity and relationship building.

The third essay with evidence of questioning is very problematic. The participant (Katie, who also agreed to be interviewed) chose to discuss sexism in *Harry Potter and the Sorcerer's Stone*. While reading the draft, which was submitted on December 2, 2003, I was intrigued by the clarity of ideas, including comments about Hermione sacrificing her values, Professor McGonagall as a negative model for females, and the fact that author Rowling is the single mother of a daughter. It was such an interesting argument that I decided to look for more information on the Internet. To my disappointment, I found an article on salon.com (Schoefer, 2000) that followed nearly the same trajectory. Below are some examples:

> *Katie*: Quidditch and its soccer like qualities interested me, the shops in Diagon Alley were fascinating, and the Sorting Hat for first year students to be assigned was intriguing. There is one thing that bothered me after further analysis and discussion of the book in class and after further thinking about it on my own; why did there seem to be so much sexism?
>
> *Schoefer*: Of course, Diagon Alley haunted me, the Sorting Hat dazzled me, Quidditch intrigued me. Believe me, I tried as hard as I could to ignore the sexism.
>
> *Katie*: One of the most obvious scenes in the book that shows the author does not look at Hermione as an equal is what I would like to call the damsel in distress scene.
>
> *Schoefer*: Like every Hollywood damsel in distress, Hermione depends on the resourcefulness of boys and repays them with her complicity.
>
> *Katie*: The male authority figure [Dumbledore] is given a completely different character [than the female McGonagall]. He is able to keep his feelings and emotions under control and she is not.
>
> *Schoefer*: Although she makes a great effort to keep her feelings under control, in a situation of crisis she loses herself in emotions because she lacks Dumbledore's vision of the bigger picture.

Katie: After further thinking the thought that the book may be considered sexist by some, especially feminist [sic] confused me even more because the author of the book, J.K. Rowling was a single mother of a girl.

Schoefer: But I remain perplexed that a woman (the mother of a daughter, no less) would, at the turn of the 20th century, write a book so full of stereotypes.

The similarities were startling. I printed a copy of the article and gave it to Katie; she explained that she had visited the website and used some of the ideas, but had not yet provided citations. There were empty parentheses in two areas, indicating that she was planning to provide citations for two quotations. Katie also claimed that she came up with the idea of sexism in *Harry Potter* and then found corresponding information on the Internet. Nevertheless, the final version of this essay was quite similar to the draft. For the purposes of this study, I have counted her essay as showing evidence of questioning, although I am still not certain about the authenticity of ideas.

The participants who noted similarities with other texts were making comparisons with other novels or stories rather than questioning. Fourteen participants discussed *Harry Potter* (one student compared it to *The Whipping Boy* and another compared it to *A Little Princess*), mainly focusing on character development. Six participants chose to discuss *A Little Princess*, although none of the essays mentioned issues of colonialism, class differences, or racial inequalities that are quite evident in the text. Instead, they tended to focus on the "sweetness" of the main character. For example,

When Sara loses everything her attitude and demeanor do not change. Although Sara is abused and worked like an animal she finds strength within herself and acts like a princess should.

Likewise,

In the beginning of the story Sara is described as a child with wonderful characteristics; she is rich, beautiful, smart, and generous. These characteristics remain in Sara until the end of the story but due to the maturity process she goes through they change and become stronger.

Similar to Cinderella and other fairy tale heroines, Sara is rewarded for her beauty, passivity, and sacrifice. Obviously, some participants continued to view the qualities of a princess as positive models.

In fact, many essays continued to highlight the important lessons participants thought readers might learn. For example, the conclusion of an essay comparing "Cinderella" to *A Little Princess* a participant remarked,

> It is not a tale of beauty, but one of graciousness, something that we can all learn and adhere to our lives. Even a little princess like Sara can learn to be more gracious.

Perhaps the "we" mentioned in "we can all learn" refers to men as well as women, but I would suspect not, especially since the entire essay focused on two female characters. It is not too far-fetched to claim that many participants believed there were gender-specific lessons for girls and boys. *A Little Princess* is a "girl" book, whereas *Harry Potter* is a "boy" book. "In the end, Harry was acknowledged for his bravery by his friends, professors, and classmates," wrote one student. She continued,

> Harry's bravery helped him get through hard situations, and it is good for children to learn about bravery so they can overcome scary situations that you face while growing up in life.

Perhaps "children" does refer to both boys and girls; nevertheless, participants did not refer to Sara as "brave" or Harry Potter as "gracious." There appear to be obvious qualities that are considered appropriate for each gender. For example, Hermione (in *Harry Potter*) transformed through the course of the novel, according to one participant. "She is no longer a selfish, bossy, know-it-all; instead she has become a kind-hearted, loyal intelligent friend." This participant also speculated on Hermione's family, arguing,

> For the most part, the background of Hermione Granger still remains a mystery, but it can be *assumed* that she is an only child. Her over-bearing personality and parental tendencies mirror that of children who have been surrounded by a mother and father only. It is evident that she is used to receiving all of the attention, and Harry and Ron label Hermione as selfish, cocky, and bossy for many reasons. (emphasis added)

As the single parent of an only child (a daughter), I had to scrutinize my own reaction to this statement prior to analyzing the statement itself. I resented the belief that a child without siblings would "automatically" be selfish, cocky, and bossy, but I realized this participant's comment reflected a particular aspect of the cultural model of family.

That is, her statement seems to reproduce assumptions from the participant's own upbringing—a trend exemplified by many of the written responses previously discussed (world building). As the data so far have shown, many of the future teachers in this study adhere to cultural models that reproduce their own upbringing—predominantly white and middle-class. And as mentioned earlier, based on information gathered from our conversations, all participants who agreed to be interviewed were white, middle-class, native English speakers.

Individual Responses

This section incorporates information gathered from the seven individual interviews, with data from the written responses interwoven as appropriate. Below is a breakdown of the seven data sets, categorized by response type, and arranged by participant. The following pseudonyms correspond to the participant numbers used in the previous tables: #2 = Eloise, #6 = Dory, #10 = Penny, #15 = T.D., #17 = Katie, #23 = Ella, and #24 = Kiera. The column on the left indicates each data set, with the entries for each out-of-class essay specifying first whether there was evidence of questioning, and second, the main idea of the essay. Note that for data set #7, the out-of-class essay related to children's and young adult novels, Katie's essay exhibited extensive questioning, but it was problematic due to the possibility of plagiarism.

RESPONSE	ELOISE	DORY	PENNY	T.D.	KATIE	ELLA	KIERA
Out-of-Class Essays							
Fairy Tales #1			Question	Question	Question	Question	Question
Main Idea Picture Books #4	Change	Surprise	Influence	Surprise	Influence	Influence	Influence
Main Idea Novels #7	Synopsis	Lesson	Synopsis	Lesson	Synopsis / Question	Synopsis	Synopsis
Main Idea	Character	Character	Character	Character	Lesson	Lesson	Lesson

RESPONSE	ELOISE	DORY	PENNY	T.D.	KATIE	ELLA	KIERA
In-Class Essays							
Critical Literacy #3	Would use	Don't know	Don't know	Would use	Would use	Would use	Would use
Controversial Issues #6	Some	All	All	All	Don't know	Don't know	All
Brief Responses							
Literary Criticism #2	Don't know	Somewhat valuable		Valuable		Somewhat valuable	
Daddy's Roommate #5	Don't know	Don't know	Would use	Would use	Don't know	Would use	Don't know

Eloise (#2). In the essay about picture books (Data Set #4), Eloise wrote, "I absolutely love Eloise even if she is a spoiled rich kid with a nanny for a mother." This comment explained her choice of pseudonym, but it also revealed her belief regarding the cultural model of a healthy family—a consistent motif in her written responses. She wrote, in the essay regarding controversial issues (Data Set #6),

> I believe it is the duty of a parent to inform their children about the things they will encounter, before they actually encounter them. I also think reading books to children about gangs and other issues should be the job of a parent. What I mean is parents shouldn't leave this up to the teachers. Parents should be reading books to their children that explain the issues they are talking about.

Eloise had definite ideas about the roles of parents and teachers, which fit neatly into the white, middle-class cultural model. When asked during the interview (December 18, 2003) why she wanted to be an elementary school teacher, she said, "It's my calling. Honestly," using the word "love" in four instances to describe her relationship with children. She also claimed, "My whole life I've worked with kids," indicating a feeling of comfort entering the profession, in a way that seems quite similar to becoming a parent. She described playing with her younger cousins: "I was carrying them all the time, playing with them, and dressing them up." This comment presents an interesting notion of children as toys or dolls.

In addition to the concept of "naturally" transitioning into a position of teacher, Eloise expressed concern about job security. In the essay regarding controversial books (Data Set #6), she wrote, "I just feel like it is better to be safe than sorry—the last thing I need is a lawsuit because of a book I decided to read to my class!" She repeated this idea when I asked her how realistic children's books should be:

> It's hard because I think that it [controversial issues] should be something that the kids are gonna learn about, but at the same time, I don't think that it should be too risky because you don't want your job on the line because of it.

There is truth in the adage "It's better to be safe than sorry." There appear to be safe topics to study, often corresponding to a superficial notion of multiculturalism. For instance, when I asked Eloise what types of books she would like to use in her future classroom, she discussed books about the various seasons and "books about how different cultures celebrate the different holidays because it's important to know about not just your own culture but all different kinds of cultures." Clearly, there are safe "differences" to discuss that adults are relatively comfortable with for various reasons, including the fact that a particular issue is personally important. In Eloise's perspective, teachers should not discuss drugs or sex, explaining that, "some [children] know more than they should, because of their parents." The key word in her statement is "should," implying she knows what is right and how parents should educate their children.

Additionally, when discussing the roles of teacher and student, as well as the purpose of education, Eloise mentioned teaching children "lifelong skills of things they're gonna have to know when they get older so that they can function in the world." She reinforced her statement by saying they need "to be able to get along in the world," indicating a belief in conformity—preparing students to fit in seamlessly with the mainstream.

Dory (#6). Dory had several years of experience working as a teacher's assistant in elementary schools, and she viewed teaching as a "steady job." She commented in the interview (December 15, 2003) that for a while she had been uncertain of her career goal, but her best friend's stepfather "gave me the idea of I should be a teacher, because

I'm really good with kids and I love them. I was like star babysitter at fourteen." Dory's response reflected a trend among participants of viewing teaching as a default career, because they seemed to be "naturally" transitioning into the position and/or the "benefits" suited their future plans for family. Dory said, "Look at all the holidays and everything" and "my future husband's gonna make money too." Like Eloise, Dory envisioned herself in a mothering role as a teacher, describing her future classroom as "warm," "homey," and "comfortable," and commenting on the importance of "getting to know your kids" and "making everyone close and comfortable with each other." When asked about her favorite books as a child, she remembered the Berenstain Bears series, because "I like the family type setting."

Furthermore, Dory's views about the role of a "healthy" parent were clear in the interview: "It is a parent's job to teach their child." When I asked her about children's books with controversial issues in the classroom, she indicated hesitation, "because you always have to think of the parents and you don't wanna get in trouble with it." She brought up *Daddy's Roommate*, explaining, "I probably wouldn't wanna leave it just on the shelf, that way it wouldn't end up in any wrong hands." Interestingly, the main idea of her in-class essay regarding controversial issues (Data Set #6) was:

> I believe that it is our job as teachers to teach these children about what is going on in the world so they can survive. Some specific topics that have caused controversy in teaching in our schools are homelessness, drug abuse, prejudice, and homosexuality. Many try to shelter their children from these topics and not realizing that it's a part of our world. When it comes down to important issues like the ones mentioned above, I believe the children should be exposed to them.

Dory seemed to contradict herself because she indicated a desire to expose students to controversial topics in the essay, but then she expressed concerns about job security, as well as a belief about parents' roles during the interview. Her responses indicate a general lack of reflection, underscored by the fact that she said "I don't know" 67 times during the interview. As was evident with most of the participants, she had not considered the purpose of education. However, after thinking for a moment, Dory decided education is about teaching the "type of skills that they [students] need as they grow up and live life," once again suggesting "getting along in the world."

Penny (#10). When I read *Daddy's Roommate* to the class and asked them to respond (Data Set #5), Penny wrote, "I like that the mom is okay with daddy's new lifestyle (choice)" but she didn't "like the fact that the dad doesn't talk to the son about being gay, he leaves it up to the mom to do it." Penny stayed after class and looked through *Heather Has Two Mommies* (Newman, 1989), which portrays a lesbian couple who conceive Heather through artificial insemination. Penny told me that she liked the way in which the book presented many different kinds of families. Two days later, in the in-class essay about controversial issues (Data Set #6), Penny wrote the following:

> In the classroom, teachers should introduce books that deal with these sensitive topics and allow the students to think about these topics and ask questions. Teachers should not bombard the students with these topics, but introduce them as showing that there are people out there who live their lives differently. In the case of *Daddy's Roommate*, a teacher could introduce the topic of homosexuality and get a feel for what the students are thinking. For myself, being gay is hard enough. If I had teachers that introduced the topic and just said it's okay and that they were sensitive to the topic, I may have felt more comfortable with coming out later in life.

Penny explained that she did not know she was gay in elementary school, but "knowing from an early age that it is okay and that teachers I looked up to so much cared, it might have been easier to deal with." Like most of the interviewees, Penny said during her interview (December 12, 2003) that her experiences in elementary school were positive. She described her teachers as "cool people," and explained, "I've always wanted to be a teacher." Her vision of an ideal classroom focused on relationships, just like Eloise and Dory.

However, Penny presented an overall perspective that was quite different from any of the participants in this study (including those who were not interviewed). Whereas most participants focused on the academic development of the individual, Penny talked about guiding students to become "more understanding." She stated, "anything can be presented in a manner that is not offensive," expressing a desire to "introduce that there's inequalities and stuff," and to help students become more aware of the "real world." Penny's family and teachers did not discuss controversial issues with her, but because of her personal experiences, she believed it was very important. If children are exposed to "sensitive topics," "when they come across it, they're a more caring person, hopefully." When I asked about the possibility of objections from parents, Penny asked, "So do I have to check with the teachers or the principals before I introduce topics?" Perhaps her enthusiasm and idealism exemplify naiveté. Regardless, unlike most of the participants who fit the "normal" cultural model of American family (white, middle-class, English-speaking, *and* hetero-sexual), Penny experienced the feeling of being different, of not iden-tifying with characters in books, of not feeling comfortable in the classroom. She explained that children "need to know they're in a safe place." We are definitely concerned with students' physical safety in schools, but perhaps we are not aware of the ways in which we compromise their emotional well-being.

Penny also pointed out the fact that many future teachers were averse to discussing controversial issues, based on our classroom dis-cussion November 18, 2003. She stated that the overall educational system seems "afraid to try new things" and that it is "closed-minded." When I first asked her about the purpose of education, she said it was "to allow children to go out into the world and be success-ful in whatever field or whatever they decide to do." But as we began a conversation about how the system should change, she realized that she was never "presented different sides of the story," and teachers never asked, "'Penny, what do you think about it?'" She stated that she wanted to achieve a balance with her students—to help them see "totally different sides of the story and then also be that friend or the person they can come to."

T.D. (#15). The only male in our class, T.D.'s background was quite different from the other six interviewees' experiences. He wanted to become a teacher because of his negative school experiences, reveal-ing in the interview (December 12, 2003) a desire to

> give back to the kids; give them something that I didn't receive, especially if there's a kid struggling. I'd rather be there and help him out and get him through it, and not have him turn out how I did and struggle all the way through.

He described himself as "one of the students that barely passed," part of "the outside group," and "just there." He recalled an event in his first grade class at a private school: "I remember getting into trouble, having him [the teacher] take me and slam me up against the cup-board." In second grade: "I remember getting slapped right in the face" by the principal. T.D. explained that the incidents "will always stay with me." When asked about the books read in elementary school, T.D. could not remember any except *Charlie and the Chocolate Factory* because he wrote a report about it. I asked about his response to the book, but he said he could not remember because "I don't remember doing the report, I remember my mom doing the report. A lot of reports were done by my mom."

Like Dory, T.D. was not particularly reflective regarding his future teaching, sometimes contradicting his own comments. For example, when we discussed how he might handle a reluctant student, T.D. clearly had not thought about it. He talked about integrating the students and calling on the struggling student to read. I suggested the student might be embarrassed, so he revised the scenario to small groups, in which the student who did not complete the assigned reading would be assisted by the other group members. Then he decided such a situation might encourage the reluctant student not to read, and we agreed that T.D. would probably learn about effective techniques in the future. Likewise, we talked about the types of books he would want in his future classroom, and T.D. decided he would like texts with a lot of pictures in order to keep readers' interest. He said,

> If it's not interesting, some kinds may look like they're reading it, but they'll get halfway through, [think] this is boring, and just skip through pages, or just go from reading it to just looking at the pictures.

However, if T.D. provides books with pictures, students will probably focus on the pictures. This seemed to be another example of not engaging in reflective thinking.

T.D. also contradicted himself when talking about children's books with controversial issues. In the in-class essay about controversial issues (Data Set #6), T.D. wrote in the first paragraph,

> Focusing on controversial issues such as homosexuality, drug use, homelessness, etc. is an iffy topic to discuss with kids, but it should not be overlooked inside or outside a classroom. Keeping a child from the negative the world produces only produces a close-minded child, and not allowing that child to view those negatives for what they are.

He ended the essay with the following:

> I am a future teacher, my job is to teach. If I can't teach what kids want to learn about or I am reprimanded otherwise, then I'm in the wrong district. A closed-minded school produces close-minded people.

Nevertheless, in the interview, T.D. said, "I don't really see a point to it [introducing controversial issues], because they're [children] not gonna see it," but when I asked if there were certain subjects to avoid, he answered, "No, because I would incorporate books about home-lessness, drugs, crimes, because they're eventually gonna learn...they're gonna see reality anyway." T.D. also claimed that "parents are brutal" and decided he would need to think further about how to handle sensitive issues in the classroom.

Perhaps most revealing was T.D.'s comment: "It's tough because you know you're not gonna reach all of them [his future students]." Regarding the purpose of education, T.D. said the goal was "to better kids for the future," "prepare them for the outside world," and "to better themselves for the future in ways that they can survive." Once again, this response indicated a focus on the individual and his or her development of skills to survive. The word "survive" implies mere existence, just "getting along in the world." The *Oxford English Dictionary* offers the following definition of "get along": "coexist or communicate in a specified manner (together, with); live harmoni-ously, be or remain on good terms (together, with)." (Brown, 1993, p. 1084). It is not far-fetched to compare "get along in the world" with "conformity," which can be defined as "action in accordance with some standard; compliance; acquiescence" (Brown, 1993, p. 477). De-spite a sincere desire to help children, some participants seemed more likely to conform to cultural models of education than to question "the norm."

Katie (#17). Unlike most students, Katie exhibited some comfort with questioning the status quo. She had the most experience with elementary school education; her mother and grandmother were both teachers, and she spent a lot of time her mother's classroom, in addi-tion to other teachers' rooms. Her father was a stay-at-home dad when she was young, but he is now a teacher. Katie loved to read as a child, recalling the titles of many favorite books. In her in-class essay about critical literacy (Data Set #3), Katie[35] was one of the few partici-pants to provide a specific example:

> In second grade while my mom was reading my little sister a bedtime story, I asked her how babies were made. I think at the age I was at most parents would have avoided the subject all together or would have come up with a

---

[35] Another excerpt from Katie's essay is above, in the section discussing Data Set #3.

stork story. No, not my mom, she flat out told me exactly how it was done. I remember feeling a bit flustered and overwhelmed thinking maybe that was a question I shouldn't have asked. However, while most kids learned lots of untrue things about sex from their friends, movies, or tv, I got the straight facts right from the beginning....Having my mom teach me about a rather uncomfortable subject also taught me that I could approach her about any-thing.

It seemed that Katie had thought about many issues relevant to her future teaching. When I asked, "What do you see as the overall goal of education, at least as it stands?" she hesitated and then said,

especially in elementary school, to be able to think on your own and to not just be fed information, to present the kids with different things and let them on their own decide what they want to take in.

I asked, "Do you see that happening in education?" Katie replied, "No. You said ideal, right? Or did you say ideal?" I had used the word "ideal" to discuss the relationship between teacher and student, which Katie described as "mutual respect," but I had not used "ideal" in the question about education. When I asked her, "what kinds of people are coming out of this educational system?" she said, "This may be a strong statement, but really manufactured, people who are really worried about meeting standards and passing tests." Katie as-serted, "you should be bettering yourself as a person." Although the focus of her comment was on the individual, Katie expressed a belief in the importance of teaching students to think for themselves. Katie also brought up an idea echoed by Ella (discussed below)—her frus-tration and dismay with the attitudes and aptitude of her fellow fu-ture teachers.

Katie did not appear to rely heavily on conventional cultural models of family and education, perhaps due to her own experiences with a stay-at-home father and a mother who believed in the princi-ples of critical literacy. However, she did reveal concerns about job security, as well as a tendency to view teaching as a default career. Katie said, "I didn't actually want to be one [a teacher] until I decided what major I was gonna be. I always wanted to be a lawyer." When I asked in the end of our interview if she might change her mind and study law, she said,

No, I took my LSATs, it was too hard, I couldn't do it anymore. It wasn't too bad but law school's really expensive so if I go and then decide I don't like it, it's a lot of money to pay back.

Perhaps the field of education seemed "natural" due to the fact that her family members were teachers and there was a certain amount of comfort in familiarity. Also, she said, "on a practicality side, I wanna get married and have a family some day, so it's a really good job for that, there's benefits, there's summers."

There was evidence, however, of a taken-for-granted belief in the traditional family, once again possibly influenced by her own up-bringing, in which her mother read bedtime stories. When I asked Katie about controversial children's books, she replied that "ideally it should be something the parents discuss with the kids." She explained, "I feel like I would never personally bring up some of the books that we discussed in class. But I might have some of them available in the class." Katie continued, "The whole thing scares me so I almost don't want to touch it at all. I want to be like all the other teachers and just pretend it's not there." When I replied, "that's one way to handle it," Katie said, "Yeah, but I don't think it's the best way. If something were to come up in class, if a kid were to bring something up, I think you should address it." I mentioned that some parents might be upset if she were to discuss homosexuality in class. She said, "I don't understand why parents would be [upset], I don't know, it's just something that is." In Katie's experience, "something that is" should be discussed because children will learn about it in other ways—perhaps in ways that are detrimental. Nevertheless, she had a realistic perspective of the current educational climate, and she realized that she would engage in a process of negotiation between staying true to her beliefs and making decisions for practical (job se-curity) reasons.

Ella (#23). Like many future teachers, Ella loves kids. She also revealed the importance of church in her life,[36] explaining in our interview (December 11, 2003) that she wrote curriculum for her Sunday school, and in her career she hoped "to ultimately create curriculum and implement curriculum." She recalled having positive experiences in elementary school, describing her kindergarten teacher as "amaz-ing," "awesome," "cool," and "fun." Ella also explained that she had very supportive parents who encouraged her to remain true to her

---

[36] Eloise also discussed the importance of her religious beliefs, as well as her experi-ences teaching Sunday school. The other participants did not choose to reveal infor-mation about their spirituality.

beliefs, even when she was questioning authority. She remembered a situation in fifth grade:

> I was very upset because they [the school] took away our baseball game. Our teacher-student baseball game. And I was very angry, it's a fifth grade thing, and they decided the teachers didn't wanna do it anymore, and so I got upset. So I started a petition, and I had all the fifth graders sign it and then I got in trouble. My parents were stoked, and the teachers were mad.

Ella said, "I had good parents," commenting on the ways in which they reinforced her actions. She continued,

> I think a lot of teachers put their foot down because it was a ten year old child....I hate [with emphasis] watching teachers pull authority over kids, it drives me crazy.

Ella perceived the appropriate relationship between teachers and students as "it's almost like an equal, not quite, I wanna say equal really bad, but it's equal in different senses."

In her essay about controversial issues in children's literature (Data Set #6), Ella argued that

> teaching a child to be a thoughtful reader should be the focus. Through this we do not advocate participation in the controversial issues, but encourage a child to be critical of the world which surrounds them.

However, during the interview, Ella remarked that she would not talk about drugs in the elementary school setting, although

> Issues such as the homosexuality issue, the homelessness issue, those I don't have a problem with, not necessarily introducing, like let's do a unit on everybody being gay, I'm not gonna do that, but if there is an obvious need to discuss something like that in the classroom because of the student situation, I'm not gonna shy away from it. I'll probably get fired. But I'm not gonna shy away from it.

She described an influential situation during her early field experience in which a first grade teacher used *Fly Away Home* (Bunting, 1991), a book about a homeless boy who lives with his father in the airport and tries to stay unnoticed. Ella explained that the teacher was not trying to provide instruction about homelessness; rather, she was using the text to teach the different types of questions a reader might ask about a book. Ella admired the teacher's introduction of a controversial issue through an activity designed to satisfy the grade level standards.

We talked about the freedom to make professional decisions and Ella commented,

> I have to be honest. I think you have an advantage when you're in a school where most of the parents aren't involved...because those are, to me, more the schools that see these issues on a daily basis.

She referred to the differences between schools in wealthier neighborhoods versus poorer neighborhoods, contending that the affluent schools had more parent involvement. By contrast, the schools in poorer areas were more likely to be influenced by problems such as homelessness and gang activity, but since there was less parent involvement, a teacher would have more freedom to discuss such issues with his or her students.

Regarding the purpose of education, Ella believed "education isn't just the classroom; I think education expands. When you walk out of the classroom door you're not done learning for the day." Like Katie, Ella was concerned about many of the future teachers she encountered:

> I'm often really scared when I look in my classes, when I look at the other people that I'm with in my classes, and if I ever have my own kids, in each of my classes there's maybe five people that I would trust my kids with being in their classroom at this point. Watching them [her peers] and how they approach our major and approach the big demanding things that we have to do....I feel like a lot of the times people use teaching or liberal studies as a default major, like "I don't know what else I'm gonna do, so I'll be a teacher" and that drives me crazy.

Clearly, Ella viewed teaching as a tremendous responsibility, requiring dedication and "passion." Referring to herself as both a student and a future teacher, Ella said, "School's a big deal. It shouldn't be dealt with lightly."

Kiera (#24). I knew Kiera prior to our class because she worked with me as an elementary school reading tutor for one semester. I discovered through the interview (December 16, 2003) that Kiera had an unusual perspective on education when she was young. She said,

> I wasn't very into school, I didn't really think of school as being such a learning experience. I honestly believed, and this is very sad, my mom laughs at

me now, for many years that I would just grow up smart. When I turned a certain age I would be smart.

Kiera remembered elementary school as "nice" and also said "I've always done the bare minimum." She recalled that she "hated reading, wouldn't pick up a book, and so for assignments even, you know, later elementary school and whatnot, I would typically just skim through, maybe read a few chapters." She could not think of any books that were interesting, stating: "I just wasn't into it. I just didn't understand why, what was the point of me reading this for you; why do I need to read this for you?" Kiera seemed to view reading assignments as chores to complete solely for the purpose of satisfying the teacher. I asked, "Well, what about [reading] for yourself?" She replied, "But I never had that intrinsic motivation."

When I asked Kiera if there were certain issues she would avoid bringing into the classroom, she replied, "I can't think of any issues that I wouldn't wanna bring in, no." In an effort to extend her thinking, I asked about the topic of abortion, and Kiera said "I don't know if I'd bring in abortion, that's not my place to." She continued, "I definitely want to incorporate racism and the ideas of being prejudice." Kiera used *The Watsons Go to Birmingham* (Curtis, 1995) for the out-of-class essay regarding novels (Data Set #7), pointing out the book as "a tool to discuss racism and the following Civil Rights Movement." She cited a passage in the book and discussed its meaning:

> Prior to the Watsons trip to Birmingham, there were a few racist remarks. Kenny was brought (by his teacher) to demonstrate his reading ability to an upper class—his brother's. Before he began, Byron's [the brother's] teacher said to the class: "All right, I have a special treat for you today. I've often told you that as Negroes the world is many times a hostile place for us." The teacher is pointing out that "Negroes" are, in a sense, the underdog so it is important to stand out. It is ashamed [sic] a teacher feels this comment needs to be said. It seems the teacher is an African American too. Therefore, the reader gets a sense of the oppression the African Americans face—in the 1960's. What is being denoted is one who grows up an African American, is not equal to other races—white's.

Kiera did not seem to understand the point of the entire book—a representation of "reality" for a young boy over forty years ago. My interpretation of the passage does not indicate that the teacher is highlighting inequality; rather, he is celebrating the achievement of a talented individual, hoping to inspire others to cultivate their own strong points.

Regarding the purpose of education, Kiera said, "to rid ignorance," which she also discussed in the in-class essay about controversial issues in children's books (Data Set #6):

> Reading and the gathering of information is a beautiful thing. Is it not important to encourage the learning process? As an educator and/or parent it is our duty to expose our youth to topics of varying importance. However, the job doesn't end there. Books that discuss or introduce controversial topics can and should be used as a stepping stone to bridge the gap of ignorance. It is then up to the parent (or educator) to further the discussion.

Kiera seemed to believe deeply in the importance of enlightening children. Yet there was a discontinuity in her responses, mainly due to her adamant dislike of reading revealed in the interview. Her statement "Reading and the gathering of information is a beautiful thing" did not coincide with her comments of hating reading and "I've always done the bare minimum." Perhaps Kiera was attempting to please her audience in the written response and felt more comfortable expressing her true beliefs during the interview.

When I asked her why she wanted to be a teacher, Kiera said, "It's the one thing I know I would be good at, the one career choice that I could make, I'm certain that I'll be good." She also said, "school should be a fun experience," and talked about wanting to engage in activities that students would enjoy, such as "art projects so that they can remember it [reading]. Why make them write so much?" Kiera recalled instances in elementary school when teachers told the students to figure out the answer to a question. She said, "What do you do when you don't know the answer? You make them figure it out. Because you don't know everything, and you can't let the kids know, you can't let on." She discussed her vision of a "good" teacher:

> So I know a lot of things, does that mean I can teach a child? Of course not. But also know this or not knowing all the content knowledge, does that really inhibit my ability to teach? I mean as long as I plan ahead what I'm going to teach, of course you have to do a little bit more research throughout the year, but I don't feel capable right now of going into a classroom teaching math, but I'm not gonna get any more math courses, I have to figure it out as I go along.

Kiera's assumption that teachers ask students to figure out an answer might be rooted in her own experiences rather than an overall trend among educators.

She was definitely a caring individual with good intentions; nevertheless, Kiera exemplified a tendency to accept appearances and make assumptions based on surface understandings. For example, in the out-of-class essay regarding picture books (Data Set #4), Kiera chose *Love You Forever* (Munsch, 1986). This book depicts a white, middle-class boy becoming a man, while his mother demonstrates unconditional love by rocking her son, even when he is too big (in real life) for her to lift onto her lap.

As an educator interested in children's literature, I have conducted research about this text and I discovered that people often have very strong opinions about it. A recent discussion thread on the Children's Literature List Serv (February 2004) offered numerous arguments about the book, ranging from personal memories of enjoyment to explanations of Munsch reading his book aloud in a humorous way—indicating a lack of seriousness about some of the less realistic scenes.

Regardless, Kiera focused on retelling the book, mainly summarizing the story and talking about the pictures. She ended the essay:

> With all this in mind, it is clear the message: no bond is more important than the one between a parent and child. The author does not talk of a second parent in either situation. What is emphasized is the relationship between mother and son.

This represented a surface-level reading of the text, and I would argue that Kiera's expressed concern about inequality might also be somewhat surface level. In other words, to translate a desire "to rid ignorance" into action requires deeper thinking and questioning, especially in terms of the taken-for-granted, such as the importance of the relationship between a white, middle-class, English-speaking mother and son. Returning to *The Watsons Go to Birmingham*, one wonders what the teacher represented in the book would say to his students about the lack of African American characters in popular picture books.

Thematic Categories

This section briefly organizes the whole-class and individual data into thematic categories. Chapter 7 elaborates on these themes and discusses the findings in terms of the research questions. I developed thematic categories by identifying ideas that were repeatedly evident

in the participants' responses, concentrating on uncovering participants' cultural models—their "taken-for-granted assumptions about
what is 'typical' or 'normal'" (Gee, 1999; p. 59) in order to discover
their "theories." According to Gee,

> Cultural models are not just based on our experiences in the world, they
> "project" onto that world, from where we "stand" (where we are socially
> positioned), certain viewpoints about what is right and wrong, and what can
> or cannot be done to solve problems in the world. (p. 74)

Cultural models are simplifications and idealizations formulated
through one's experiences. Based on the purposes of this study, the
most appropriate categorization emerged through the concept of cultural models, specifically the cultural models of family and of education—with a degree of overlap between the two.

Cultural Model of Family. Overall, the standard of reference for these
participants tends to be oneself, reflecting the model of a white, English-speaking, heterosexual, middle-class family, exemplified by
Olivia, with a hard-working father and a mother with time to spend at
home. There is an expectation that parents read to their children and
teach them about sensitive issues. However, it is the parent who de-
cides what issues are discussed.

Cultural Model of Education. Based on one's own experiences, there
is a definite understanding by these participants of what education
looks like, what "good" teaching looks like, and what is taught and
not taught. Sensitive or controversial issues were evaluated based on
the participant's own experiences and beliefs, indicating an unquestioned assumption that he or she knew what was "right" for children.
There was a belief in the importance of multiculturalism, although it
was on a relatively surface level. Also, there was tendency to view
teaching as a default career, with some participants indicating a
"natural transition" into the position. For the most part, the participants thought education was about functioning or surviving in the
world, with a focus on individual development. School should be
"fun," but the focus is on "getting along in the world" and all that
term implies—conformity, compliance, and fitting in.

Overlap Between Cultural Models. There was definitely overlap between the two cultural models, including the concepts of childhood
innocence, adult authority, and what is "right" (using oneself as the

standard). Participants believed that stories influence readers, and they often pointed out the importance of lessons within stories— perceiving them as "tools," without regard for entertainment value or literary quality. Also, there appeared to be implicit models of appropriate gender roles. Whereas Harry Potter exemplified a "good" boy (brave and determined), a princess was the model for a "good" girl. One participant began her essay about fairy tales (Data Set #1):

> With a nickname "princess" growing up, it is no wonder that I am and have always been a fan of fairy tales. Some of my fondest childhood memories are reading fairy tales with my mom before bedtime. As she read each page, I would imagine myself as the beautiful princess that gets swept off her feet by prince charming....Fairy tales have long been a part of our society, for they influence and shape our expectations and standards of behavior.

For the most part, such an influence was perceived by participants as positive. The overlap between the two cultural models indicates an interrelatedness, which suggests that individuals are either "inside" or "outside."

Cultural Model of Family	Overlap	Cultural Model of Education
◆ White, middle-class, English-speaking, heterosexual ◆ Mother and father live with child ◆ Mother reads to child ◆ Parents teach "sensitive" issues	◆ Self as standard (knows what is right) ◆ Childhood innocence ◆ Adult authority ◆ "Appropriate" gender roles ◆ Stories influence ◆ Importance of lessons	◆ Purpose = getting along in the world ◆ Teaching as default career (natural transition) ◆ Surface level multiculturalism ◆ Use of controversial issues depends on own beliefs ◆ Innate knowledge of what is appropriate to teach

The most significant result of adherence to these cultural models would be a tendency toward exclusion, due to viewing oneself as the standard. According to Gee (1999), "Cultural models often involve us in exclusions that are not at first obvious and which we are often unaware of making" (p. 59). Such a lack of awareness was evident in the participants' written and verbal responses in this study. Certainly, individuals should be free to express their opinions, which can be as different as the four narrators in *Voices in the Park* (Browne, 1998). Yet it is also important to engage in reflection—gathering as much information as possible and thinking seriously about one's own beliefs, particularly in hypothetical situations related to one's future career. Most of the future teachers in this study had not thought much about many of the topics we discussed, despite information provided in class and opportunities to explore ideas through writing. Both in written responses and interviews, participants sometimes contradicted themselves and often simply said, "I don't know." The combination of ingrained assumptions (situated meanings and cultural models) and lack of reflection seemed to be the norm rather than the exception. The implications of these findings are discussed in the next chapter.

◆ CHAPTER 7
Discussion of Findings

The "standard" versions of fairy tales such as "Cinderella," "Snow White," and "Sleeping Beauty," complete with passive heroine and happily-ever-after ending, permeate our culture, and the "Disneyfication" (Giroux, 1997) of society can be considered an enormous influence. For example, Tchaikovsky's "The Sleeping Beauty Waltz" (1891) was adapted by Disney for the movie *Sleeping Beauty* (1959), becoming the famous song "Once Upon a Dream." The 1959 version continues to be popular, despite stock characters and stereotypes, perhaps because of the apparent timelessness of the movie.

Movie viewers and readers typically adopt a "willing suspension of disbelief"[37] when presented with fairy tales and other fantasy-like scenarios. The visual representation of fairy tales (and other animated movies) often reflects a timeless world, in which there are few recognizable props to indicate a particular era. That is, most films clearly depict the reality of a certain time period through the use of clothing, hairstyles, vehicles, and other props. An exception would be the recent *Lord of the Rings* trilogy, which presents a fantasy world, similar to those represented in animated movies—without reference to a particular time period. This quality of timelessness seems important because it contributes to the willing suspension of disbelief by not seeming outdated with regard to the setting or the cinematic techniques.

Such conditions can also be created in theatre, although television and movies can reach a much wider audience. Unless, of course, the theatre involves Disney. Everyone (except Grumpy) knows that Disneyland is the "happiest place on earth." So who would not want to see the latest extravaganza: "Snow White: An Enchanting New Musical," "live on stage at the Fantasyland Theatre"? It is free with the price of admission, but you can receive preferred show seating: "**just**

---

[37] The term "willing suspension of disbelief" was first used by Samuel Taylor Coleridge in his autobiography (1817).

purchase a Vacation Package![38] The "new" musical has its own website, complete with a screensaver to download for your computer and
"enchanted merchandise." The Snow White Costume and Shoes,
which cannot be purchased online—you must go to the "Snow White
Cart outside the Fantasyland Theatre"—will be irresistible for girls:
"Mirror, Mirror on the Wall, Who's the Fairest of Them All? Now
your little princess can play the part of Snow White, in the Snow
White Costume and Shoes." For boys, there are Grumpy and Dopey
tee shirts—depending on whether they feel mad or stupid because
they have to see the musical.

I realize my tone is a bit sarcastic, but I am trying to make a point.
This is serious business, serious marketing, and serious stereotyping.
The website offers a "fun fact" that *"Snow White and the Seven
Dwarfs* was released in 1937. It is called 'The One that Started it All'
because it was Disney's first animated feature." Just as everyone loves
Disneyland, everyone loves *Snow White*. You can:

> Sing along to all your favorite songs from the classic film like: "Whistle
> While You Work," "Heigh-Ho" and "Some Day My Prince Will Come;"
> Marvel at the breathtaking sets, sensational scenery and extraordinary cos-
> tumes; Be dazzled by the spectacular special effects. Experience the heart-
> pounding suspense, side-splitting comedy and tear-jerking romance of this
> beloved story. Fall under the spell of this enchanting story all over again at
> the Fantasyland Theatre. (Disneyland, 2004)

Falling under the spell seems like an appropriate statement—very
truthful advertising. In the chapter "Are Disney Movies Good for
Your Kids?" (1997), Giroux answered his own question with "no,"
explaining that "The power and influence of Disney is so pervasive in
American society, parents, educators, and others need to find ways to
make Disney accountable for what it produces" (p. 65).

I am not suggesting that we ban Disney, and I believe that Disney
offers entertaining stories, delightful fantasy worlds, and a welcome
escape from "reality." In other words, it is important to get beyond
black and white polarities into the gray area of possibilities. It is possible to enjoy Disney and simultaneously maintain a critical stance.
One focus of critical literacy is to "make the familiar strange," and
since Disney is already familiar to most of us, our task is to *consider*
other possibilities, to problematize the taken-for-granted. According
to Steinberg & Kincheloe (1997), we are allowing Disney and other

---

[38] The boldface indicates "click here." This show debuted in February 2004.

distributors of media to write the curriculum and engage in cultural pedagogy. The above-mentioned Disney production of *Snow White* is closely based on the version released in 1937, a year in which the Hindenburg caught fire and exploded, Spam was introduced, Amelia Earhart vanished in the South Pacific, and a first-class postage stamp cost three cents. Our world has changed considerably in 67 years, but much of the material we present to children and the cultural models to which the mainstream adheres seem to remain philosophically static.

The participant in this study who referred to Cinderella and Snow White as role models for young girls to "hold out hope that maybe one day their lives too will change and their prince will come" has learned her lessons well. To what degree will she reproduce this cultural pedagogy in her future classroom? It is impossible to predict how participants will present children's literature to their future students; however, it is possible to describe the current thinking of these preservice teachers. Below are the five research questions guiding this study, followed by a brief discussion based on the findings.

Question 1: How Do Future Teachers Read and Interpret Children's Literature?

The purpose of this question was to describe how future teachers think about and respond to children's literature. My assumption was that future teachers would respond to children's literature in different ways, which was accurate in terms of the topics they chose to discuss (see question #2). However, there was an overall tendency to "read" children's literature through the perspective of an imagined or idealized child, focusing on speculation regarding how the text would influence the reader and the lessons children would/could/should learn. This was especially true of the picture books and young adult novels. Participants engaged in more "adult" interpretations of fairy tales and controversial children's books (such as *Daddy's Roommate*), perhaps due to the discussions in English 306A, as well as the "obvious" inappropriateness of texts with sensitive issues. The perspectives adopted by participants in reading and interpreting children's literature reinforced the cultural model of adult authority.

Question 2: What Do Future Teachers *Choose* to Focus on When They Respond in Writing to Children's Literature?

The purpose of this question was to determine the topics that future teachers believe are most important to discuss. My assumption was that future teachers would have different ideas concerning what topics and elements of children's literature are important. Once again, the importance of lessons—both implicit and explicit within the text—was an overarching theme, with the related assumption that stories influence (child) readers. The majority of written responses drew on cultural models of "normal" family and traditional education. Moreover, even when participants framed their essays around a discussion of character, such as Harry Potter or Sara (*A Little Princess*), they tended to interweave commentary regarding positive (often gender-specific) qualities, and the ways in which characters and situations represented positive role models and behavior for readers.

Question 3: As Evidenced in Their Writing, to What Degree Do Future Teachers Recognize Stereotypes and Underlying Images in Children's Literature?

The purpose of this question was to discover how future teachers seek out stereotypical images and the types of images they uncover. My assumption was that some future teachers would pay more attention to stereotypes and underlying images than others. The discussion of stereotypes was most evident in Data Set #1, the essay regarding fairy tales, perhaps because these images were pointed out in English 306A. However, participants overwhelmingly ignored stereotypes in picture books and young adult novels,[39] while demonstrating adherence to cultural models of education and a "normal" family. Even within the fairy tale responses, some participants highlighted what

---

[39] For example, in my interpretation, Sara (*A Little Princess*) is presented as too good to be true, suffering tremendous hardship—always with a positive attitude. Additionally, she serves as a sort of surrogate wife to her father, who is described as a "rash, innocent young man" (p. 11) and "boyish" (p. 13), sometimes referring to his daughter as "my little missus" (p. 74). Moreover, when Sara finds the perfect doll, she says, "'I should like her always to look as if she was a child with a good mother.'" Along these lines, girls in our culture are generally encouraged to play with dolls and pretend (practice?) to be mothers beginning at an early age. These are just a few elements of *A Little Princess* that are presented as reality, and unquestioned by participants in this study.

they considered positive gender-specific qualities, including deference to adult authority.

Question 4: Do They Think about Children's Literature in a Critical Way That Might Lead to Self-reflection? Does This Exercise Lead to Inquiry about Themselves and/or Action?

The purpose of this question was to detect how future teachers' transactions with various texts, combined with classroom information about critical literacy, influences their thinking and behavior. My assumption was that future teachers would practice self-reflection to varying degrees. Likewise, I believed that some would adopt new ways of reading (and responding) that would influence how they think about children's literature. Some participants indicated that they were learning to view children's literature in new and different ways, mainly due to discussions in English 306A. However, with a few exceptions, participants indicated an overall lack of reflective thinking. For example, they seemed to struggle with identifying their own beliefs when forced to think about whether they would introduce controversial texts in their future classrooms. Did any of the interviewees exhibit serious reflection and genuine questioning? Eloise, Dory, T.D., and Kiera seemed uncertain, indecisive, and likely to conform to prevailing opinions. I believe Penny,[40] Katie, and Ella questioned to various degrees, and they appeared to be engaging in reflection, perhaps as a result of being asked to think about concepts they had not previously considered.

Question 5: To What Degree Do Future Teachers Adopt a Stance of Critical Literacy?

The purpose of this question was to describe the ways in which future teachers demonstrate a desire to practice critical literacy on some

---

[40] Penny seemed particularly engaged in self-transformation, which was evident as she worked through her ideas about the purpose of education, shifting from "getting along in the world" to teaching students how to think critically. In a note to me on the final day of class, Penny wrote: "I just wanted to thank you for allowing me to express myself and be comfortable with whom I am. You really don't know how much it means to me….You have proven to me once again that being a teacher really can touch people's lives."

level. My assumption was that some future teachers would be interested in using critical literacy whereas others would disagree with it or perceive it to be impractical. I would argue that most of the participants thought critical literacy would be a good strategy immediately after reading about it. However, based on their subsequent responses, most participants who previously indicated an interest in critical literacy reverted to ingrained cultural models of education and family. For the most part, the purpose of education seemed to focus on "getting along in the world" and participants overwhelmingly indicated that parents should teach children about sensitive issues. Hence, although critical literacy was perceived as an interesting concept, it was ultimately regarded as impractical and/or inappropriate in the "real" world.

Of course, "our conclusions are always tentative" (Gee, 1999, p. 79), and I cannot predict for certain whether or not these participants will utilize critical literacy in the future. Yet the participants gravitated toward "safety" and tended to adhere to cultural models, pointing out apparent "unhealthy" situations or attempting to impose a sense of "normalcy" when it was perceived as lacking. For instance, some participants lamented situations representing single-parent households. Additionally, in her discussion regarding the importance of friendship in Harry Potter, one student wrote: "Before attending Hogwarts, Harry was excluded from people and events, but after attending Hogwarts, Harry is able to live a *normal* childhood with the company of loyal friends" (emphasis added). Although Harry's foster family the Dursleys represent a "normal" family in appearance, they treat Harry horribly. In the absence of a loving family, loyal friends (and mentors) are an appropriate substitute. The key concept, of course, is normalcy—whether referring to a family, institutions such as education, or larger society.

Gee pointed out that cultural models—what we view as normal— are simplifications. He wrote, "The simplifications in cultural models can do harm by implanting in thought and action unfair, dismissive, or derogatory assumptions about other people" (Gee, 1999, p. 59). Moreover, cultural models "can become emblematic visions of an idealized, 'normal,' 'typical' reality" (Gee, 1999, p. 60) and, as mentioned earlier, we are usually unaware that we are using cultural models. Therefore, the need to reflect on our ways of thinking is crucial for a variety of reasons. Perhaps most important for teachers is, "The values of mainstream culture are, in fact, often complicit with the oppression of non-mainstream students' home cultures and other social identities" (Gee, 1996, p. 89). Unreflective adherence to cultural models of education and a "healthy" family may result in ethnocentrism, unquestioned white privilege, and reproduction of the status quo.

What about those on the outside of these cultural models? The cultural model of a "normal" family signified by participants in this study assumes that both the mother and father live with the child; they are typically white, middle-class, English-speaking, and heterosexual; the mother reads to the child; and the parents teach their children about sensitive issues, as appropriate. Perhaps with time and experience, some of the participants in this study will modify their cultural models, engaging in alternate world-building processes when they are challenged by someone or by a new experience, or if they discover their cultural models clearly don't "fit" (Gee, 1999). The cultural model of education maintained by the participants is more problematic because the personal stakes are higher. Whereas an individual may be able to create a "normal," idealized family to some degree, the institution of public education is nearly immutable and individuals entering the system have little power to create meaningful, large-scale change (UNESCO, 2003).

Moreover, inductees to an institution have many reasons to perpetuate the status quo, mainly in efforts toward self-preservation. Therefore, due to the nature of institutions as well as the predominant cultural model of education, it seems likely that social reproduction would be the rule rather than the exception. The cultural model of education signified by many participants in this study assumes that the purpose of education is "getting along in the world"; teaching is a default career—a natural transition for them from student into teacher; they have innate knowledge of what is appropriate to teach; the introduction of controversial issues depends on their own beliefs; and they view multiculturalism on a relatively surface level, in which comfortable and safe "differences" are discussed.

The power inherent in membership within these cultural models is amplified for educators, regardless of whether one's students are inside or outside of the two cultural models. According to Gee (1999),

> Your own Discourse grid is the limit of your understanding, and *it is the fundamental job of education* to give people bigger and better Discourse maps, ones that reflect the working of Discourses throughout society, the world, and history in relationship to each other and to the learner. (p. 23; emphasis added)

In other words, educators have a responsibility to reflect on their own worldviews, to learn as much as possible about alternate perspectives, and to help students become aware of the various possibilities. What are the options for unreflective educators when they enter a school setting? Perhaps they will take their cues from surrounding colleagues (do what others around them do), fall back on patterns learned through their own experiences as students (drawing on the cultural model of education), and/or do what they are told (implicitly or explicitly) by authority figures. Many factors point toward perpetuation of the status quo.

I would argue that an individual is located either inside of both cultural models of family and education or outside of both cultural models due to the overlap, and for the most part, the participants in this study located themselves inside both models. The intersection between the two cultural models includes the concepts of (a) childhood innocence, (b) adult authority, (c) knowing what is "right" (using oneself as the standard), (d) appropriate gender roles, (e) importance of lessons in children's books, and (f) the influence of texts on readers. Keeping in mind the fact that cultural models are simplifications and we tend to be unaware of our adherence to them, it is evident that these intersecting factors would be perceived as the norm. You might be considered a radical, a trouble-maker, or spoilsport if you ventured to question "conventional wisdom."

Childhood Innocence

What if a student witnesses his father murdering his mother?[41] Such a scenario may seem farfetched based on our own experiences, but childhood innocence is essentially a cultural construction.

Adult Authority

Children should obey adults. What if a student is sexually abused by an adult who forced her to obey? Many adults were trained as children to respect and obey their elders, and they continue to expect

---

[41] An article in the *San Diego Union Tribune* (3/17/04) reported that a nine-year-old boy in Adelanto, California, was "eating cookies and drinking milk when his father shot him and his mother Sunday." The boy "remained motionless on the floor until his father shot and killed himself" (Associated Press, p. A6).

such behavior, especially in the school setting. However, children can learn to question authority in a respectful manner.

Knowing What Is "Right"

Using oneself as the standard. I know what is right because I have "good" and appropriate values. What if I'm a gay teacher and I'm "out" in the classroom? Some parents and colleagues would disagree that I have "good" values, especially if I have controversial texts, such as *Daddy's Roommate* (Willhoite, 1990), in the classroom library.[42] This idea ties into the concept of childhood innocence—to what degree do we expose children to "reality"? And who's reality do we present?

Appropriate Gender Roles

What if a young boy wears pink to school and wants to play with a baby doll? How should a classroom teacher handle such a situation, especially in terms of the other students' reactions? We seem to be comfortable stretching stereotypical gender roles, but there are limits, especially within mainstream ideology. For example, *Heather Has Two Mommies* (Newman, 1989) portrays a lesbian couple who conceive Heather through artificial insemination. Similar to *Daddy's Roommate*,[43] depictions of same sex adults caring for children disrupts cultural models of a "normal" family. This relates to surface-level multicultural education, in which only comfortable and safe (for adults) differences are presented.

---

[42] An article in the *Wilmington Star* (2004, March 18) described a mother and father's outrage when their seven-year-old daughter brought home *King & King* (De Haan & Nijland, 2002) from the school library. This book is about a prince who is required to marry, and instead of picking from an assortment of princesses, he chooses another prince. The father said, "I was flabbergasted. My child is not old enough to understand something like that, especially when it is not in our beliefs." The school principal was also quoted: "We have a lot of diversity in our schools. What might be inappropriate for one family, in another family is a totally acceptable thing." The young girl's parents are thinking about transferring their daughter to a private Christian school. Nevertheless, the parents refuse to return the book because they "want assurances it won't circulate among other children."

[43] Both *Daddy's Roommate* (Willhoite, 1990) and *Heather Has Two Mommies* (Newman, 1989) were listed on the "The 10 Most Targeted Books of the 90s" in positions two and nine, respectively (The Freedom Forum).

Importance of Morals or Lessons in Children's Texts

What if readers internalize the "wrong" lesson? That is, what if they do not "learn" the lesson intended by adults who provide the book? If reading is a transaction between reader and text, the individual's prior experience and knowledge inform his or her interpretation. By focusing on the reader's own response, rather than the author's "intended" message, individuals are better situated to become more empathetic toward others and to develop a greater sense of responsibility for their own behaviors (Rosenblatt, 1995).

Influence of Texts on Readers

What about the power of brand-name labels and advertisements, which saturate our surroundings—on clothing, television, food, radio, billboards, magazines, stadiums, even schools? It is hypocritical to claim that books and movies influence children, while simultaneously ignoring the power of other texts in the environment. This is why critical literacy is a crucial component of education—to assist students in learning to read their *entire* worlds.

These intersecting concepts of the cultural models of education and a "normal" family are products of world building. They are constructions that require extensive thinking and reflection—for all of us, but especially for people involved with children.

During the process of my research, I was compelled to read many books: for information, for inspiration, for pleasure, and for agitation—to recognize (re-cognize) what is truly important to me. I recently read for the first time Ray Bradbury's *Fahrenheit 451*, which was originally published in 1953—over 50 years ago, yet incredibly relevant today. A mindless, futuristic society is kept unreflective and conformable as television pervades every aspect of life. Firemen no longer extinguish fires, but start them—whenever an individual is found in the possession of books, which are illegal and dangerous (intellectuals are outlaws). Bradbury presents a frightening scenario, yet it is not unbelievable because our society shows evidence of heading in this direction, as many people live "for pleasure, for titillation" (Bradbury, 1953, p. 63), becoming increasingly more alike. Where is the impetus to question cultural models and ingrained beliefs? In the in-class essay about controversial issues (Data Set #6), one participant wrote the following:

> Controversial books should not be brought into classrooms because the topics are too risky and often opinion-based. Introducing topics such as homosexuality and prejudice in the classroom may cause more harm than good because of *differing views* of teachers, parents, and students. (emphasis added)

Fahrenheit 451 is relevant today because books are still considered dangerous, and more importantly, because differing views are sometimes disregarded or discouraged.

Is school a place to introduce new ideas and encourage individual thinking? Based on the responses of many participants in this study, I would argue that the focus of school is "getting along in world," with the implied notion of conformity and mere survival. It is important to point out the fact that the connotations of "getting along in the world" in this study are being highlighted through a lens of critical literacy and discourse analysis. The idea of "getting along in the world" certainly suggests the development of interpersonal skills and students' abilities to work together effectively.[44] Once again, the goal in this case is to problematize the taken-for-granted and to "make the familiar strange." Nevertheless, I would suggest that most of the future teachers in this study are not likely to practice critical literacy, unless they receive extensive guidance, opportunities for reflection, and ongoing modeling and support in favor of critical literacy.

---

[44] Shannon (personal communication, April 8, 2004) pointed out the implications of "getting along" in a democracy, stating that discomfort with "disagreement and diversity works against a democratic position."

CHAPTER 8

Implications, Limitations, and Future Research

Implications

The participants in this study had not thought about many of the issues related to critical literacy, despite discussions and writing in class. Preservice teachers need opportunities to think about, reflect on, and understand their own views, as well as the reality of their future school settings, deciding (before entering the classroom) how they might handle particular situations.

Related to the importance of reflection, which includes questioning one's ingrained perspectives (a difficult task), are the ways in which we teach students to read—both texts and their worlds. In 1990, Luke and Freebody presented the four resources model of reading, in which readers adopted the following roles: code breaker (coding competence), meaning maker (semantic competence), text user (pragmatic competence), and text critic (critical competence). Recently, Luke and Freebody (1999)[45] expanded on and clarified the model, referring to the various components as a "family of practices" because "while literacy is an aspect of an individual's history, capability, and possibilities, it is also a feature of the collective or joint capabilities of a group, community, or society." They explained that effective literacy should allow learners to: break the code of written texts; participate in understanding and composing meaningful written, visual, and spoken texts; use texts functionally; and critically analyze and transform texts. (See Appendix F for further information.)

Luke and Freebody also claimed that "literacy was never a matter of deficit but principally an issue of economic and social access to the cultural institutions charged with literacy education and practice." The crucial element of their model is "necessity, not sufficiency" because none of the components by themselves are "sufficient for literate citizens and subjects." Luke and Freebody explained that "while

---

[45] See also Luke (2000).

students who have a high degree of congruence with the culture of the teachers perform well in various types of programs, students who lack such congruence perform particularly poorly in programs described as 'meaning based.'" In other words, students who are socially similar to their teachers are better at "doing school," partly because they adhere to the same cultural models.

Once again, what about the students on the outside? Luke and Freebody advocate using differing literacy teaching approaches, claiming that "effective teachers know this and monitor the progress of their students in order to make appropriate adaptations." For students both on the inside and on the outside of the cultural models, it is important to go beyond breaking the code, understanding, and using texts functionally to engage in critical analysis and transformation of texts. This involves

> acting on knowledge that texts are not ideologically natural or neutral—that they represent particular points of views while silencing others and influence people's ideas—and that their designs and discourses can be critiqued and redesigned in novel and hybrid ways. (Luke & Freebody, 1999)

Students on the inside may become better situated to become more empathetic toward others and to develop a greater sense of responsibility for their own behaviors (Rosenblatt, 1995). Students on the outside may feel acknowledged ("my voice is being heard"), empowered ("I am capable"), and valued ("I am important").

However, educators must be truly invested in the concept of critical literacy in order to teach effectively with this theory; otherwise, one is simply going through the motions. A person would have to embrace the philosophy and appropriate it because critical literacy is not a set of techniques, but a mind-set. Luke and Freebody (1999) reinforced the fact that the Australian educational system is more receptive to critical pedagogy, and Luke (2000) explained that most Australian teacher education programs now include functional grammar and genre study, critical literacy and text analysis, second-language acquisition models, and Vygotskian psychology as core components. The inclusion of such subject matter in United States teacher education programs could be a step toward transformative practice. Likewise, explicit, ongoing opportunities for future teachers to reflect on their own beliefs in a variety of ways could prepare them to be more effective, socioculturally conscientious decision-makers.

Limitations Related to Theory

An extremely important caveat for this study is the reminder that critical literacy is only one component of effective literacy education. Luke and Freebody (1999) advised,

> We have attempted to avoid and resist the "commodification" of critical literacy as an educational and political solution for all that ails us. In our view, critical literacies—in all their varied print and multimedia, practical and theoretical, cultural and political forms—refer to openings in the curriculum that enable teachers, students, and communities to explore alternative ways of structuring practices around texts to address new cultural and economic contexts and new forms of practice and identity.

Critical literacy should not be viewed as the best or only way of reading, especially when considering the importance of pleasure; that is, the value of purely aesthetic experience. Sometimes *Olivia* is just about a cute, spunky little pig with endless self-esteem, a fabulous imagination and enough energy to fuel a small city, rather than one of many examples of a white, middle-class, heterosexual family. There are appropriate times and places for each type of literacy, although sometimes these various literacies are intertwined.

Moreover, Luke (personal communication, April 6, 2004) reemphasized the danger of "commodification" of critical literacy—we must consider the local context of a situation rather than unreflectingly attempting to employ a generic model of questioning or rebellion. Luke (2004) also pointed out the complexities of critical literacy, reinforcing the notion of venturing beyond black and white dichotomies, such as oppression versus liberation and hope versus despair, toward the gray area of possibilities. Freire's work represented a less complex situation of binary dialectics, which was explicable in terms of his political context (Luke, personal communication, April 6, 2004). It is important to remember that Freire "maintained that educators should not regard his work as a recipe book to be followed. He demands that we critically appropriate from, recontextualize, and thus reinvent his ideas to fit the spaces and places where we work" (Leistyna, Lavandez, & Nelson, 2004, p. 8).

Another valid objection to critical pedagogy is the disconnection between theory and practice (see for example, Ellsworth, 1989). In other words, critical literacy may seem like an interesting or useful theory but how can we possibly act on such a philosophy when faced with daunting restrictions such as No Child Left Behind, influences of the powerful publishing industry, and the prevalence of a "one size fits all" standards approach? According to Leistyna, Lavandez, and Nelson (2004),

> As students are diverted or lured away from critically reading historical and existing social formations, especially those that maintain abuses of power, they so often become the newest wave of exploited labor power and reproducers, whether they are conscious of it or not, of oppressive social practices. (p. 8)

An important solution is that "teacher education programs need to assist prospective teachers in developing critical languages to explain the world around and within them—the *ways* and *how* of what is happening in society" (Leistyna, Lavandez, & Nelson, 2004, p. 8). Another consideration is education of the public to increase awareness because they essentially "own" the system. It is difficult to step back "from the world as we are accustomed to seeing it" (Kincheloe, 2004, p. 64), and most "owners" of public education are products of the system. However, an effort to educate parents (perhaps alongside students or with take-home activities) in principles of critical literacy, starting with accessible, relevant materials such as messages in the popular media, would be worthwhile.

Luke mentioned (2004) that sometimes the most receptive adherents of critical pedagogy are those who have experienced oppression or "Otherness," and Sleeter, Torres, and Laughlin (2004) pointed out:

> Those who are in privileged positions often object to social justice education and consider it as a type of indoctrination. They question the educators' right to change the consciousness of students. Raising questions about what students take for granted, however, is different from indoctrination. (pp. 83-84)

Since the majority of preservice teachers are white, female, monolingual and middle-class (Bartolomé, 2004), it would seem "natural" for them to resist critical literacy due to their unquestioned or unrecognized positions of privileged. Moreover, Shannon (personal communication, April 7, 2004) explained that young teachers might have conservative values about education partly due to the fact that schools have been increasingly framed as dysfunctional institutions, with teachers being asked to accept responsibility for achievement gaps among demographic groups. Moreover,

> Given the social class, racial, cultural, and language differences between teachers and students, and our society's historical predisposition to view culturally and linguistically diverse students through a deficit lens that positions them as less intelligent, talented, qualified, and deserving, it is especially urgent that educators critically understand their ideological orientations with respect to these differences, and begin to comprehend that teaching is not a politically or ideologically neutral undertaking. (Bartolomé, 2004, p. 99)

The suggestion of infusing teacher preparation programs with opportunities for inquiry and reflection of students' taken-for-granted beliefs is not meant to entail indoctrination into one particular perspective or theory. Rather, the purpose is to guide future teachers through a process of learning about a variety of "canons of knowledge" and to introduce them to different ways of thinking (Kincheloe, 2004). As mentioned earlier regarding various definitions of "getting along in the world," diversity and disagreement are necessary elements of democracy. In 1916, Dewey wrote the following:

> I appeal to teachers in the face of every hysterical wave of emotion, and of every subtle appeal of sinister class interest, to remember that they above all others are consecrated servants of the democratic ideas in which alone this country is truly a distinctive nation—ideas of friendly and helpful intercourse between all and the equipment of every individual to serve the community by his own best powers in his own best way. (Dewey, 1980b, p. 210)

However, Shannon (2004), pointed out the contradictions of democratic "freedom" within the current educational system:

> We are free to choose, but not free to develop our choices. How do we reform schools and literacy education in order to fit our criteria of how we wish to live together? The future of communities, schools, and reading education is not merely a set of variables to be loaded into someone's prediction equation. The future is what is to be decided—to be made. Our *possibilities* are influenced, but not fixed, by the past, and the practices of democracy become the means through which we can express this freedom to make our future. (p. 7; emphasis added)

A key word in Shannon's statement is *"possibilities,"* which can represent that complex gray area between black and white. Possibilities are chances, with connotations of risk, gamble, potential, and hope. Ayers, Mitchie and Rome (2004) explained, "Perhaps the biggest challenge, then becomes holding on to hope, and that can be exceedingly difficult—especially when the discourse surrounding teaching and schools is unendingly pessimistic" (p. 127). Bartolomé (2004) used the term "realistic yet hopeful" (p. 120) to describe the exemplary educators in her study. Critical literacy might seem like an ideal concept in theory, but what about in real-life classroom practice? This is where hope and vision are necessary—realistic *hope* for positive transformation and a *vision* of "what could be" (Kincheloe, 2004). Although some would argue for complete revolution,[46] "ordinary" people can foster positive change through relatively small (though not insignificant), thoughtful actions (Meyerson, 2001).

Limitations Related to Research Design and Methodology

Regarding the methods employed in this study, the findings might have varied with different interviewees, or if all participants had been interviewed. I believe an important question I could have asked would be why participants agreed to be interviewed because their reasons might have revealed more about their cultural models and overall beliefs, especially regarding their identities as students. Concerning the written data, the questions and essay prompts were relatively open-ended, mainly in order to solicit participants' "true" thinking. I was hoping to elicit their ideas about what was important to discuss. However, there were a variety of ways in which the prompts could have been constructed, leading to different types of responses. Additionally, the English 306A professor's lectures probably influenced participants' responses. For example, the latest group of writing students I taught had a different professor for English 306A, and he focused heavily on folklore and more obscure children's stories. Whereas the other instructor expected students to learn details such as specific dates and authors' biographical information, the subsequent instructor seemed more interested in common themes.

In addition to the influence of the English 306A professor, I believe I had an impact on the participants, despite an attempt to present information as objectively as possible. That is, I tried to provide students with as much information as possible, encouraging them to make their own decisions—an attempt to model critical literacy. However, I realize that my own subjectivity and advocacy were

---

[46] See, for example, the work of Marxist theorists such as McLaren; specifically "Teaching In and Against the Empire: Critical Pedagogy as Revolutionary Praxis" (2004).

transparent throughout the study, partly due to the topics I chose to present (critical literacy, controversial children's books), and the obvious fact that I was conducting research on preservice teachers responses to children's literature through a framework of critical literacy. Moreover, I recognized a younger version of myself in at least one participant—Dory, who said "I don't know" 67 times during the interview. I identified with her lack of reflection because I was able to recall myself in the same situation prior to deciding to go to college. Additionally, I viewed all of the participants I interviewed as valuable, caring individuals who truly hoped to make a difference in their future students' lives. Some of the participants who were not interviewed seemed intent mainly on getting through their program, and since I did not get to know them as well as the interviewees, I cannot comment accurately on their attitudes toward teaching. Nevertheless, due to an overall affinity for the participants, I experienced some actual pain when reviewing and trying to make sense of their responses. At times I felt like I was judging the participants, and I had to step away temporarily and refocus on analyzing their responses. The cycle of analyzing data while simultaneously experiencing emotions regarding the participants was the most difficult aspect of this study.

Future Research

I have learned that questions inevitably lead to more questions, and the findings from this study are no different. I believe my five original research questions have tentative, adequate answers, the most important being that the future teachers in this study are not likely to practice critical literacy, unless they receive extensive guidance, opportunities for reflection, and ongoing modeling and support in favor of critical literacy.

To counter some of the limitations of this study, it would be appropriate for an outsider to interview participants; that is, to conduct a similar study in which the researcher is not the participants' instructor. Likewise, replicating this study with a different English 306A professor would be worthwhile, especially in order to find out how participants respond to fairy tales. It would also be useful to conduct this study with two classes—a treatment group and a control group, in which the treatment group receives explicit information about critical literacy, to determine whether the brief exposure to critical literacy has any impact. Likewise, this study could be conducted at another university in which participants receive ongoing critical literacy information and modeling, which is interwoven throughout their academic program. In other words, replicate this study at an institution that explicitly advocates principles of critical pedagogy and emphasizes reflection.

Other possibilities include tracking the participants in the current study, following them through their teacher preparation programs into the classroom in order to determine how their cultural models change or remain the same, and whether they are leaning closer to or farther away from the principles of critical literacy. This would involve observation, which might be best conducted by a researcher other than myself. Finally, since the data collection involved written responses and individual interviews, I believe that this study could be replicated using literature circles and/or book clubs.

CHAPTER 9
Suggestions for Practice

Kincheloe (2004) advocated "empowerment of teachers in an era where teacher professionalism is under assault" (p. 50). He argued that "Teacher educators, teachers, and teacher education students must not only understand the complexity of good teaching, but stand ready to make this known to political leaders and the general population" (p. 50). According to Kincheloe,

> Only with a solid foundation in various mainstream and alternative canons of knowledge can they [teachers] begin to make wise judgments and informed choices about curriculum development and classroom practice" (p. 50).

Specifically, Kincheloe (2004) suggested investigation into the following: (a) the context in which education takes place; (b) the historical forces that have shaped the purposes of schooling; (c) the ways dominant power uses schools for anti-democratic ideological self interest; (d) how all of this relates to the effort to develop democratic, transformative pedagogy; and (e) the specific ways all of these knowledges relate to transformative classroom teaching in general and to their particular curricular domain in particular. Teachers must "become researchers of educational contexts" (p. 64) and they should be "encouraged to confront why they think as they do about themselves as teachers—especially in relationship to the social, cultural, political, economic, and historical world around them" (p. 58). Through such rigorous examination, we are more likely to practice "reflexive awareness," in which we step back "from the world as we are accustomed to seeing it" (p. 64).

Bartolomé (2004) also discussed the importance of helping educators to examine their own assumptions, values, and beliefs, through what she referred to as "political clarity" and "ideological clarity." Reporting the findings of a study at a high school "approximately 18 miles north of the Mexican border" in southern California, Bartolomé examined the practices and perspectives of four "exemplary" educators who created a "comfort zone" in which students were academically and socially successful. These teachers questioned dominant ideologies to varying degrees, but they also reported "having engaged in what I label as 'cultural border crossing' where they personally experienced being positioned as low status, or witnessed someone else's subordination" (Bartolomé, 2004, p. 102). She explained that "a border crosser, while embracing the cultural 'Other,' must also divest from his/her cultural privilege that often functions as a cultural border itself" (p. 109). Bartolomé suggested that such border-crossing experiences can be replicated or simulated through teacher preparation coursework and practicum.

Likewise, Sleeter, Torres, and Laughlin (2004) delineated useful activities for future teachers, explaining the ways in which they provided explicit scaffolding for students in order to make the instruction transparent. Torres described two projects requiring students to "find first-hand hard data about representation of minority groups in media and textbooks, so there was less chance to deny that such things would ever happen in this society" (p. 85.). Students engaged in individual inquiry as well as small group and whole group study to reveal misrepresentation as "systematic replication with different minority groups and cultural contexts" (p. 86). Sleeter discussed community-based field experiences in which future teachers found "themselves seeing many conditions related to oppression that they might not have believed exist on a significant scale" (p. 87). Students developed relationships with people in the field that eventually built a trusting environment in which these future teachers began "to ask questions some would not have dreamed of verbalizing earlier" (p. 87). Sleeter also described the "Why?" project:

> Students are each to pose an authentic question related to race language, social class, gender, or disability, and over the semester search for an understanding of that question that reflects the point of view of a group other than their own, to whom the question might pertain. (p. 87)

Laughlin utilized participatory research in which students engaged in individual case study assignments and simultaneous group synthesis tasks, and participants "incorporated into their final project a recommendation for action, which was to be applied to their own professional and personal context for growth" (p. 92). The researchers believed that "we engage our students by sharing power" (p. 92), and this perspective is evident in all of the activities. In addition to providing explicit scaffolding, modeling, and support, the researchers compiled students' papers into a class book, which served as "textbooks" during the latter part of the semester or as models and sources of information for subsequent classes. The main limitation of these activities appeared to be the relatively brief time frame: "One semester is not sufficient to carry out an inquiry project, process the results at cognitive and emotional levels (anger, guilt, etc.) and then try to become proactive advocates for more democratic social practices and schooling" (Sleeter, Torres, & Laughlin, 2004, p. 86).

Other specific suggestions for practice include gradually introducing topics for discussion because initiating an investigation into critical pedagogy with extremely personal concepts such as white privilege is more likely to engender resentment and resistance. Harste (personal communication, April 6, 2004) explained,

> I have found it easier to work with materials that are more distant to future teachers than to hit them on things that are too close to home. They can unpack the implicit message in "Little Red Riding Hood" rather than unpack the messages inherent in belonging to a sorority, for example.

Finally, Kincheloe mentioned the importance of educating the public, claiming that education professors should write for public consumption and speak to public groups (personal communication, April 8, 2004). Through such efforts, we can nurture an environment in which individuals are aware that "no teacher, no concerned citizen is ever fully educated; they are always 'in process,' waiting for the next learning experience" (Kincheloe, 2004, p. 52). Hence, my reason for wanting to share my research and experiences with the public. My hope is that some of this information will be useful to various audiences—teachers, students, parents, and the general public.

In my own experiences as a teacher and parent, I have discovered the value of "teachable moments." That is, when I perceive a specific need, I strive to find ways to set up effective learning situations, usually when I notice unthinking behavior. It is important to avoid blaming or shaming; rather, introduce new ideas and possibilities in a spirit of learning together. This highlights the value of dialogue, in which we learn through the process of speaking and listening to each other.

Most of my examples are from college-level teaching, but the overall thought process is the same. For example, immigration—both legal and illegal—is a highly debated topic in San Diego, since we are located very close to the Mexican border. Young children who cross the border to attend school may experience negative comments from teachers as well as fellow students (who may be influenced by their parents' ideas). In such a situation, a teacher could introduce Gloria Anzaldúa's bilingual picture book *Friends from the Other Side/Amigos Del Otro Lado* (1993). This book depicts a young boy who crosses the Rio Grande with his mother, living in hiding to avoid the Border Patrol vans. Neighborhood children call the boy "mojado" and "wetback," although a young girl becomes his friend. Regardless of one's belief about immigration, it would be worthwhile to show students how others might feel. In this case, children might "see" a young boy much like them who is different only because he comes from another place.

However, when designing lessons based on the needs of students, careful planning is mandatory. In addition to avoiding blame and shame, it is important to consider the appropriateness of the material to be used. Likewise, depending on the situation, students will need varying degrees of scaffolding (background information to help them understand the material) and follow-up activities. Most importantly, students need opportunities to reflect on their own beliefs before and after the activities. Below are three "lessons" I developed recently, generated from events in the classroom and based on my perceptions of students' needs. I am sharing them to demonstrate my thinking processes and implementation of the lessons. Of course, there are many ways to address situations that emerge within a classroom, and the following are simply examples of the choices I made.

Bums

In a college-level developmental writing class, we were working on how to structure a cause-and-effect essay. I suggested the topic of homelessness, since we could probably come up with supporting examples from our own experiences in the world. I solicited ideas from the students regarding some possible causes for homelessness (losing one's job, substance abuse, etc.) and we generated specific examples to support these ideas. Then I asked about some potential effects of homelessness and one student mentioned "Bumfights,"[47] which are

---

[47] The website (www.bumfights.com) boasts: "Already illegal in some countries, this is the video series the U.S. Congress tried to ban. Worldwide, Bumfights has established itself as the hardest, rawest, most hilariously shocking video series on the planet." These videos were filmed mostly in the San Diego area by three young men.

controversial "real life" videos depicting "real bums trad[ing] blows on the street." I started to comment that the producers of these videos paid homeless people to perform dangerous stunts, when a young African American student said, "Oh, there's a homeless guy that lives under the bridge by my work. A bunch of guys [from work] beat him up one day and now he walks funny." She laughed after saying this.

I have learned how to avoid reacting to students' comments, especially with my facial gestures, but inside I was boiling. Instead of singling out this student, I shifted the conversation and asked the entire class why people commit hate crimes. Nobody had much of an answer (apparently they had not thought much about it), although a few comments were essentially, "that stuff doesn't happen much any more" and "racism really isn't a problem." It was interesting that they equated hate crimes with racism. Regardless, the overall response of the class seemed to be, "it doesn't affect my life." I agreed that in many ways we live in a more tolerant world, but terrible acts of violence and injustice still occur; in fact, perhaps closer to home than we realize. I told them I had a video about hate crimes and they were interested.

The next class meeting, I provided background information to the video *Culture of Hate: Who Are We?* (Harvey, 2002), which was filmed in the rural town of Lakeside in San Diego County. I showed the location on the map, pointing out that it was only about twenty miles away. This documentary presents white-power teenagers with swastika tattoos who practice Heil Hitler salutes. Three of the boys murdered a Mexican migrant worker for no apparent reason. And perhaps the most poignant element is the audience's gradual awareness that these young people have no idea why they want to be white supremacists. A 15-year-old-girl responds with "I don't know" when asked why she allowed her boyfriend to shave a swastika on the back of her head. Viewers see the utter senselessness of this culture of hate, and hopefully, their understanding of the world will grow.

Immediately after watching the video, I asked students to freewrite for ten minutes about their reactions, comments, and any questions. The majority of students indicated that they were surprised to know such groups existed, especially in San Diego County. They were outraged by the selfishness and brutality exhibited by the teenagers, and many tried to understand what would cause such behavior. As a class, we discussed the video and brainstormed possible causes (such as parental neglect and bullying by others).

I do not imagine this one lesson prompted miraculous shifts in students' perspectives. However, I suspect that students will pay more attention when they hear about hate crimes and the young woman will not laugh so easily at another's misfortune. In terms of adding more content to the curriculum, I considered the information from the video as evidence to use in a cause-and-effect essay, which was our original task. In other words, we shifted our topic to hate crimes and thought of possible causes and effects. After choosing to focus on causes, we were then able to use events from the video as specific examples to support our points about some causes of hate crimes.

Obviously, this activity was specific to my context—the students, our location, and the particular issue that arose in the classroom. And this is precisely why critical literacy can be so powerful: it is generated through students' needs and a unique context. Below are two more examples.

"Retards"

Just before the semester began, I received a typed note from a young man in a freshman composition class (I'll call him Jake). He explained that he had Tourette's Syndrome and this would be his first semester in college. Jake stated that although his parents did not believe he should attend college, he wanted to challenge himself and he promised he would try his best. He also explained his condition and some ways that he manages it, such as sitting in the front row and leaving the room if he needed a break. During the first week of class, I noticed students snickering whenever Jake would speak—he tended to stammer, say "um" a lot, and sometimes ramble, but his comments were intelligent. I encouraged him to raise his hand whenever he started to blurt out a comment, and he never made offensive noises or comments.

I understood that my job was to provide an effective learning environment for *all* students, which was difficult due to the circumstances. At times, I wanted to discuss Jake's condition with the class when I noticed them laughing or clearly making fun of him. Fortunately, Jake never seemed to notice the students' rude behavior because he sat in the front row. Once when I asked students to work in pairs, Jake faced the student next to him and requested that they work together several times. The student pretended not to hear Jake and got up to work with someone else. It was clear that Jake was "different," so I did not understand why students could behave with such coldness and lack of empathy. In fact, I was shocked and disappointed.

One day, for no apparent reason, Jake got frustrated and started banging his head against the desk. I noticed many of the students laughing and I calmly invited to Jake to take a break outside, which he did. Later, I contacted Disabled Student Services and asked for advice with the situation. They suggested talking to the entire class, but I did not want to put Jake in an embarrassing situation. And after all, it was the other students who needed a "lesson," not Jake.

We were about to study the narrative form in composition, so I searched for a story about a college student with a disability. I discovered an anthology of stories edited by an anthropology professor with Asperger's Syndrome: *Aquamarine Blue: Personal Stories of College Students with Autism* (Prince-Hughes, 2002). I chose Jim's story, which explains what it feels like to be "different" and how he has learned to adjust in order to be a successful college student. I presented the story as an example of narration and asked students to read silently. When they were finished, I prompted them to write their reactions, anything they learned, and their thoughts about the author's technique.

Once again, my goal was to fit this lesson into the context of our regular coursework in order to avoid blaming or preaching. Immediately after reading the story, Jake came up and asked me if he could keep it. He said he really liked it, which of course, I was happy to hear. In this case, I chose not to have a whole class discussion about the story. Instead, I read students' writing and wrote comments as a mini-dialogue, trying to gauge from their individual responses how I could best facilitate further thinking about the topic. Students' responses ranged from having no connection or interest in the story to feeling profoundly moved or enlightened by the challenges Jim had to face. I thought it was best to avoid making explicit connections to Jake, hoping students would see the similarities. Certainly, this activity did not prompt a dramatic shift in all students' perspectives. However, although I cannot claim a cause-and-effect relationship, I did notice more students reaching out to include Jake in group work. As I mentioned earlier, the activities I selected were specific to the context because my goal was to address a need that emerged from the classroom.

Murderers

In an advanced critical thinking and composition class, the textbook I use is *Thinking Critically: A Concise Guide* (Chaffee, 2004), which includes a section about a woman, Mary Barnett, who left her six-month-old baby home alone, left the state, and went on a drinking binge. The baby slowly died and Barnett received a 15-year prison sentence. Students are asked to evaluate the claims and support of both the prosecution and defense. In class, we debated whether Barnett was solely responsible, if a postpartum depression defense was reasonable, and other issues related to the case. Then we discussed murder in general, trying to decide if there are ever cases in which murder is acceptable or "right." Of course, we did not reach any consensus.

Meanwhile, I assigned an essay that was structured as follows: describe a belief you have and explain how you think it developed. Then describe the opposite viewpoint and how someone may have developed it. I provided a model for students using my belief that cheating is wrong. I explained my belief and showed how my opinion developed early due to my parents' behavior and teaching. Then I discussed the ways in which my belief became stronger through my experiences as a student, parent, and teacher. I cautioned students several times not to select a belief that was so strong they could not envision the opposing view.

Nearly every student who turned in a first draft version of this essay focused only on his or her belief. Some stretched a bit and explained why the opposing view was wrong. Of course, my response was that I had not explained or demonstrated the assignment well enough. I rephrased the writing prompt and provided anonymous examples on the overhead of the few essays that addressed the opposing view. Then I pointed out the ways in which the essays could be revised to provide a balanced discussion of the overall belief. Likewise, I made comments on students' papers indicating where their own beliefs were clear and how to present the other side. When I read the final drafts, I noticed that a few students revised their essays to reflect a more balanced discussion. However, the majority of the papers focused on students' own beliefs and/or negated the opposing view if it was discussed.

I felt like a failure because I was unable to help students think critically through this activity. I spent a lot of time reevaluating my understanding of the goals of this course, what I knew about teaching and learning, and how I could facilitate authentic change in perspective. Somehow it all came together when I remembered our discussions about murder.

Without any sort of introduction, I asked students to describe a murderer and they generated a list right away, which I wrote on the board: evil, insane, violent, monster, etc. Then I asked what we should do with murderers and students shouted out "kill 'em," "lock 'em up and throw away the key," "life in prison," although a few suggested rehabilitation. Then, once again without introduction, I showed the documentary *What I Want My Words to Do to You: Voices from Inside a Women's Maximum Security Prison* by Eve Ensler (2003). The prisoners, who are mainly serving long terms for murder, are involved in a writing workshop in which they recount their crimes, reveal their feelings, and share personal thoughts and experiences. The end of the film shows a performance at the prison in which actresses such as Glenn Close, Marisa Tomei, and Rosie Perez read the women's writing.

After the film, I immediately asked students to write their responses (I provided no other prompt—just "write your reactions.") Without exception, every student wrote that his or her perspective of prisoners and/or murders had changed due to this movie. Students now saw these criminals as real people with feelings who might be worth saving through rehabilitation (such as Ensler's writing workshop). They certainly did not condone the murders, but students now saw how it is possible that one mistake can change your entire life. I was deeply moved by the students' responses because I witnessed a profound change in their thinking. Although their perspectives had changed in only one area (views about murder and punishment), I hope the lesson helped them understand that we may have unexamined beliefs. And we continued to work on this throughout the semester.

I consider internal change to be "transformation" in a Freirean sense; however, the component of critical literacy that is missing in the above activities is social action. I am hoping to add this in the near future as I incorporate service learning activities into advanced composition classes. Our college has a well-established service learning program, and I plan to develop assignments in which students interact with members of the community (similar to Sleeter and Laughlin, above). There are other methods of facilitating social action, such as letter writing (to the newspaper, school administrators, government officials, etc.) and any activity intended to promote positive change. Two excellent texts that illustrate social action are *Freedom Writers with Erin Gruwell* (1999), in which a first-year high school teacher helped 150 teenagers transform themselves and others through writing, and *Text, Lies & Videotape: Stories about Life, Literacy, and Learning* (Shannon, 1995), which uses his family's experiences to demonstrate critical literacy in "real life."

I use the term "real life" to indicate the world outside of school, and I would like to share an example from my own experience. My daughter became interested in social protest art in high school, so it was natural that UC Berkeley would be one of her choices for college. As she was preparing to send applications, I mentioned that she might try using the "legacy" preference. Our great aunt, Katherine Towle, had been Dean of Students at Berkeley and we were her only descendants. After more discussion, my daughter decided not to mention the legacy as a matter of principle. Why? Partly because Katherine Towle was involved with suppressing the Berkeley Free Speech Movement in 1964, and my daughter did not want to be associated with such a viewpoint. But the main reason was, "I wanted to be accepted by college based on my own merit and achievement, rather than the value of someone's last name." She was not accepted by UC Berkeley, but she is currently in her second year at UC San Diego, with a double major in art history and photography.

When I compare the type of thinker my daughter is at 19 years old with myself at the same age, I am amazed at the difference. She has informed opinions and she acts upon them, unlike me, who did not know how to reflect, question, or challenge the status quo. I was, as some of the participants in my study, merely "getting along in the world." However, this behavior can be modified if a person is motivated, and motivation is the key because we will not change unless without genuine desire.

◆ FINAL THOUGHTS

Clearly I am a proponent of critical literacy and as I maintained in my article (McDaniel, 2004), I continue to believe that we need more models of questioning behavior for young children. However, the literary quality and aesthetic value of the books must be considered because a reader's level of engagement and degree of pleasure are significant factors (Rosenblatt, 1994; Sipe, 1999). Some readily available examples of quality literature include *Click Clack Moo, Cows that Type* (Cronin, 2000), in which the cows use a typewriter (hence, "click, clack, moo") to protest their poor working environment, and the farmer eventually concedes to their demands. *Sister Anne's Hands* (Lorbiecki, 1998), which was mentioned earlier, depicts a situation of racism in the 1960s, although the conclusion seems overly idealistic, as a seven-year-old white girl transcends racist attitudes toward her African American teacher during the course of one year.

Additionally, in *Sitti's Secrets* (Nye, 1994), readers are presented with an example of social action through a young American girl's decision to write to the U.S. president after visiting her grandmother in a Palestinian village on the West Bank. Another picture book, *Whitewash* (Shange, 1997), is based on a series of true incidents, portraying a young African American girl being attacked by a gang of racist youths who paint her face white and call her a "mud" person. Unlike *Sister Anne's Hands*, this book presents a more realistic, and therefore more troubling, account of transformation. The young girl heals slowly with the help of family and friends, although readers may understand that the protagonist will never be the same again (loss of childhood "innocence"). Reviewers have labeled this book "shocking" and "inappropriate" for younger children, which may explain why *Whitewash* is out of print. It seems that many books promoting critical literacy are neither widely used nor popular, perhaps because bestsellers likely represent adults' choices, since they purchase the literature.

However, as mentioned earlier, I recommend that more children's book authors and publishers create *engaging* texts that promote critical literacy. I would not suggest attempting to include all seven crite-ria[48] (see Chapter 4) in a single text, but to incorporate one or two in an appealing manner that invites repeated readings. Nevertheless, I suspect that more realistic content, despite engaging literary style, would incite resistance. Leland and Harste (1999), who have re-searched and written about critical literacy extensively in the United States, discussed teachers' and parents' desires to avoid controversial literature:

> We find this stance problematic. First, it helps to maintain schools as places that are often disconnected from children's everyday experiences—places where nothing real or important ever happens or is addressed. Second, this view underestimates the capacity of children to understand and deal with complex problems and issues. (p. 4-5)

Perhaps less focus on adults' desires and more investigation into chil-dren's voluntary choices of reading material and their responses to literature would be helpful.

Neither language nor texts are neutral (Apple, 1992; Fairclough, 1995; Gee, 1996; Gee, 1997; Gee, 1999; Jaworski & Coupland, 1999; Luke, 2000; Luke & Freebody, 1999), and the taken-for-granted—more than the sensational, shocking, or unusual—merits serious scrutiny precisely because of its apparent ordinariness and outward appropri-ateness. Gee (1999) explained how situations or contexts, which we create, understand, and reproduce through language, are repeated over time. "Such repetition tends to 'ritualize,' 'habitualize,' or 'freeze' situations to varying degrees" (p. 82), and this repetition is crucial in the formation of institutions, which continue the cycle of repetition and reinforcement (Gee, 1999). I understand this concept in terms of the statement, "that's how we've always done it," perhaps in re-sponse to the question, "why is it done this way and not some other way?" Situations and contexts are particularly transparent for some-one visiting a different culture or country—so-called "culture shock"—or for others who are "outsiders" in some way.

---

[48] Exploring difference; giving a voice to traditionally marginalized people; demon-strating social action; investigating dominant systems of meaning that operate in our society to position people and groups of people; avoiding inappropriately happy endings for complex problems; helping readers question why certain groups are posi-tioned as "others"; and depicting multiple perspectives.

An example might help to illustrate the cycle of repetition and re-inforcement, resulting in cultural reproduction. Many of us learned in kindergarten (or earlier) to form two lines—boys and girls—whenever our teacher planned to lead us from one point to another on campus. This was how it was done and we probably did not question it—we simply learned to get in line behind someone of our own gender when the order was given. Repetition solidified this practice as "normal," and I would speculate that many teachers automatically (without thinking) continue this ritual. This example is not meant to imply that separating boys and girls is wrong, although it is clear that we institutionalize gender differences at an early age. My intent is to demonstrate the ways in which we *unreflectively* reproduce cultural practices.

A related concern is the reproduction of images and texts within our culture. How much of the material intended for children is *unreflectively* created, based on repetition and habit? Returning to the discussion of standard fairy tales from the beginning of this chapter, most individuals learn at an early age to predict the plot and conclusion of these stories: "Once upon a time...stuff happens...they live happily ever after." It is the anomaly that we tend to notice—a story that disrupts the typical plotline or conclusion—rather than the standard version.

After writing students in English 306W (composition for future teachers) have turned in their final drafts of the fairy tale essays, I like to read the book *Jane and the Dragon* (Baynton, 1988) to them. Jane is not a princess, although she lives in the castle with her father and mother, who is a lady-in waiting. Jane hates sewing but loves to watch the knights practicing their swordplay. Nobody supports her desire to be a knight, except the court jester, who gives Jane his little suit of armor and she begins practicing secretly. One day, a terrible green dragon descends on the kingdom and snatches the prince. All of the knights are "away at a jousting carnival," but a small knight in armor gallops away after the dragon. Jane bravely confronts the dragon and a long battle ensues, in which both Jane and the dragon could have killed each other but chose not to. The dragon admits that he really does not enjoy hurting people but says, "it's expected of me," and sobs, "I want to be loved." Jane promises to visit the dragon every Saturday, returns to the kingdom with the prince, and is granted her wish to become a knight once everyone recovers from shock. The book ends with the king giving a ball in Jane's honor:

"You must choose a partner, Jane," said the King, "and lead the dancing."
      All the handsome young men waited, each one hoping to be chosen.
      But Jane took the jester's hand and led him onto the floor.
      "Thank you for the armor," said Jane.
      "Thank you for the dream," said the jester.
      And together they danced and danced and danced.

Students usually laugh several times during the reading of this story,
and once I finish, I ask them what was funny, but they are not certain.

      In fact, I notice that the students especially laugh when the dragon
says he wants to be loved, perhaps because his behavior is noticeably
undragonlike, particularly when he begins to sob. Jane is unprincess-
like, with frizzy red hair, freckles, and no desire to "live happily ever
after" in the fairy tale sense. This story does not depend on any character being "the bad guy," and most importantly, Jane takes charge of
her own happiness—she is not seeking to simply survive or "get
along in the world;" she wants to thrive. *Jane and the Dragon* disrupts
the concepts of childhood innocence, adult authority, and appropriate
gender roles in an engaging manner. Perhaps we could categorize the
book as literary nonviolent resistance to the status quo.

      Challenging the status quo is risky, but silence can be even more
dangerous.[49] Just as the 52-year-old *Fahrenheit 451* (Bradbury, 1953)
resonates today, especially regarding the "danger" of books, voices
from the past can be powerful reminders regarding the detriments of
conformity. Mark Twain (1835-1910) wrote candidly about society,
often using satire, a literary form that can be misunderstood sometimes by readers. His comments on conformity and lack of reflection
are worth considering:

   ♦   "Whenever you find yourself on the side of the majority, it is
       time to reform (or pause and reflect)" (*Notebook*, 1904).

---

[49] Consider, for instance, the words attributed to Martin Niemoller, German Protestant pastor (1892-1984) regarding the Holocaust: "In Germany they first came for the
Communists, and I didn't speak up because I wasn't a Communist. Then they came
for the Jews, and I didn't speak up because I wasn't a Jew. Then they came for the
trade unionists, and I didn't speak up because I wasn't a trade unionist. Then they
came for the Catholics, and I didn't speak up because I was a Protestant. Then they
came for me—and by that time no one was left to speak up." There are various versions of this quotation, but the devastating effect of silence is quite clear.

- "Truth is stranger than fiction, but it is because Fiction is obliged to stick to possibilities; Truth isn't" (*Following the Equator*, 1897).

- "Loyalty to petrified opinion never yet broke a chain or freed a human soul" ("Consistency," speech, 1887).

- "Education consists mainly in what we have unlearned" (*Notebook*, 1898).

- "Customs do not concern themselves with right or wrong or reason" ("The Gorky Incident," 1906).

Twain's *The Adventures of Huckleberry Finn,* originally published in 1885, is consistently listed as a frequently challenged book because, "Despite Twain's positive treatment of the relationship between Huck and Jim [a slave], this American classic is perennially challenged because of its offensive language" (The Freedom Forum). I wonder how Twain would react to the charge.

He could cite a passage from his 1885 letter to Francis Wayland:

> I do not believe I would very cheerfully help a white student who would ask a benevolence of a stranger, but I do not feel so about the other color. We have ground the manhood out of them, and the shame is ours, not theirs, and we should pay for it.

However, I do not believe he would use this tactic—it would be too easy. I imagine his first response would be that the book was intended for adults, not children. Then he might refer people to the "Notice" on the first page, hoping to point out the tongue-in-cheek tone:

> Persons attempting to find a motive in this narrative will be prosecuted; persons attempting to find a moral in it will be banished; persons attempting to find a plot in it will be shot.

Finally, he might say, "Don't explain your author, read him right and he explains himself,"[50] and then refuse to discuss the matter further.

Why does any of this matter? Because clearly, some people are very serious about literature, especially if they go to the trouble of

---

[50] Letter to Cordelia Welsh Foote of Cincinnati, 12/2/1887.

challenging a book; obviously, books are dangerous. Whether their opinion is right or wrong is irrelevant. But authors are also serious—about writing; they might not always adopt a serious tone, but writers have something important to say: the "truth" as they perceive it. Authors, teachers, parents, and other adults are certainly entitled to their own opinions. And students are entitled to learn the skills to develop their own opinions. Breaking the code of texts, understanding and composing texts, and using texts functionally are not sufficient. Students also need to learn how to critically analyze and transform texts—and they are dependent on adults for this guidance (Luke & Freebody, 1999). Critical literacy is one way to help students of all types to read their worlds and learn to thrive; there is more to life than simply "getting along in the world."

Self-Reflection: Necessary and Ongoing #7

Gabriel, who I discussed in the first chapter, contacted me a few months ago and asked if he could interview me for a class he is taking at the university. Of course, I agreed, and he met me in my office with a list of prepared questions. He said that he is thinking about becoming a teacher and wanted to ask about my perspective. One question was, "What is most rewarding about teaching?" No need to think about that one. I replied, "Students." The next question was, "What is most frustrating about teaching?" I needed a few seconds to think before responding. However, clearly the answer was "Students."

Teaching and parenting are challenges, but the rewards are incredible. The feeling of excitement and satisfaction when students "get it" is indescribable. The best part for me is the fact that we never get to a point in which we are the perfect parent or teacher. Just like writing, there is always room for improvement, always something that can be revised or polished. Critical literacy provides a framework for those of us who seek to continually improve because we are called on to question ourselves and the world, reflect, learn from our children and students, and then act upon our newfound understanding. It is truly a way of thinking and a way of life.

APPENDIX A

Questions to Explore the Relationship
Between the Text, the Author,
the Reader, and the World (Apol, 1998)

1. What does this text ask of you as a reader? What does it assume about your beliefs, values, experiences? Are you as a reader willing to go along with those assumptions? Are there aspects of the text you wish or feel compelled to resist or refuse?

2. What happens if various elements of the text are transposed (i.e., race, gender, economic class)? Think in terms of patterns of dominance and submission in the text—what if these patterns were reversed? How would the story or its message change?

3. Consider the ending. How does the ending relate to the rest of the book? What kind of reading does the ending support? Does it reify values that otherwise have been questioned? Does it undermine values that have not been examined?

4. Try to identify the overt message of the text, its surface ideology—the "lesson" to be learned. Then try to determine the text's unspoken, underlying message—the passive ideology of the author or the times, the assumptions on which the text depends. How do these messages interact? Are the text's "official" ideas contradicted by unconscious assumptions? If they are, what might that mean?

5. Think not only about what the text says, but about what it does not say as well. Who are the people who "do not exist" in the story? Whose voices are given prominence? Whose voices are not heard? What might the silent or silenced voices say?

6. Which parts of the story seem absolutely "obvious" or "natural" to you—so much a part of "the way things are" that you may have difficulty identifying them at all? Since all literature

constructs a *version* of reality, why do you think these ideas seem so convincingly realistic?

7. How might this text be read by readers from another time or place—readers from a hundred years in the past? Readers from a hundred years in the future? Readers from another geographic area or culture? What would those readers find strange? What would they find "normal"? What would they find inspiring, shocking, or offensive?

8. How else might this text be read? Are there other viable interpretations that could be made? Are there radical or subversive interpretations you can defend? What do the multiple readings have in common? Where do they diverge?

9. What patterns do you see in this text—repeated within the text itself or echoing from other texts you've read? How does this text "speak" to other literature? Which texts is it like or unlike?

10. Which of your own experiences, assumptions, or beliefs do you feel most strongly when you interact with this literature? How can an awareness of your own cultural background impact the way you read this text?

APPENDIX B

Developing Questions to Analyze Formal Essays Using Apol (1998)

Simplifying Each Question
Does the Participant:

1. Question any basic assumptions of the text?

2. Question power (dominance and submission).

3. Question the ending.

4. Go beyond the overt message to the text's unspoken, underlying message—the passive ideology of the author or the times.

5. Question the absences/gaps/silences in the text.

6. Address elements that represent the norm/status quo?

7. Discuss elements that reflect contemporary culture and/or place?

8. Consider alternate interpretations.

9. Identify similarities with other texts ("texts" in a broad sense, including popular culture).

10. Consider the influence of his/her own culture when responding to the text.

Collapsing the Questions:

- Removed question 1 because it fits into overarching question.

- Removed question 3 because it doesn't seem relevant.

- Combined questions 4 and 7; rephrased and simplified.

- Combined questions 5 and 6

- Removed question 8 because it fits into the remaining questions.

Resulting Questions.
Does the Participant:

1. Show evidence of questioning the text (overarching question)?

2. Question power (dominance and submission)?

3. Address the text's unspoken, underlying message, such as influences of the author's values, contemporary culture and/or place?

4. Question the absences/gaps/silences in the text (what is missing) or what is represented as normal?

5. Identify similarities with other texts ("texts" in a broad sense, including popular culture)?

6. Consider the influence of his/her own experiences and/or culture when responding to the text?

APPENDIX C
Out-of-Class Essays

#	Data Set #1: Fairy Tales	Data Set #4: Picture Books	Data Set #7: Novels
1	Fairy tales often create a false reality for young girls that involve gender roles and stereotypes about growing up to become a woman that are not appropriate to today's society.	*And the Dish Ran Away with the Spoon* teaches children the importance of teamwork and dedication to friends, and it is also entertaining.	Harry Potter's passage throughout the book follows the predictable pattern of the hero's journey with an interesting magical twist. Harry is transformed from an ordinary Muggle to a keen wizard throughout his journey as a hero.
2	The reason fairy tales have evolved over the decades is because they change as society does.	*Eloise* is an entertaining book.	Sara (*A Little Princess*) goes on a hero's journey. She realizes through the reality of her hardships that the magic you see is only found inside and you have to make it, it doesn't just appear.
3	Along with the help of the movies and people like Walt Disney, it is no wonder girls have such high expectations as adults looking for their mates.	The use of B&W instead of color in Chris Van Allsburg's *Zathura* makes readers use their imagination.	*A Little Princess* should be called *Cinderella in London* due to the many similarities.
4	The moral of the story not only provides people with a plot and point of the legend, but shapes behaviors and thoughts throughout life.	*The True Story of the Three Little Pigs* has a message of not giving up.	As he goes through the hero's journey, Harry Potter's heroism and humility are evident.

#	Data Set #1: Fairy Tales	Data Set #4: Picture Books	Data Set #7: Novels
5	How can a fairy tale have such an impact of society's views on love and romance and geared mainly towards girls than boys?	*The Three Pigs/Los Tres Cerdos* demonstrates the Chicano culture through use of language, illustrations, and humor.	*Harry Potter* reveals the importance of friendship.
6	Fairy tales that have an element of surprise are more interesting than the common fairy tale.	*Stand Tall, Molly Lou Mellon* has an important message: it's okay to be different and you should always try your best.	Harry Potter is very determined.
7	Fairy tales have set the standards for the unrealistic expectations of women today.	*Clifford and the Grouchy Neighbors* is a didactic story with the purpose of teaching tolerance.	Harry Potter is transformed through the Hero's Journey.
8	19th-century fairy tales show defined gender roles reflecting stereotypes of values, beliefs, and social behaviors accepted and appreciated in contemporary society through the main characters' traits, which are always rewarded.	*Olivia* is a story that portrays an idealized childhood through the support and love of her family, and a positive environment allowing the main character to acquire a positive personality which enhances her learning development.	Due to her suffering, Sara develops and matures through the course of the story.
9	I believe that we as a society influence fairy tales. A fairy tale's content can also be modified according to the audience which the story is geared toward.	*The Big Box* uses conflict, character vs. society, to allow the reader to judge if children can actually handle their freedom.	*The Watsons Go to Birmingham* presents discrimination based on intellectual ability, social class, and skin color.
10	Fairy tales present readers with unrealistic gender roles and stereotypes that become ingrained in	*Dr. Seuss' Oh the Places You'll Go!* uses color (dark & light) to depict moods—serious and happy—	Harry Potter, Hermione, and Ron develop a strong friendship through the course of the story.

#	Data Set #1: Fairy Tales	Data Set #4: Picture Books	Data Set #7: Novels
	children's minds.	hardships and successes that readers will encounter.	
11	In "The Little Mermaid," Hans Christian Andersen has broken many of the boundaries set up by many successful writers before him (doesn't adhere to traditional fairy tale elements).	*The Giving Tree* reminds readers that money and things with materialistic value do not provide happiness, but love can.	Harry Potter is a tale of good vs. evil using specific literary elements, and the archetypal Hero's Journey is evident.
12	Fairy tales reflect society—they nicely portray the characteristics seen in real-life children.	*Tell Me Again About the Night I Was Born* takes a tough subject (adoption) and turns it into an issue of love, family, and happiness	Hermione transforms from a cocky know-it-all to intelligent, loyal friend.
13	Fairy tales influence and shape our expectations and standards of behavior; the morals of stories are important.	*The Jolly Postman or Other People's Letters* shows different perspectives of famous children's stories.	Through each experience Byron and Kenny share, both brothers learn from what the other has to teach, resulting in a deep friendship and bond the two boys gradually develop toward one another.
14	"Cinderella" has changed over time to meet its diverse and growing society.	*Wilfrid Gordon McDonald Partridge* discusses the importance of relationships between young and old.	*A Little Princess* is a fairy tale (like "Cinderella").
15	Fairy tales intended for girls are predictable, whereas tales for boys are unpredictable.	*The House That Crack Built* uses illustrations and repetition to point out the nature of choosing a wrong path.	*Harry Potter* is a Hero Journey.
16	Not only do fairy tales influence people's standards of behavior; they are also a response to the everyday life of a	*The Very Hungry Caterpillar* teaches children the days of the week, numbers 1-5, and the life cycle of a butterfly. It also	Harry Potter proves to be brave by showing courage and heroism.

#	Data Set #1: Fairy Tales	Data Set #4: Picture Books	Data Set #7: Novels
	society.	teaches them about nutrition.	
17	Fairy tales are important because they build imagination, which is useful for surviving and getting along better in the world.	In *The Spider and the Fly*, there is a whole other story in the pictures than what is in the text.	The roles played by the female characters in Harry Potter are stereotypical; there is sexism.
18	Society is reflected and shaped by fairy tales: morals, romantic love, marriage, and gender roles influence us.	*Miss Spider's Tea Party* is about prejudice.	*Harry Potter* and *The Whipping Boy* have similarities and differences.
19	The writers brought into their stories the real life society, ideas, and beliefs relevant in their era, making it easier for the people of their time to form connections with the stories.	*Swimmy* conveys the ideas that everyone has a place in the world and that in order to excel one must believe in oneself.	*A Little Princess* is similar to the typical Cinderella story.
20	The reality is the need to realize that these fairy tales are for entertainment purposes and should not be seen as ultimate truth regarding love.	Draft: *Two Bad Ants* talks about making choices. Final: *Two Bad Ants* is educational and entertaining.	*A Little Princess* and *Harry Potter* each have a distinct application of magic.
21	Through the ages, the stories that are told and written have been indicative of the societal attitudes and thoughts occurring during that period of time, which is evident even in books containing child-like stories.		

#	Data Set #1: Fairy Tales	Data Set #4: Picture Books	Data Set #7: Novels
22	Fairy tales are created to reflect the time and culture they were created in.	The David series of picture books (David Shannon) show a tragic cry for help by a neglected young boy.	*Harry Potter* follows the Hero's Journey framework to a tee.
23	"Cinderella," the timeless tale of "rags to riches," has left an inescapable impression upon the society of its time. But, in the same instances, has reflected the values and mind-set of that same society.	*Voices in the Park* takes readers to a place where difference is far from invisible.	A child can self-identify with characters in books; authors often create protagonists with positive qualities and antagonists with negative qualities.
24	Fairy tales are teaching unrealistic morals.	*Love You Forever* demonstrates a mother's unconditional love.	*The Watsons Go to Birmingham* is educational and deals with oppression and racism.
25	Fairy tales touch upon numerous morals and values that parents most often attempt to instill in their children.	*No David* is an effective tool for children because it displays youthlike images, realistic and age-appropriate behaviors, as well as common consequences relating to those behaviors.	*The Whipping Boy* shows the breakdown of social barriers (between rich and poor).

APPENDIX D
In-Class Essays

#	Data Set #3: Critical Literacy	Data Set #6: Controversial Issues
1	Yes, but for older children (3rd/4th grade), not younger children because it will ruin their reading pleasure.	Introducing topics such as homosexuality and prejudice in the classroom may cause more harm than good because of differing views of teachers, parents, and students.
2	Yes, I will use it.	There are some topics like homelessness and prejudice that are safe to talk about; but others such as drug abuse and homosexuality should be left to the child's parents to discuss with them.
3	Yes; all teachers should use it.	I believe that students should be exposed to such topics.
4	Yes; I will use it.	I think children can and should be exposed to sensitive issues.
5	Yes.	I feel that teaching our children about controversial topics is okay because children are aware of these things whether we know it or not.
6	Agree & disagree; need to be truthful but on an age-appropriate level.	I believe children should be exposed to controversial issues.
7	Yes, teachers should use it.	Should books that contain sensitive topics be left off of the book list for school? Yes.
8	Yes, but in third grade after they've learned the basics of reading.	It is not the teacher's role to teach other kinds of subjects such as religion, values, customs or other controversial topics.
9	Yes, I agree overall, but students should also enjoy books. Overanalyzing sometimes ruins books. Critical literacy should be used in older elementary grades.	It is up to parents to decide how the issue will be addressed according to their life experiences and beliefs.

#	Data Set #3: Critical Literacy	Data Set #6: Controversial Issues
10	Yes, but we must also protect their innocence.	Children, even young children, should be introduced to sensitive topics.
11	Yes.	Certain books, depending upon age appropriateness and content, are not meant for the classroom.
12	No. They need to learn to decode first and read for enjoyment. They need to use their imaginations when young, not search for deep meaning.	Whether you are a parent, teacher, or both, you should realize that trying to protect children from things that are offensive teaches them nothing.
13	Yes, I will use it.	I will teach my students not only the basic subjects but other potentially controversial issues.
14	Yes, but imagination is important and they shouldn't be forced to interpret a text in one particular way.	I believe that children should be introduced to sensitive topics, but as a teacher you should not take complete control.
15	Yes.	Controversial issues should not be overlooked inside or outside a classroom.
16	Yes.	Books with controversial issues can be read to children, then used in a meaningful way.
17	Yes; this is how I was raised.	Should these controversial books be banned? No, I really do not think so. Should these controversial books be taught in the classroom as required reading? I still can't decide and think it should be a class by class basis.
18	Yes; will use as a teacher.	Banning books is wrong...However she later says, "I have to agree with the mother who found the book Boys & Sex in her 10 year old son's school library that it probably should not have been available to him."
19	Yes.	The censorship and the banning of books in children's literature is a destructive aspect of society in that it goes against the first amendment, shelters the youth from issues in soci-

#	Data Set #3: Critical Literacy	Data Set #6: Controversial Issues
		ety, and decreases the need for parent participation in the lives of their children.
20	Teachers should incorporate critical literacy and reading for pleasure—the lesson's goal determines which method will be used.	Although I feel that it is not necessarily a teacher's job to teach a child about every right and wrong, I do believe that teachers should be allowed the material to present their students various issues—moral or controversial—that exist.
21	Yes.	Censorship of books should not be allowed for various reasons.
22	Yes.	Censoring what children read is an outright crime.
23	Yes.	When a young mind is exposed to sensitive issues they need a way to filter through these tough topics....Teaching a child to be a thoughtful reader should be the focus.
24	Yes.	Most controversial topics should be discussed.
25	No; we need to maintain children's innocence.	Children deserve the right to preserve their innocence, and if a parent feels they want their child to know a specific topic, then it should be discussed at home—not at school.

APPENDIX E
Brief Written Responses

#	Data Set #2: Literary Criticism	Data Set #5: *Daddy's Roommate*
1	Likes topical/historical; structuralist takes away from work; feminist often goes too far.	
2	Reads for enjoyment; never thought about analyzing stories; it's sometimes interesting and sometimes disturbing.	Surprised there's a book for kids that is so graphic and to the point.
3	Likes topical/historical; also, reader response to figure out something new about self.	Well-done and appropriate. Not sure at which age I would read this book.
4	Doesn't usually use a literacy approach when reading; has been using structuralist approach for 306A.	A very sweet story.
5	Critical approaches are new; likes to apply the different approaches to discover different views.	It's good but a bit too much for kids.
6	Critical approaches are interesting but she's definitely noticing different people have different interpretations.	Very surprised they would write a book like that.
7	Likes moral/intellectual; difficult to categorize various approaches because not good to have a black & white interpretation.	Good for all kids to read.
8	Likes to focus on connection to own experiences.	It's the parents' responsibility to teach these subjects and not the teacher.
9	Likes topical/historical (prefers "older" versions of stories?)	I don't think it is an issue that should be talked about in the classroom.
10	Important for readers to come up with their own ideas when reading.	It's good but I think the dad should've talked to the son about being gay instead of the mom.
11	Critical approaches are new; prefers reader response; least likes psychoanalytic.	I was shocked.

#	Data Set #2: Literary Criticism	Data Set #5: *Daddy's Roommate*
12	Some interpretations are valid; others aren't. Overanalyzing can ruin the work.	I'm just surprised there's a book like this made for children.
13		Children may be confused.
14	Fairy tale analysis seemed true (uncovering authors' culture), but picture book analysis is taking the fun out of the reading.	I would want to use in a classroom but would have to find out if I'd get into trouble.
15	Various interpretations provide readers with new perspectives.	It will give kids an open mind.
16		It's an appropriate book for children who are learning to deal with a similar situation.
17		It's not inappropriate but many parents would want to approach this topic on their own and not have a book educate their child.
18	We should interpret what we read on our own; finds her own interpretations are sometimes "wrong"; but some of the interpretations are interesting.	It's good.
19		Shocked because I didn't think that a children's book would focus on that issue.
20		The story is good for young children to read.
21	We all have some way of critically analyzing what we read; interpretations help broaden our understanding.	
22	Likes topical/historical (she is history minor); the other interpretations seem ridiculous.	It's an excellent book but I wouldn't read it in a classroom.
23	Each interpretation is workable if you back it up (with evidence); Some are far-fetched; likes historical.	It's a great book but I doubt it will ever find its way into a school curriculum.
24		
25	Psychoanalytical is most closely connected with the author's initial message.	I was more surprised than anything.

APPENDIX F

Further Notes on the Four Resources Model—Luke & Freebody (1999)

Effective literacy draws on a repertoire of practices that allow learners, as they engage in reading and writing activities, to

- break the code of written texts by recognizing and using fundamental features and architecture, including alphabet, sounds in words, spelling, and structural conventions and patterns;

- participate in understanding and composing meaningful written, visual, and spoken texts, taking into account each text's interior meaning systems in relation to their available knowledge and their experiences of other cultural discourses, texts, and meaning systems;

- use texts functionally by traversing and negotiating the labor and social relations around them—that is, by knowing about and acting on the different cultural and social functions that various texts perform inside and outside school, and understanding that these functions shape the way texts are structured, their tone, their degree of formality, and their sequence of components;

- critically analyze and transform texts by acting on knowledge that texts are not ideologically natural or neutral—that they represent particular points of views while silencing others and influence people's ideas—and that their designs and discourses can be critiqued and redesigned in novel and hybrid ways.

◆ SELECTED REFERENCES

Children's Books that Can Be Used to Promote Critical Literacy

Anzaldúa, G., and Méndez, C. (1993). *Friends from the other side/Amigos del otro lado*. Emeryville, CA: Children's Book Press.

Baynton, M. (1988). *Jane and the dragon*. London: Walker Books.

Browne, A. (1998). *Voices in the park*. New York, NY: DK Publishing, Inc.

Bunting, E. (1994a). *A day's work*. New York, NY: Clarion Books.

Bunting, E. (1991). *Fly away home*. New York, NY: Clarion Books.

Bunting, E. (1996). *Going home*. New York, NY: HarperCollins.

Bunting, E. (1994b). *Smoky night*. San Diego, CA: Harcourt Brace.

Bunting, E. (1980). *Terrible things: an allegory of the Holocaust*. New York, NY: Harper and Row.

Bunting, E. (1990). *The wall*. New York, NY: Clarion Books.

Cronin, D. (2000). *Click, clack, moo: cows that type*. New York, NY: Simon & Schuster Books for Young Readers.

De Haan, L., and Nijland, S. (2002). *King & King*. Berkeley, CA: Tricycle Press.

Lin, G. (1999). *The ugly vegetables*. Watertown, MA: Charlesbridge Publishing.

Lorbiecki, M. (1998). *Sister Anne's hands*. New York, NY: Dial Books for Young Readers.

Macaulay, D. (1990). *Black and white*. Boston, MA: Houghton Mifflin.

Newman, L. (1989). *Heather has two mommies*. Boston, MA: Alyson Wonderland.

Nye, N.S. (1994). *Sitti's secrets*. New York, NY: Four Winds Press.

Ringgold, F. (1991). *Tar beach*. New York, NY: Crown Publishers, Inc.

Scieszka, J. (1989). *The true story of the three little pigs*. New York, NY: Viking.

Shange, N. (1997). *Whitewash*. New York, NY: Walker Publishing Company.

Smith, D.J. (2002). *If the world were a village.* Tonawanda, NY: Kids Can Press Ltd.

Willhoite, M. (1990). *Daddy's roommate.* Los Angeles, CA: Alyson Wonderland.

Young, E. (1992). *Seven blind mice.* New York, NY: Philomel Books.

Texts Related to Critical Literacy

Bartolomé, L.I. (2004). Critical pedagogy and teacher education: Radicalizing prospective teachers. *Teacher Education Quarterly, 97-122.*

Bean, T.W., & Moni, K. (2003). Developing students' critical literacy: Exploring identity construction in young adult fiction. *Journal of Adolescent & Adult Literacy, 46(8)*, 638-648.

Boutte, G.S. (2002). The critical literacy process: Guidelines for examining books. *Childhood Education, 78*, 147-152.

Cadiero-Kaplan, K., and Smith, K. (2002). Literacy ideologies: Critically engaging the language arts curriculum. *Language Arts, 79*, 372-381.

Comber, B. (2001). Critical literacy: Power and pleasure with language and literacy in the early years. *Australian Journal of Language and Literacy, 24(3)*, 168-181.

Comber, B., and Simpson, A., eds. (2001). *Negotiating critical literacies in classrooms.* Mahwah, NJ: Lawrence Erlbaum Associates, Publishers.

Flint, A.S. (2000). Envisioning the possible: Building a critical literacy curriculum. *Primary Voices K-6, 9(2)*, 30-33.

Freedom Writers with Erin Gruwell. (1999). *The Freedom Writers diary: how a teacher and 150 teens used writing to change themselves and the world around them.* New York, NY: Broadway Books.

Freire, P. (2000). *Pedagogy of the Oppressed*, 30th Anniversary Edition. New York: Continuum International Publishing Group, Inc. Originally published in 1970.

Freire, P., and Macedo, D. (1987). *Literacy: Reading the word and the world.* South Hadley, MA: Bergin and Garvey Publishers.

Hadden, J.E. (2000). A charter of educate or a mandate to train: Conflicts between theory and practice. *Harvard Educational Review, 70(4)*, 524-537.

Harris, Violet J. (1999). Applying critical theories to children's literature. *Theory into Practice, 38*, 147-154.

Harste, J.C. (2000). Supporting critical conversations in classrooms. In Pierce, K.M., ed. *Adventuring with Books: A Booklist for Pre-K—Grade 6*. Urbana, IL: NCTE. (pp. 507-554).

Kincheloe, J.L., and McLaren, P. (2000). Rethinking critical theory and qualitative research. In Denzin, N.K., and Lincoln, Y.S., eds. *Handbook of qualitative research, 2nd ed.* Thousand Oaks, CA: Sage Publications, 279-313.

Kohl, H. (1995). *Should we burn Babar? Essays on children's literature and the power of stories*. New York, NY: The New York Press.

Kohl, H. (2002). Developing teachers for social justice. *Radical Teacher, 65*, 5-10.

Leistyna, P., Lavandez, M., and Nelson, T. (2004). Critical pedagogy: Revitalizing and democratizing teacher education. *Teacher Education Quarterly*, 3-15.

Leland, C., & Harste, J. (1999). Is this appropriate for children? Books that bring realistic social issues into the classroom. *Practically Primary, 4(3)*, 4-5.

Longfellow, L. (2002). Critical moves with the Wiggles. *Practically Primary, 7(3)*, 12-14.

Luke, A. (2000). Critical literacy in Australia: a matter of context and standpoint. *Journal of Adolescent & Adult Literacy, 43(5)*, 448-461.

Luke, A. (2004). Two takes on the critical. In Norton, B., and Toohey, K., eds. *Critical pedagogies and language learning*. Cambridge: Cambridge University Press.

Luke, A., and Freebody, P. (1999). Further notes on the four resources model. Reading Online. *http://www.readingonline.org/research/lukefreebody.html*.

Luke, A., and Freebody, P. (1997). Shaping the social practices of reading. In Muspratt, S., Luke, A., and Freebody, P., eds. *Constructing critical literacies: Teaching and learning textual practice*. Cresskill, NJ: Hampton Press, 185-225.

Macedo, D., and Freire, A.A. (2001). (Mis)understanding Paulo Freire. In Richardson, V., ed. *Handbook of research on teaching, 4th ed.* Washington, D.C.: American Educational Research Association, 106-110.

McDaniel, C.A. (2004). Critical literacy: A questioning stance and possibility for change. *The Reading Teacher*.

McLaren, P. (2002). *Life in schools: An introduction to critical pedagogy in the foundations of education*. Boston, MA: Pearson Education.

Morgan, W. (1997). *Critical literacy in the classroom: The art of the possible*. New York, NY: Routledge.

Rogers, R. (2002). "That's what you're here for, you're suppose to tell us": Teaching and learning critical literacy. *Journal of Adolescent & Adult Literacy, 45(8)*, 772-787.

Shannon. D. (1998). *No, David!* New York, NY: The Blue Sky Press.

Shannon, P. (1995). *Text, lies, & videotape: Stories about life, literacy, and learning*. Portsmouth, NH: Heinemann.

Shannon, P. (2004, in press). The practice of democracy and Dewey's challenge. *Language Arts*.

Shor, I., and Pari, C. (1999). *Critical literacy in action: Writing words, changing worlds*. Portsmouth, NH: Boynton/Cook Publishers, Inc.

Stephens, J. (1992). *Language and ideology in children's fiction*. London: Longman.

Williams, S. (2002). Reading *Daddy's Roommate*: Preservice teachers respond to a controversial text. *New Advocate, 15(3)*, 231-236.

Wink, J. (1999). *Critical pedagogy: Notes from the real world*. New York, NY: Longman.

Films that Can Be Used to Promote Critical Literacy (for Older Students)

♦ *Blue-Eyed*. Participants are separated based on eye color. The blue-eyed members are subjected to pseudo-scientific explanations of their inferiority, culturally biased IQ tests and blatant discrimination.

♦ *Crash*. Several characters of different racial backgrounds collide in one incident, The different stereotypes society has created for those backgrounds affect their judgment, beliefs, and actions.

♦ *Culture of Hate: Who Are We?* (PBS). Investigates San Diego's East County white power gangs and racist teens to understand the motivation behind racism and hate crimes. It takes a humanistic look at this complex issue, and finds child abuse, poverty, and a changing social climate in the United States to be contributing factors.

♦ *Doublespeak* (Films for Humanities). Looks at how the English language has been inflated and manipulated to distort, obfuscate, or cover up meaning, or to replace meaning altogether. Illustrations are drawn from ordinary conversation, advertising, the workplace, and the Iran-Contra hearings, which offer a case study of governmental doublespeak.

◆ *El Norte*. Portrays the life of a Mayan brother and sister who are forced to leave Guatemala, their homeland, in search of survival in El Norte (The North). But they discover that the U.S.-Mexico border is a virtual war zone. The film ends in the tragedy that represents the reality of life for many Native people, whose status as "illegal aliens" is less than the humanity that they deserve.

◆ *Ethnic Notions* (California Newsreel). Marlon Riggs' Emmy-winning documentary that takes viewers on a disturbing voyage through American history, tracing for the first time the deep-rooted stereotypes that have fueled anti-black prejudice. Through these images we can begin to understand the evolution of racial consciousness in America.

◆ *Faces of the Enemy* (California Newsreel). Using documentary footage, interviews, political cartoons, and examples of propaganda, this powerful documentary examines the universal images used in mass persuasion and analyzes the psychological roots of enmity.

◆ *Hotel Rwanda*. The true-life story of Paul Rusesabagina, a (Hutu) hotel manager who housed over a thousand Tutsi refugees during their struggle against the Hutu militia in Rwanda.

◆ *Invisible Children*. In 2003, three young filmmakers from California went to Africa and ended up making a documentary about children being abducted to become rebel soldiers and those trying to escape rebel capture. *www.invisiblechildren.com*.

◆ *Maria Full of Grace*. A pregnant Colombian teenager becomes a drug mule to make some desperately needed money for her family.

◆ *Orwell Rolls in His Grave*. Questions whether the bleak, feverishly regulated world of author George Orwell's *1984* is no longer a dire fictional account of government power gone wrong but a creeping reality of recent American media trends.

♦ *Skin Deep* (California Newsreel). A multi-racial group of college students in a weekend racial sensitivity workshop discuss affirmative action, self-segregation, internalized racism and cultural identity.

♦ *The Ballad of Gregorio Cortez*. Recounts the true story of the largest manhunt in Texas history. In June 1901, six hundred Texas Rangers chased Gregorio Cortez, a Mexican-American ranch hand, for 11 days across 450 miles of terrain. Was Cortez a cold-blooded killer or an innocent man fleeing injustice? You decide.

♦ *The Persuaders* (PBS Frontline). Examines the "persuasion industries" — advertising and public relations. To cut through consumers' growing resistance to their pitches, marketers have developed new ways of integrating their messages into the fabric of our lives, using sophisticated market research techniques to better understand consumers and turning to the little-understood techniques of public relations to make sure their messages come from sources we trust.

♦ *We Shall Overcome*. Traces the story of how an old slave spiritual was transformed into a labor organizing song before becoming the well-known anthem of the civil rights movement.

♦ *What I Want My Words to Do to You*. Eve Ensler's documentary about an exploratory writing class that was held over a period of four years at a maximum security prison in New York. During these classes, the women were encouraged to write about specific topics dealing with their incarceration, as well as all the things that contributed to their crimes.

◆◆◆ REFERENCES

ALA (American Library Association.) (2003). The most frequently challenged books of 1990-1999. http://www.ala.org.

Altieri, J.L. (1996). Children's written responses to multicultural texts: a look at aesthetic involvement and the focuses of aesthetically complex responses. *Reading Research and Instruction, 35,* 237-48.

Alvermann, D.E., Moon, J.S., and Hagood, M.C. (1999). *Popular culture in the classroom: Teaching and researching critical media literacy.* Newark, DE: International Reading Association.

Angelou, M. (1993/1970). *I know why the caged bird sings.* New York, NY: Bantam Books.

Anzaldúa, G., and Méndez, C. (1993). *Friends from the other side/Amigos del otro lado.* Emeryville, CA: Children's Book Press.

Apple, M.W. (1992). The text and cultural politics. *Educational Researcher, 21,* (4-11, 19).

Apol, L. (1998). "But what does this have to do with kids?" Literary theory in children's literature in the children's literature classroom. *Journal of Children's Literature, 24*(2), 32-46.

Arato, A., and Gebhardt, E. (1978). *The essential Frankfurt School reader.* New York, NY: Urizen Books.

Ashliman, D.L. (1987). *A guide to folktales in the English language: based on the Aarne-Thompson classification system.* New York, NY: Greenwood Press.

Associated Press. (2004, March 17). Boy, 9, plays dead, survives shooting. *San Diego Union Tribune*, A6.

Athanases, S.Z. (1998). Diverse learners, diverse texts: exploring identity and difference through literary encounters. *Journal of Literacy Research, 30*(2), 273-296.

Ayers, W., Mitchies, G., and Rome, A. (2004). Embers of hope: In search of a meaningful critical pedagogy. *Teacher Education Quarterly.* 123-130.

Baez, B. (2000). Diversity and its contradictions. *Academe, 86*(5), 43-47.

Bang, M. (1991). *Picture this: How picture books work*. New York, NY: SeaStar Books.

Banks, J.A., and Banks, C.A.M. (2001). *Multicultural education: Issues and perspectives, 4th ed*. New York, NY: John Wiley & Sons, Inc.

Bartolomé, L.I. (2004). Critical pedagogy and teacher education: Radicalizing prospective teachers. *Teacher Education Quarterly*, 97-122.

Basile, G. (1634-1636/1996). Sun, Moon, and Talia. In Hallett, M. and Karasek, B., eds. *Folk and fairy tales*. Peterborough, Ontario, Canada: Broadview Press, 1996. 36-40.

Baynton, M. (1988). *Jane and the dragon*. London: Walker Books.

Bean, T.W., and Moni, K. (2003). Developing students' critical literacy: Exploring identity construction in young adult fiction. *Journal of Adolescent & Adult Literacy, 46(8)*, 638-648.

Bean, T.W. and Stevens, L.P. (2002). Scaffolding reflection for preservice and inservice teachers. *Reflective Practice, 3*(2), 205-218.

Bennett, C., Cole., D., and Thompson, J. (2000). Preparing teachers of color at a predominately White university: A case study of Project TEAM. *Teaching and Teacher Education, 16*, 445-464.

Berlak, A. (2002). Education teachers in California (or drowning in alphabet soup). *Radical Teacher, 64*, 9-13.

Berliner, D.C. (2000). A personal response to those who bash teacher education. *Journal of Teacher Education, 51*(5), 358-71.

Beyer, L.E. (2000). The value of critical perspectives in teacher education. *Journal of Teacher Education, 52*(2), 151-163.

Bishop, K., & Van Orden, P. (1998). Reviewing children's books: a content analysis. *Library Quarterly, 68(2)*, 145-183.

Blume, J. (1999). Places I never meant to be: a personal view. *American Libraries, 30*, 62-68.

Bottigheimer, R.B. 1998. An important system of its own: Defining children's literature. *The Princeton University Library Chronicle, 59*, 190-210.

Boutte, G.S. (2002). The critical literacy process: Guidelines for examining books. *Childhood Education, 78*, 147-152.

Boyd, P.C., Boll, M., Browner, L., & Villaume, S.K. (1998). Becoming reflective professionals: An exploration of preservice teachers' struggles as they translate language and literacy theory into practice. *Action in Teacher Education, 19*(4), 61-75.

Bradbury, R. (1980/1953). *Fahrenheit 451*. New York, NY: Ballantine Books.

Breault, R.A. (2003). Dewey, Freire, and a pedagogy for the oppressor. *Multicultural Education, 10(3)*, 2-6.

Bridwell, N. (1989). *Clifford and the grouchy neighbors*. New York, NY: Scholastic, Inc.

Briggs, L., and Pailliotet, A.W. (1997). A story about grammar and power. *Journal of Basic Writing, 16(2)*, 46-61.

Briggs, R. (2000). *Snowman*. New York, NY: Random House.

Broadfoot, P. (2000). Comparative education for the 21st century: Retrospect and prospect. *Comparative Education, 36(3)*, 357-371.

Brookhart, S.M. and Freeman, D.J. (1992). Characteristics of entering teacher candidates. *Review of Educational Research, 62*, 37-60.

Brown, L., ed. (1993). *The new shorter Oxford English dictionary on historical principles*. New York, NY: Oxford University Press.

Brown, M.W. (1947/1975). *Goodnight moon*. New York, NY: HarerTrophy.

Browne, A. (1998). *Voices in the park*. New York, NY: DK Publishing, Inc.

Bunting, E. (1994a). *A day's work*. New York, NY: Clarion Books.

Bunting, E. (1991). *Fly away home*. New York, NY: Clarion Books.

Bunting, E. (1996). *Going home*. New York, NY: HarperCollins.

Bunting, E. (1994b). *Smoky night*. San Diego, CA: Harcourt Brace.

Bunting, E. (1980). *Terrible things: an allegory of the Holocaust*. New York, NY: Harper and Row.

Bunting, E. (1990). *The wall*. New York, NY: Clarion Books.

Burnett, F.H. (1995/1905). *A little princess*. New York, NY: Penguin Putnam, Inc.

California Department of Education. Recommended literature for K-12. *http://www.cde.ca.gov/literaturelist*.

Cadiero-Kaplan, K., and Smith, K. (2002). Literacy ideologies: Critically engaging the language arts curriculum. *Language Arts, 79*, 372-381.

Carle, E. (1987). *The very hungry caterpillar*. New York, NY: Philomel Books. Originally published in 1969.

Chaffee, J. (2004). *Thinking critically: a concise guide*. Boston, MA: Houghton Mifflin.

Chambless, M.S., and Bass. J.F. (1995). Effecting changes in student teachers' attitudes toward writing. *Reading Research and Instruction, 35*, 153-159.

Children's Literature Association (ChLA). (2004). Children's and young adult literature and culture links. http://ebbs.english.vt.edu /chla/links.html.

Children's Literature List Serv. (February, 2004). http://www.rci .rutgers.edu/~mjoseph/childlit/about.html.

Comber, B. (2001). Critical literacy: Power and pleasure with language and literacy in the early years. *Australian Journal of Language and Literacy, 24(3)*, 168-181.

Comber, B., and Simpson, A., eds. (2001). *Negotiating critical literacies in classrooms.* Mahwah, NJ: Lawrence Erlbaum Associates, Publishers.

Cook-Sather, A. (2002). Authorizing students' perspectives: Toward trust, dialogue, and change in education. *Educational Researcher, 31(4)*, 3-14.

Cossett, R., and Pipkin, G., eds. (2003). *Silent no more: Voices of courage in American schools.* Portsmouth, NH: Heinemann.

Courlander, H., ed. (1955). *Ride with the sun: an anthology of folk tales and stories from the United Nations.* New York, NY: Whittlesey House.

Creighton, D.C. (1997). Critical literacy in the elementary classroom. *Language Arts, 74(6)*, 438-448.

Creswell, J.W. (1998). *Qualitative inquiry and research design: choosing among five traditions.* Thousand Oaks, CA: Sage Publications, Inc.

Cronin, D. (2000). *Click, clack, moo: cows that type.* New York, NY: Simon & Schuster Books for Young Readers.

Cunningham, J.W., and Fitzgerald, J. (1996). Epistemology and reading. *Reading Research Quarterly, 31(1)*, 36-60.

Curtis, C.P. (1995). *The Watsons go to Birmingham—1963.* New York, NY: Bantam Doubleday Dell Books for Young Readers.

D'Andrade, R.G., and Strauss, C., eds. (1992). *Human motives and cultural models.* New York, NY: Cambridge University Press.

De Haan, L., and Nijland, S. (2002). *King & King.* Berkeley, CA: Tricycle Press.

Denzin, N.K., & Lincoln, Y.S., eds. (2000). *The handbook of qualitative research, 2nd ed.* Thousand Oaks, CA: Sage Publications.

Dewey, J. (1980a). *Democracy and education.* In J. Boydston, ed. *The middle works of John Dewey, Vol. 9.* Carbondale: Southern Illinois University Press. (Originally published in 1916).

Dewey, (1980b). Nationalizing education. In J. Boydston, ed. *The middle works of John Dewey, Vol. 9*. Carbondale: Southern Illinois University Press. (Originally published in 1916).

Disneyland. (2004). A new musical at Disneyland park. http://disneyland.disney.go.com/dlr/special/snow?CMP=ILC-DLRHomeWNSnowComing.

Doyle, M. (1997). Beyond life history as a student: preservice teachers' beliefs about teaching and learning. *College Student Journal, 31*, 519-531.

Draper, S. M. (2000). *Teaching from the Heart*. Portsmouth: Heineman.

Draper, M.C., Barksdale-Ladd, M.A., & Radencich, M.C. (2000). Reading and writing habits of preservice teachers. *Reading Horizons, 40*, 185-203.

Dutro, E. (2003, May). *"What are you and where are you from?" Exploring literacy, identity and culture in a diverse urban classroom*. Paper presented at the interactive research symposium at the University of San Diego, San Diego, CA.

Edmundson, P.J. (1990). A normative look at the curriculum in teacher education. *Phi Delta Kappan, 71*, 717-722.

Eisenberg, K.N. (2002). Gender and ethnicity stereotypes in children's books. *Dissertation Abstracts International, 63(01)*, p. 585.

Ellsworth, E. (1989). Why doesn't this feel empowering? Working through the repressive myths of critical pedagogy. *Harvard Educational Review, 59(3)*, 297-324.

Ensler, E. (Producer). (2003). *What I want my words to do to you: Voices from inside a women's maximum security prison*. [Documentary]. United States: PBS Home Video.

Erickson, F. (1986). Qualitative methods in research on teaching. In Wittrock, M.C., ed. *Handbook of research on teaching, 3rd ed*. New York, NY: Macmillan, pp. 119-161.

Evans, R.W., Avery, P.G., and Pederson, P.V. (1999). Taboo topics: Cultural restraint on teaching social issues. *The Social Studies, 90*, 218-224.

Fairclough, N. (1995) *Critical discourse analysis: The critical study of language*. New York, NY: Longman.

Falconer, I. (2000). *Olivia*. New York, NY: Antheneum Books for Young Readers.

Falk-Ross, F.C. (2001). Toward the new literacy: Changes in college students' reading comprehension strategies following reading/writing projects. *Journal of Adolescent & Adult Literacy, 45(4)*, 278-288.

Fleischman, S. (2003/1986). *The whipping boy*. New York, NY: Harper-Collins Children's Books.

Flint, A.S. (2000). Envisioning the possible: Building a critical literacy curriculum. *Primary Voices K-6, 9(2)*, 30-33.

Florio-Ruane, S., and Lensmire, T.J. (1990). Transforming future teachers' ideas about writing instruction. *Journal of Curriculum Studies, 22(3)*, 277-289.

Fontana, A., and Frey, J.H. (2000). The interview: From structured questions to negotiated text. In Denzin, N.K., and Lincoln, Y.S., eds. *Handbook of qualitative research, 2nd ed.* Thousand Oaks, CA: Sage Publications, 645-672.

Fox, M. (1991). *Wilfrid Gordon McDonald Partridge*. La Jolla, CA: Kane/Miller Book Publishers.

Fox, M. (2001). Politics, literature, and green shoes: Current realities in whole language. *Mem Fox* (website). http://www.memfox.net/teachers/politics_&_green_shoes.html.

Freedom Forum. (2000). From Harry Potter to "Blubber,'": 100 books make list of the most challenged of the '90s. http://www.freedomforum.org.

Freedom Writers with Erin Gruwell. (1999). *The Freedom Writers diary: how a teacher and 150 teens used writing to change themselves and the world around them*. New York, NY: Broadway Books.

Freire, P. (2000). *Pedagogy of the Oppressed*, 30th Anniversary Edition. New York: Continuum International Publishing Group, Inc. Originally published in 1970.

Freire, P., and Macedo, D. (1987). *Literacy: Reading the word and the world*. South Hadley, MA: Bergin and Garvey Publishers.

Fu, D., and Lamme, L. (2002). Writing lessons with Gavin Curtis. *Journal of Children's Literature, 28(1)*, 63-71.

Galda, L., Ash, G. E., and Cullinan, B. E. (2000). Children's literature. In Kamil, M.L., Mosenthal, P.B., Pearson, P.D., and Barr, R., eds. *Handbook of reading research, vol. III*. Mahway, NJ, Lawrence Erlbaum Associates, Publishers, 361-379.

Garrison, W.H. (2003). Democracy, experience, and education: promoting a continued capacity for growth. *Phi Delta Kappan, 84(7)*, 525-529.

Gee, J.P. (1996). *Social linguistics and literacies: Ideology in discourses*, 2nd Edition. London: Routledge Falmer.

Gee, J.P. (1997). Dilemmas of literacy: Plato and Freire. In Freire, P., Fraser, J.W., Macedo, D., McKinnon, T., and Stokes, W.T., eds. *Mentoring the mentor: A critical dialogue with Paulo Freire.* New York: Peter Lang Publishing, Inc., 229-241.

Gee, J.P. (1999). *An introduction to discourse analysis: Theory and method.* New York, NY: Routledge.

Gee, J.P. (2001). Reading as situated language: A sociocognitive perspective. *Journal of Adolescent & Adult Literacy, 44(8),* 714-725.

Geertz, C. (1973). Religion as a cultural system. In *The interpretation of cultures.* New York, NY: Basic Books, Inc. 87-125.

Ginsburg, M.B., and Newman, K.K. (1985). Social inequalities, schooling, and teacher education. *Journal of Teacher Education, 36(2),* 49-54.

Giroux, H.A. (1993). Literacy and the politics of difference. In Lankshear, C., and McLaren, P.L., eds. *Critical literacy: Politics, praxis, and the postmodern.* Albany, NY: SUNY Press, 367-377.

Giroux, H.A. (1997). Are Disney movies good for your kids? In Steinberg, S.R., and Kincheloe, J.L., eds. *Kinderculture: The corporate construction of childhood.* Boulder, CO: Westview Press, 53-67.

Giroux, H.A. (1999). Schools for sale: Public education, corporate culture, and the citizen-consumer. *The Educational Forum, 63(2),* 140-149.

Gish, K.W. (2000). Hunting down Harry Potter: An exploration of religious concerns about children's literature. *The Horn Book,* 262-271.

Graff, G. (2000). Teaching politically without political correctness. *Radical Teacher, 58,* 26-30.

Graff, H.J. (2001). Literacy's myths and legacies: From lessons from the history of literacy, to the question of critical literacy. In Freebody, P., Muspratt, S., and Dwyer, B., *Difference, silence, and textual practice: Studies in critical literacy.* Cresskill, NJ: Hampton Press, 1-29.

Grimm, J., and Grimm, W. (1812-1815). Snow white. In David, A., and Meek, M.E., eds. *The twelve dancing princesses and other fairy tales.* Bloomington, IN: Indiana University Press, 54-63.

Grindler, M. C., Stratton, B. D., & McKenna, M. C. (1995). Bookmatching in the classroom: How action research reached the lives of children through books. *Action in Teacher Education, 16(4),* 50-58.

Grisham, D.L. (2001). Developing preservice teachers' perspectives on reader response. *Reading Horizons, 41(4)*, 211-238.

Hadden, J.E. (2000). A charter of educate or a mandate to train: Conflicts between theory and practice. *Harvard Educational Review, 70(4)*, 524-537.

Hade, D.D. (1997). Reading multiculturally. In Harris, V.J., ed. *Using multiethnic literature in the K-8 classroom*. Norwood, MA: Christopher-Gordon Publishers, 233-256.

Harris, Violet J. (1999). Applying critical theories to children's literature. *Theory into Practice, 38*, 147-154.

Harste, J.C. (2000). Supporting critical conversations in classrooms. In Pierce, K.M., ed. *Adventuring with Books: A Booklist for Pre-K—Grade 6*. Urbana, IL: NCTE, 507-554.

Harvey, L. (Producer & Director). (2002). *Culture of hate: Who are we?* [Documentary]. United States: KPBS.

Heins, M. (2001). Not in front of the children: "Indecency," censorship, and the innocence of youth. New York, NY: Hill and Wang.

Herendeen, S. (2003). District removes book after parent's objection. *Modesto Bee Online*. http://www.modestobee.com.

Hermann-Wilmarth, J. (2003, December). *Ideology and reality: The intersection of school ideologies and gay and lesbian children's literature*. Paper presented at the National Reading Conference, Scottsdale, AZ.

Hoewisch, A.K. (2000). Children's literature in teacher-preparation programs. *Reading Online*. http://www.readingonline.org/critical/hoewisch/index.html.

Hoey, M. (2001). *Textual interaction: An introduction to written discourse analysis*. New York, NY: Routledge.

Holland, D.C. (1992). How cultural systems become desire: a case study of American romance. In D'Andrade, R., and Strauss, C., eds. *Human motives and cultural models*. New York, NY: Cambridge University Press, 61-89.

Holland, D.C. (1998). Figured worlds. In Holland, D., Lachicotte, Jr., W., Skinner, D., and Cain, C. *Identity and agency in cultural worlds*. Cambridge, MA: Harvard University Press, 49-65.

Hourihan, M. (1997) *Deconstructing the hero: Literary theory and children's literature*. London, England: Routledge.

Howard, E. (1988). Facing the dark side in children's books. *The Lion and the Unicorn, 12(1)*, 7-11.

Hunt, P. (1991). *Criticism, theory, and children's literature*. Cambridge, MA: Blackwell.

James, A., and Prout, A. (1997). *Constructing and reconstructing childhood: Contemporary issues in the sociological study of childhood.* Washington, D.C.: Falmer Press.

Jaworski, A., and Coupland, N., eds. (1999). Introduction. *The discourse reader.* New York, NY: Routledge, 1-44.

John-Steiner, V., and Mahn, Holbrook. (1996). Sociocultural approaches to learning and development: A Vygotskian framework. *Educational Psychologist, 31,* 191-206.

Johnson, G. (2002). Moving towards critical literacies in conversations about the teaching of English. *Australian Journal of Language and Literacy, 25(1),* 49-61.

Kiefer, B.Z. (1995). *The potential of picturebooks: From visual literacy to aesthetic understanding.* Englewood Cliffs, NJ: Prentice-Hall.

Kimball, R. (1990). *Tenured radicals: How politics has corrupted our higher education.* Chicago, IL: Ivan R. Dee, Publisher.

Kincheloe, J.L. (2004). The knowledges of teacher education: Developing a critical complex epistemology. *Teacher Education Quarterly,* 49-66.

Kincheloe, J.L., and McLaren, P. (2000). Rethinking critical theory and qualitative research. In Denzin, N.K., and Lincoln, Y.S., eds. *Handbook of qualitative research, 2nd ed.* Thousand Oaks, CA: Sage Publications, 279-313.

Kirk, D. (1994). *Miss Spider's tea party.* New York, NY: Scholastic, Inc.

Kohl, H. (1995). *Should we burn Babar? Essays on children's literature and the power of stories.* New York, NY: The New York Press.

Kohl, H. (2002). Developing teachers for social justice. *Radical Teacher, 65,* 5-10.

Langer, J.A., and Flihan, S. (2000). Writing and reading relationships: Constructive tasks. In Indrisano, R., and Squire, J.R., eds. *Perspectives on writing: Research, theory, and practice.* Newark, DE: International Reading Association, 112-139.

Langford, L. (2001). A building block towards the information literate school community. *Teacher Librarian, 28,* 18-21.

Leistyna, P., Lavandez, M., and Nelson, T. (2004). Critical pedagogy: Revitalizing and democratizing teacher education. *Teacher Education Quarterly,* 3-15.

Leland, C., and Harste, J. (1999). Is this appropriate for children? Books that bring realistic social issues into the classroom. *Practically Primary, 4(3),* 4-5.

Lewis, C. (2000). Critical issues: Limits of identification: the personal, pleasurable, and critical in reader response. *Journal of Literacy Research, 32(2),* 253-266.

Lewis, C., Ketter, J., and Fabos, B. (2001). Reading race in a rural context. *Qualitative Studies in Education, 14(3),* 317-350.

Lewison, M., Leland, C., and Harste, J. (2000). "Not in my classroom!" The case for using multi-view social issues books with children. *The Australian Journal of Language and Literacy, 23,* 8-20.

Lin, G. (1999). *The ugly vegetables.* Watertown, MA: Charlesbridge Publishing.

Longfellow, L. (2002). Critical moves with the Wiggles. *Practically Primary, 7(3),* 12-14.

Lorbiecki, M. (1998). *Sister Anne's hands.* New York, NY: Dial Books for Young Readers.

Lortie, D.C. (1975). *Schoolteacher.* Chicago: University of Chicago Press.

Loughran, J. 1997. Teaching about teaching: principles and practice. In Loughran, J., and Russell, T., *Teaching about Teaching: Purpose, Passion, and Pedagogy in Teacher Education.* Washington, DC: Falmer Press, 57-69.

Lowery, R.M. (2002). Grappling with issues of gender equity: Preservice teachers' reflections on children's books. *Journal of Children's Literature, 28(2),* 25-31.

Luke, A. (2000). Critical literacy in Australia: a matter of context and standpoint. *Journal of Adolescent & Adult Literacy, 43(5),* 448-461.

Luke, A. (2004). Two takes on the critical. In Norton, B., and Toohey, K., eds. *Critical pedagogies and language learning.* Cambridge: Cambridge University Press, 21-29.

Luke, A., and Freebody, P. (1999). Further notes on the four resources model. *Reading Online.* http://www.readingonline.org/research/lukefreebody.html.

Luke, A., and Freebody, P. (1997). Shaping the social practices of reading. In Muspratt, S., Luke, A., and Freebody, P., eds. *Constructing critical literacies: Teaching and learning textual practice.* Cresskill, NJ: Hampton Press, 185-225.

Lurie, A. (1998). *Don't tell the grown-ups: the subversive power of children's literature.* Boston, MA: Little Brown.

Macedo, D. (2000). Introduction. *Pedagogy of the oppressed*. 30ᵗʰ Anniversary Edition. New York: Continuum International Publishing Group, Inc. Originally published in 1970. 11-27.

Macedo, D. (2003, February). *Language, culture and pedagogy for democratic education*. Presentation at San Diego State University, San Diego, CA.

Macedo, D., and Freire, A.A. (2001). (Mis)understanding Paulo Freire. In Richardson, V., ed. *Handbook of research on teaching, 4ᵗʰ ed*. Washington, D.C.: American Educational Research Association, 106-110.

Mallette, M.H., Kile, R.S., Smith, M.M., McKinney, M., & Readence, J.E. (2000). Constructing meaning about literacy difficulties: preservice teachers beginning to think about pedagogy. *Teaching and Teacher Education*, 16, 593-612.

Many, J.E., Howard, F., and Hoge, P. (2002). Epistemology and preservice teacher education: How do beliefs about knowledge affect our students' experiences? *English Education, 34(4)*, 302-22.

Marciano, D.L. (2001). Interpretations of schooling in contemporary children's picture books. *Dissertation Abstracts International, 62 (05)*, p. 1759.

Marriott, D.M. (2003). Ending the silence. *Phi Delta Kappan, 84(7)*, 496-501.

Maxson, M.M., & Sindelar, R. (1998). Images revisited: examining preservice teachers' ideas about teaching. *Teacher Education Quarterly, 25(2)*, 5-26.

May, J. (1995). *Children's literature and critical theory: reading and writing for understanding*. New York, NY: Oxford University Press.

McDaniel, C.A. (2001). Children's literature as prevention of child sexual abuse. *Children's Literature in Education, 32(3)*, 203-224.

McDaniel, C.A. (2002). An analysis of children's picture books through a framework of critical literacy. Unpublished manuscript.

McDaniel, C.A. (2004). Critical literacy: A questioning stance and possibility for change. *The Reading Teacher*.

McGillis, R. (1996). *The nimble reader: literary theory and children's literature*. New York, NY: Twayne Publishers.

McGinley, W., Kamberelis, G., Mahoney,T., Madigan, D., Rybicki, V., & Oliver, J. (1997). Revisioning reading and teaching literature through the lens of narrative theory. In Rogers, T., and Soter, A.Ol, eds. *Reading across cultures: Teaching literature in a diverse society*. 42-68.

McKinnon, T. (1997). The dilemmas of lived multiculturalism. In Freire, P., Fraser, J.W., Macedo, D., McKinnon, T., and Stokes, W.T., eds. *Mentoring the mentor: A critical dialogue with Paulo Freire.* New York, NY: Peter Lang Publishing, Inc., 293-302.

McLaren, P., Martin, G., Farahmandapur, R., & Jaramillo, N. (2004). Teaching in and against the Empire: Critical pedagogy as revolutionary praxis. *Teacher Education Quarterly, 31*(1), 131-153.

Meyerson, D.E. (2001). Tempered radicals: How people use difference to inspire change at work. Boston, MA: Harvard Business School Press.

Moll, L.C., ed. (1990). Introduction. *Vygotsky and education: Instructional implications and applications of sociohistorical psychology.* New York, NY: Cambridge University Press, 1-27.

Moll, L.C. (1994). Literacy research in community and classrooms: A sociocultural approach. In Ruddell, R.B., Ruddell, M.R., and Singer, H., eds. *Theoretical models and processes of reading, 4th ed.* Newark: DE, International Reading Association, 179-207.

Morgan, W. (1997). *Critical literacy in the classroom: The art of the possible.* New York, NY: Routledge.

Morrison, T. (1999). *The big box.* New York, NY: Hyperion Books for Children.

Muise, M.R. (2001). Teacher do you know me? Teacher, do you care? Making teacher education critical. *Dissertation Abstracts International, 62(12),* 4047.

Munsch, R. (1986). *Love you forever.* Buffalo, NY: Firefly Books.

Murrell, P.C. (1997). Digging again the family wells: A Freirian literacy framework as emancipatory pedagogy for African American children. In Freire, P., Fraser, J.W., Macedo, D., McKinnon, T., and Stokes, W.T., eds. *Mentoring the mentor: A critical dialogue with Paulo Freire.* New York, NY: Peter Lang Publishing, Inc., 19-58.

National Call to Action. (2004). Homepage. *The national call to action: A movement to end child abuse and neglect.* http://www. nationalcalltoaction.com.

NCTE (National Council of Teachers of English). (2001). The student's right to read. NCTE website. http://www.ncte.org/censorship/right2read.shtml.

Necochea, J., and Cline, Z. (2002). School reform without a heart. *Kappa Delta Pi Record, 38(3),* 102-105.

Newman, L. (1989). *Heather has two mommies.* Boston, MA: Alyson Wonderland.

Nichols, W.D., Rupley, W.H., & Webb-Johnson, G. (2000). Teachers role in providing culturally responsive literacy instruction. *Reading Horizons, 41(1)*, 1-18.

Nodelman, P. (1988). *Words about pictures: The narrative art of children's picture books*. Athens: The University of Georgia Press.

Nodelman, P. (1996). *The pleasures of children's literature*. White Plains, NY: Longman.

Nodelman, P. (2002). Critical theory. *Bibliography of children's literature criticism*. University of Winnipeg. http://www.uwinnipeg.ca/~nodelman/resources/theory.html.

Nye, N.S. (1994). *Sitti's secrets*. New York, NY: Four Winds Press.

Otis-Wilborn, A.K., Marshall, J.D., and Sears, J.T. (1988). Commitment: A reflection of the quality of preservice teachers. *Peabody Journal of Education, 65*, 107-129.

PABBIS (Parents Against Bad Books in Schools). (2004). http://www.pabbis.com.

Pajares, M.F. (1992). Teachers' beliefs and educational research: cleaning up a messy construct. *Review of Educational Research, 62(3)*, 307-332.

Pajares, F., and Johnson, M.J. (1994). Confidence and competence in writing: The role of self-efficacy, outcome expectancy, and apprehension. *Research in the Teaching of English, 28(3)*, 313-331.

Paterson, K. (1987/1977). *Bridge to Terabithia*. New York, NY: Harper/Trophy.

Paterson, K. (1997). Interview. In West, M.I. *Trust your children: voices against censorship in children's literature*. New York, NY: Neal-Schuman Publishers, Inc., 2-10.

Patton, M.Q. (2002). *Qualitative research and evaluation methods, 3rd ed.* Thousand Oaks, CA: Sage Publications.

Pavonetti, L.M. (2002). It seems important that we should have the right to read. *Journal of Children's Literature, 28*, 9-15.

Petruzzi, A. (1998). Hermeneutic disclosure as freedom: John Dewey and Paulo Freire on the non-representational nature of education. *Proceedings of the Midwest Philosophy of Education Society, 1997-1998*.

Philion, T. (1998). Three codifications of critical literacy. In Fleishcer, C., and Schaafsma, D., eds. *Literacy and democracy: Teacher research and composition studies in pursuit of habitable spaces*. Urbana, IL: National Council of Teachers of English, 53-81.

Plato. (1992). The allegory of the cave. In Grube, G.M.A., trans. *The republic*. Indianapolis, IN: Hackett Publishing Company, 186-193.

Polkinghorne, D.E. (1988). *Narrative knowing and the human sciences*. Albany, NY: State University of New York Press.

Potter, B. (1902/2000). *The tale of Peter Rabbit*. London, England: Penguin Group.

Prince-Hughes, D., ed. *Aquamarine blue: Personal stories of college students with autism*. Athens, OH: Swallow Press, 66-75.

Reichman, H. (1988). *Censorship and selection: issues and answers for schools*. Chicago, IL: America Library Association and Arlington, VA: American Association of School Administrators.

Richardson, V. (1996). The role of attitudes and beliefs in learning to teach. In Sikula, J., Buttery, T.J., and Guyton, E., eds. *Handbook of research on teacher education, 2nd ed*. New York, NY: Macmillan Library Reference, 102-119.

Ringgold, F. (1991). *Tar beach*. New York, NY: Crown Publishers, Inc.

Risko, V. J., Roskos, K., & Vukelich, C. (2002). Prospective teachers' reflection: Strategies, qualities, and perceptions in learning to teach reading. *Reading Research and Instruction, 41* (2), 149-176.

Roberts, E.V. (1995). *Writing about Literature, 8th ed*. Englewood Cliffs, NJ: Prentice Hall.

Rogers, R. (2002). "That's what you're here for, you're suppose to tell us": Teaching and learning critical literacy. *Journal of Adolescent & Adult Literacy, 45(8)*, 772-787.

Rosenblatt, L.M. (1986). The aesthetic transaction. *Journal of Aesthetic Education, 20(4)*, 122-128.

Rosenblatt, L.M. (1994). The transaction theory of reading and writing. In Ruddell, R.B., Ruddell, M.R., and Singer, H., eds. *Theoretical Models and Processes of Reading*. Newark, DE: International Reading Association, 1057-1092.

Rosenblatt, L.M. (1995/1965). *Literature as exploration*. New York, NY: Modern Language Association.

Rowling, J.K. (1997). *Harry Potter and the sorcerer's stone*. New York, NY: Scholastic, Inc.

Rudman, M. K. (1995). *Children's literature: An issues approach*. White Plains, NY: Longman.

Salinas, B. (1998). *The three pigs (Los tres cerdos: Nacho, Tito, and Miguel)*. Oakland, CA: Pinata Publications.

Saul, W., and Wallace, K. (2002). Centering the margins: White pre-service teachers' responses to *Roll of Thunder*. *Teaching Education, 13(1)*, 41-53.

Scapp, R. (1997). The subject of education: Paulo Freire, postmodernism, and multiculturalism. In Freire, P., Fraser, J.W., Macedo, D., McKinnon, T., and Stokes, W.T., eds. *Mentoring the mentor: A critical dialogue with Paulo Freire*. New York, NY: Peter Lang Publishing, Inc., 283-291.

Scieszka, J. (1989). *The true story of the three little pigs*. New York, NY: Viking.

Schoefer, C. (2000). Harry Potter's girl trouble. *Salon.com*. http://archive.salon.com/books/feature/2000/01/13/potter/print.html.

Schuster, E.H. (2003). *Breaking the rules: Liberating writers through innovative grammar instruction*. Portsmouth, NH: Heinemann.

Scott. S. (2004, March 18). Schoolbook's gay theme upsets parents. *Star-News Online*. http://www.wilmingtonstar.com

Semali, L.M., and Pailliotet, A.W., eds. (1999). *Intermediality: The teachers' handbook of critical media literacy*. Boulder, CO: Westview Press.

Sendak, M. (1997). Interview. In West, M. *Trust Your Children: Voices Against Censorship in Children's Literature*. New York, NY: Neal-Schuman Publishers, Inc., 124-129,

Sendak, M. (1970). *In the night kitchen*. New York, NY: HarperCollins Publishers.

Sendak, M. (1993). *We are all in the dumps with Jack and Guy*. New York, NY: HarperCollins Publishers.

Seuss, D. (1957/1985). *The cat in the hat*. New York, NY: Random Houes, Inc.

Shange, N. (1997). *Whitewash*. New York, NY: Walker Publishing Company.

Shannon. D. (1998). *No, David!* New York, NY: The Blue Sky Press.

Shannon, P. (1995). *Text, lies, & videotape: Stories about life, literacy, and learning*. Portsmouth, NH: Heinemann.

Shannon, P. (2004). The practice of democracy and Dewey's challenge. *Language Arts, 82*(1), 16-25.

Shor, I. (1999, Fall). What is critical literacy? *Journal for Pedagogy, Pluralism & Practice*. Retrieved June 2, 2002 from http://www.lesley.edu/journals/jppp/4/shor.html. (Note: This essay is a revised version of the "Introduction" to *Critical literacy in action: Writing words, changing worlds*. Portsmouth, NH: Boynton/Cook Publishers, Inc.).

Shor, I., and Pari, C. (1999). *Critical literacy in action: Writing words, changing worlds.* Portsmouth, NH: Boynton/Cook Publishers, Inc.

Siegel, M., and Fernandez, S.L. (2000). Critical approaches. In Kamil, M.L., Mosenthal, P.B., Pearson, P.D., and Barr, R., eds. *Handbook of reading research, vol. III.* Mahwah, NJ: Lawrence Erlbuam Associates, 141-151.

Silent No More. (2004). Child sexual abuse: A basic introduction. Silent No More. http://www.silent-no-more.org/childabuse.html.

Silverstein, S. (1964). *The giving tree.* New York, NY: Harper Row Publishers.

Sipe, L.R. (1999). Children's response to literature: author, text, reader, context. *Theory into Practice, 38(3),* 120-129.

Sleeter, C.E. (2001). Preparing teachers for culturally diverse schools: Research and the overwhelming presence of whiteness. *Journal of Teacher Education, 52(2),* 94-106.

Sleeter, C.E. (2003). Reform and control: An analysis of SB 2042. *Teacher Education Quarterly, 30(1),* 19-30.

Sleeter, C.E., Torres, M.N., and Laughlin, P. (2004). Scaffolding conscientization through inquiry in teacher education. *Teacher Education Quarterly,* 81-96.

Sloan, G. (2002). Reader response in perspective. *Journal of Children's Literature, 28(1),* 22-30.

Smith, J. (1997). Students' goals, gatekeeping, and some questions of ethics. *College English, 59,* 299-320.

Soles, D. (1998). Problems with confrontational teaching: A reply to Virginia Anderson. *College Composition and Communication, 49(2),* 267-269.

Solochek, J.S. (2003). Parent challenges children's library book. *St. Petersburg Times* online. http://sptimes.com.

Soto, G. (1990). *Baseball in April and other stories.* San Diego, CA: Harcourt, Inc.

Sperling, M., and Freedman, S.W. (2001). Review of writing research. In Richardson, V., ed. *Handbook of research on teaching, 4th ed.* Washington, D.C.: American Educational Research Association, 370-389.

Stapinski, H. (2003). The battle over book banning. *FamilyFun.com.* http://familyfun.go.com.

Stephens, J. (1992). *Language and ideology in children's fiction.* London: Longman.

Steinberg, S.R., and Kincheloe, J.L. (1997). Introduction: No more secrets—kinderculture, information saturation, and the postmodern childhood. In Steinberg, S.R., and Kincheloe, J.L., eds. *Kinderculture: The corporate construction of childhood*. Boulder, CO: Westview Press, 1-30.

Strauss, C. (1992). Motives and models. In D'Andrade, R., and Strauss, C., eds. *Human motives and cultural models*. New York, NY: Cambridge University Press. 3-11.

Tappan, M.B., and Brown, L.M. (1996). Envisioning a postmodern moral pedagogy. *Journal of Moral Education, 25(1)*, 101-109.

Tatar, M. (1998). Sex and violence: the hard core of fairy tales. In Tatar, M., ed. *The classic fairy tales*. New York, NY: W.W. Norton. 364-373.

Taylor, C. (illustrated by Dicks, J.T.) (1992). *The house that crack built*. San Francisco, CA: Chronicle Books.

Thacker, D. (2000). Disdain or ignorance? Literary theory and the absence of children's literature. *The Lion and the Unicorn, 24*, 1-17.

Thompson, K. (1955). *Eloise*. New York, NY: Simon and Schuster.

Thoreau, H.D. (1849/1986). Civil disobedience. *Walden and civil disobedience*. New York, NY: Penguin Books, 383-413.

Titscher, S., Meyer, M., Wodak, R., and Vetter, E. (2000). *Methods of text and discourse analysis* (Jenner, B., Trans.).Thousand Oaks, CA: Sage Publications.

Tomlinson, Carl. (1995). Justifying violence in children's literature. In S. Lehr, ed. *Battling dragons: issues and controversy in children's literature*. Portsmouth, NH: Heinemann, pp. 39-50.

Twain, M. (1994/1885). *Adventures of Huckleberry Finn*. Mineola, NY: Dover Publications, Inc.

UNESCO (2003). Managing Innovation and Change. http://portal.unesco.org/education

Van Allsburg, C. (1985). *The polar express*. New York, NY: Houghton Mifflin Company.

Vandergrift, K. (2004). Special interest page. http://www.scils.rutgers.edu/~kvander.

Villanueva, V. (1997). Considerations for American Freireistas. In Villanueva, V., ed. *Cross-talk in comp theory: A reader*. Urbana, IL: National Council of Teachers of English, 621-637.

Voices in Action. (2004). Male survivors of child sexual abuse. *Voices in Action*. http://www.voices-action.org/Male%20Survivors.htm.

Warren, C.A.B. (2002). Qualitative interviewing. In Gubrium, J.F., and Holstein, J.A., eds. *Handbook of interview research: Context and method*. Thousand Oaks, CA: Sage Publications, 83-102.

Waxman, S. (1989/1976). *What is a girl? What is a boy?* New York, NY: Thomas Y. Crowell.

Wertsch, J.V. (1998). *Mind as action*. New York, NY: Oxford University Press.

Westheimer, J., and Kahne, J. (1998). Educating for action: preparing youth for participatory democracy. In Ayers, W., Hunt, J. and Quinn, T. (eds.). *Teaching for social justice: A democracy and education reader*. New York, NY: The New Press/Teachers College Press, 1-20.

Whitbeck, D.A. (2000). Born to be a teacher: What am I doing in a college of education? *Journal of Research in Childhood Education, 15(1)*, 129-136.

Whitin, D.J. and Whitin, P. (1998). Learning is born of doubting: Cultivating a skeptical stance. *Language Arts, 76*, 123-129.

Wiesner, D. (1999). *Sector 7*. New York, NY: Houghton Mifflin Company.

Willhoite, M. (1990). *Daddy's roommate*. Los Angeles, CA: Alyson Wonderland.

Williams, S. (2002). Reading *Daddy's Roommate*: Preservice teachers respond to a controversial text. *New Advocate, 15(3)*, 231-236.

Wilson, E.A. (1994, November-December). Critical literacy and the language of difference and power: A difficult concept for first year preservice teachers. Paper presented the Australian Association for Research in Education Conference, New South Wales.

Wink, J. (1999). *Critical pedagogy: Notes from the real world*. New York, NY: Longman.

Wollman-Bonilla, J.E. (1998). Outrageous viewpoints: teachers' criteria for rejecting works of children's literature. *Language Arts, 75(4)*, 287-295.

Yenika-Agbaw, V. (1997). Taking children's literature seriously: Reading for pleasure and social change. *Language Arts, 74(6)*, 446-453.

Young, E. (1992). *Seven blind mice*. New York, NY: Philomel Books.

Young, J.P. (2000). Boy talk: Critical literacy and masculinities. *Reading Research Quarterly, 35(3)*, 312-337.

Young, J.P. (2001). Displaying practices of masculinity: Critical literacy and social contexts. *Journal of Adolescent & Adult Literacy, 45(1),* 4-14.

Zipes, J. (1999). *When dreams come true: Classical fairy tales and their tradition.* New York, NY: Routledge.

❖ INDEX

Studies in the Postmodern Theory of Education

General Editors
Joe L. Kincheloe & Shirley R. Steinberg

Counterpoints publishes the most compelling and imaginative books being written in education today. Grounded on the theoretical advances in criticalism, feminism, and postmodernism in the last two decades of the twentieth century, Counterpoints engages the meaning of these innovations in various forms of educational expression. Committed to the proposition that theoretical literature should be accessible to a variety of audiences, the series insists that its authors avoid esoteric and jargonistic languages that transform educational scholarship into an elite discourse for the initiated. Scholarly work matters only to the degree it affects consciousness and practice at multiple sites. Counterpoints' editorial policy is based on these principles and the ability of scholars to break new ground, to open new conversations, to go where educators have never gone before.

For additional information about this series or for the submission of manuscripts, please contact:

Joe L. Kincheloe & Shirley R. Steinberg
c/o Peter Lang Publishing, Inc.
29 Broadway, 18th floor
New York, New York 10006

To order other books in this series, please contact our Customer Service Department:

(800) 770-LANG (within the U.S.)
(212) 647-7706 (outside the U.S.)
(212) 647-7707 FAX

Or browse online by series:
www.peterlang.com